I Love Dessert

but NOT

Sugar, Wheat, Milk, Gluten, Corn, Soy, Unhealthy Fat…

Nicolette M. Dumke

I LOVE DESSERT BUT NOT SUGAR, WHEAT, MILK, GLUTEN, CORN, SOY, UNHEALTHY FAT...

Published by
Adapt Books
Allergy Adapt, Inc.
1877 Polk Avenue
Louisville, Colorado 80027
303-666-8253

©2010 by Nicolette M. Dumke
Printed in the United States of America

Publisher's Cataloging-in-Publication
(Provided by Quality Books, Inc.)

Dumke, Nicolette M.
    I love dessert but not sugar, wheat, milk, gluten, corn, soy, unhealthy fat-- / Nicolette M. Dumke.
    262 p. 24.6 cm.
    Includes bibliographical references and index.
    LCCN 2009902985
    ISBN-13: 978-1-887624-18-3
    ISBN-10: 1-887624-18-X

    1. Desserts. 2. Food allergy--Diet therapy--Recipes.
3. Celiac disease--Diet therapy--Recipes.   I. Title.

TX773.D86 2010   641.8'6
                          QBI09-600043

Dedication

To my Sweetie Pies
Mark, Joel and John

You add the lemon zest of fun,
the rich dark chocolate of love,
the sweetness of memories and
the spicy anticipation of future joys
to my life.

Disclaimer

The information contained in this book is merely intended to communicate food preparation material and information about possible treatment options which are helpful and educational to the reader. It is not intended to replace medical diagnosis or treatment, but rather to provide information and recipes which may be helpful in implementing a diet prescribed by your doctor. Please consult your physician for medical advice before embarking on any treatment or changing your diet.

The author and publisher declare that to the best of their knowledge all material in this book is accurate; however, although unknown to the author and publisher, some recipes may contain ingredients which may be harmful to some people.

There are no warranties which extend beyond the educational nature of this book, either expressed or implied, including, but not limited to, the implied warranties of merchantability, fitness for a particular purpose, or non-infringement. Therefore, the author and publisher shall have neither liability nor responsibility to any person with respect to any loss or damage alleged to be caused, directly or indirectly, by the information contained in this book.

If you do not wish to be bound by the above, you may return this book to the publisher for a full refund.

Table of Contents

Foreword 6

I Love Dessert 7

Simple Pleasures, Special Bonds 9

Desserts Designed for Special Diets 11

Make It Easy: Tricks and Tools of the Dessert Trade 13

Know Your Ingredients. 19

Recipes
  Simple Fruit Desserts 34
  Puddings. 39
  Cobblers, Crisps, Crumbles and Other Fruit Desserts. 45
  Pies 62
  Cakes and Frostings. 74
  Ice Cream, Sherbet and Sorbet 97
  Dessert Waffles, Pancakes and Cones. 114
  Sweet Breads, Coffee Cakes, Buns and Doughnuts 120
  Cookies. 153
  Sauces and Toppings 189
  Confections, Snacks and Miscellaneous Recipes 197
  Especially for Guests 205

References
  Sources of Special Ingredients and Products 228
  Table of Measurements 235
  About Sweeteners, Health and Life 236
  About Spelt. 241
  References: Helpful Books and Websites 243
  Index to Recipes by Grain Use. 245
  General Index 250

Foreword

"Dessert" is not a bad word – at least it doesn't need to be. However, somehow we have taken the custom of ending a meal on a sweet note and, like a snowball rolling down hill, expanded it in so many ways the end result borders on the obscene – with way too many calories, too much fat (and often the wrong kinds of fat, too), overly sweetened, and very often the serving is over-sized as well. On the other hand, Nickie Dumke, in this book, has used fresh fruits and whole grains to create delicious, health enhancing desserts. They are pleasantly sweetened, but not outrageously so. You're on your own to keep the portion size under control!

Favorite desserts at our house include "Blueberry Cobbler," (for a recipe, see page 54), any fruit crisp (recipes are on pages 45 to 46), and fresh fruits eaten out of hand like in-season tree ripened peaches, black cherries or Rainier cherries, any and all berries, or grapes. And clearly it matters more to your total health what you eat day in, day out, much more than if you have an occasional splurge for a special occasion.

If our family has a tradition regarding desserts while traveling it is to say, "No, thank you." Yet several years ago when we were on a three-generation family vacation with our daughter and two granddaughters who were in their early teens, we consented to a dessert splurge. We ordered a gigantic ice cream sundae called a "volcano" with about ten scoops of three flavors of ice cream, three or four sauces (which were the "lava"), some nuts, and a few wafers stuck into the edges. Oh, and of course, it was topped with a mountain of whipped cream. To get the picture, let me explain that this ONE monster dessert was served with five spoons! When everyone was totally satisfied, enough of the sundae for a few more servings remained. We all remember this event because it was unusual for us and great fun for all. I don't think anyone's health suffered as a result of the splurge. We don't live like that normally and we haven't repeated it in the seven years since. We have only pleasant memories – and not one bit of guilt.

Many family traditions and memories revolve around food – birthday cakes, wedding cakes, Thanksgiving feasts, Christmas and Easter dinners, anniversaries, and on and on it goes. Many of those traditions can be "cleaned up" so subtly no one notices – at least, not enough to complain. I thank Nickie for doing the work necessary to produce truly delicious yet health enhancing desserts.

I can see my family is in for some new traditions, and I hope yours is, too. Enjoy!

Marjorie Hurt Jones, RN
Author of *The Allergy Self-Help Cookbook*

I Love Dessert

Desserts are the sweet threads of the warp and weft of our lives. Because they are connected to so many significant events, they are unique among foods. Birthdays, holidays, graduations, anniversaries – all celebrate with dessert. Even ordinary occasions become special accompanied by sweet treats. Without desserts, we miss more than food; we miss being a part of special events. If you are on a special diet, you don't have to be deprived. With this book, you too can enjoy delicious fun.

I only eat dessert occasionally, but dessert still is a significant part of my life and my history. My childhood memories are laced with desserts (in spite of coming from a nutrition-aware limited-sugar family). When my grandmother babysat us, we almost always made chocolate chip cookies together. I often came home from school to the spicy aroma of applesauce cooking on the stove or a tantalizing something sweet baking in the oven. My sister and I each got a beater to lick when my mother made a dessert that required a mixer. I even remember many times sitting in front of the window in the oven door watching cakes magically rising as they baked.

Desserts connect friends as well as families. In my early teens we went on a mountain picnic with friends. There we found some wild chokecherry bushes and picked every ripe berry we could find. At home we made them into chokecherry jam with our mothers. This jam found its way into coffee cakes and sandwiches and repeatedly reminded us of our delightful day in the mountains. Because desserts are a special part of friendships, I always enjoy making a homemade treat to share when I visit a friend. Everyone has Christmas memories of cookies connecting friends who participate in cookie exchange parties.

Desserts bind me to many friends who are important contributors to this book. My tasters tell me if the spices in the pfeffernuse are really like what they had growing up in a German community and if something is too sweet, not sweet enough, too hard, too soft, or too crumbly. Of course, each person has different standards for what makes a good dessert, and these vary with how limited their diets are and what grains they are used to eating. A wide variety of input from their different perspectives is invaluable for this book because its readers have diverse dietary needs. Thus, this book provides a broad range of desserts to hopefully make it possible for anyone on almost any diet to find a recipe for making an important occasion more special.

Although we may cook dinner because we have to, we cook dessert because we want to. It is a special way of expressing love, of nurturing ourselves and others who will eat the dessert. Creative activities like making dessert are good for the mind, the emotions, and the soul. The anticipation and planning that goes into making dessert for a special occasion is part of the fun.

Dessert is one of the simple pleasures of life which have sustained people during difficult times. I hope that as many of us face challenges, we will take advantage of opportunities to enjoy desserts, made with family members or friends if possible, and use them as a way to build relationships and enrich our lives.

Simple Pleasures, Special Bonds

In good times and bad, having fun helps us maintain our sanity and have a positive outlook. At the time of this writing the world is experiencing a recession. Perhaps this should be a call for us to return to simpler ways of enjoying life. Rather than taking an expensive vacation or buying a new "toy" for enjoyment, consider having some inexpensive fun with family and friends. Dessert can be a part of simple fun and building significant bonds and special memories with other people.

My parents grew up during the Great Depression. Their families had very little money but they considered themselves among the fortunate because they usually had enough food. Because food was almost all they had, they used it for having fun as well as for physical nourishment. My mother told stories about making homemade ice cream with her parents and siblings during summers in the 1930s. Grandpa would fill the ice cream maker with ice and rock salt, Grandma would mix cream, sugar, and vanilla, and all of the kids would take turns cranking. Everybody had a lot of fun, nobody did so much of the work that his arm got sore, and the ice cream was delicious.

My parents began dating during high school and planned to marry after my father finished college. Unfortunately, life became grim when World War II began. My father was anxious about getting good grades so he could keep his educational deferment. When all deferments were suspended, he enlisted in the Navy and my parents decided to marry immediately so my mother could accompany him for his Naval training. The boarding house where they lived in San Francisco for a few months before his ship left had a peach tree in the back yard. They picked peaches and made a cobbler together. As my father kept peeling peaches and encouraging my mother to put just another peach or two into the cobbler, it became so large that it ran all over the oven. They always said it was delicious, however, and this experience became one of their most cherished memories. Whenever we had fresh peaches when I was a child, my mother would say to my father, "Remember the peach cobbler?" Then they would reminisce about how that was the best cobbler they had ever eaten. If my father had been killed, my mother would at least have had her memories of the peach cobbler and their early days together to sustain her for the rest of her life. Dessert helped them cope and enjoy life in spite of the fact that they were living under a dire threat.

When I was a child in the 1950s, the family who lived two houses west of us had a cherry tree in their yard. Every summer when the tart cherries ripened, both mothers, three daughters, and occasionally one son sat under that tree and pitted cherries (using hairpins) for hours on end. Sometimes the older lady who lived one house farther west also joined us. We enjoyed talking to each other while we worked, and each family took a share of the pitted cherries home to make pies, cobblers, and preserves.

During my high school years I remember sitting at the kitchen sink for hours with my mother and peeling apples from the tree in our yard for pies and applesauce. In my late teens my grandmother taught me to make Italian sweet bread, rich with eggs and anise. These experiences all stand out as high points among my memories.

When I had children, the tradition of having fun together with food continued. My two sons helped me in the kitchen from very early ages. I have pictures of each of them at about age 1½ standing on a chair helping wash fruits and vegetables in the kitchen sink. In one of these pictures, asparagus stalks are flying through the air to the other side of the double sink! Such fun! They were kneading bread by age two. Our photo album shows them at age three adding decorations to Christmas cookies. They baked cookies with my mother when she babysat them during their elementary school years. This last Christmas, my older son's school break from graduate school began several days after my younger son returned home from college. We waited until everyone was home to make our Christmas cookies because they enjoy baking cookies together and carrying on a tradition that spans the generations and binds together our family – past, present, and future.

Desserts create and enhance bonds with friends as well as family. Several members of my dentist's staff have food allergies, and as I have "unloaded" extra desserts on them while working on recipes for this book, we have developed friendships. I actually look forward to going to the dentist now (especially if all I need is a cleaning).

Sometimes we want to say "Thank you" or "You are special to me" in a tangible way. Giving a homemade dessert is an ideal way to do this. If we buy a small gift, the other person may feel obligated to reciprocate, which can be financially burdensome. However, home-baked goodies say "I value you enough to spend time making something that will bring you pleasure" with no strings attached. When a friend or family member is down, a dessert made with love brings comfort.

A special diet does not have to bring an end to desserts for you. My hope is that this book will bring simple pleasures into your life and help you to create bonds with others and to build special memories that will cheer you for the rest of your life.

Desserts Designed for Special Diets

When you are told that you must follow a special diet, you may feel that your days of enjoying what you eat have come to an end. I felt this way just considering the possibility of being on a food allergy diet as I spent two consecutive days having food allergy testing many years ago. The nurse did not tell me what the test results were until all of the testing was completed. I knew I was reacting to many foods, but I didn't know what they were as I left the doctor's office the first day. Because I feared that I would never do this again, I stopped at Baskin Robbins on the way home and had a scoop of my favorite ice cream.

After I had been on my food allergy diet for a few weeks, feeling better convinced me that it was very much worth the discipline of staying on the diet faithfully. However, there were occasions where I felt that I was missing out when those around me ate a favorite food. I began experimenting with alternative ingredients to make something similar to the foods I missed and discovered that it is possible to stay on a special diet and do what needs to be done for optimal health without being deprived.

This book contains a wide variety of desserts designed to fit a wide variety of special diets. For example, if you are gluten-intolerant, you will find many desserts that you can use, but they are different in design than the recipes in most gluten-free cookbooks. The recipes in this book do not contain a myriad of allergenic additives, sugar, shortening, and the like so they can also be used by those who are lactose intolerant or avoid milk due to allergy. There are also recipes for those are allergic to eggs or avoid them because of cholesterol, those who avoid sugar because of diabetes or *Candida* problems, or those who limit the fats they consume, especially saturated or unnatural trans fats. If you have multiple health problems necessitating more than one type of dietary restriction, you will probably find recipes that you can use in this book.

If your restrictions are moderate, there are recipes just for you. Those who are allergic to wheat but not gluten-intolerant can make desserts with a variety of grains using these recipes. If you tolerate spelt, there is a chapter of recipes "especially for guests" that are so normal in taste and texture no one will know they do not contain wheat or sugar. Most of the recipes in this book are free of dairy products and eggs, but if you can tolerate them, some of the recipes in the "Especially for Guests" chapter and a few in other chapters are enhanced by these ingredients. None of the recipes in this book calls for soy, corn, hydrogenated fats, or other common allergens that are in almost all prepared foods but that we can easily cook without; nor do any recipes contain wheat or sugar.

If you cannot have grains at all, you can still have dessert. The all-fruit, ice cream, sherbet, sorbet, and pudding recipes in this book are grain and gluten-free. There are recipes for baked goods made with non-grains such as amaranth, quinoa, and buckwheat; cobblers with nut-coconut toppings; and even waffles made with only a starch (such as tapioca), nuts or seeds and water and which are delicious topped with fresh fruit, ice cream (non-dairy if needed), sorbet and/or a dessert sauce. Almost everyone can find something they can eat in this book. Although your diet may not allow you to eat dessert often, especially if it is a diet for diabetes or *Candida*, you probably will not have to be deprived on your birthday. However, be sure to **ask your doctor** about the specifics of your diet, what you must avoid absolutely, and what you can eat occasionally or routinely. Have him or her consider stevia-sweetened desserts if your options are quite limited.

Some of the special ingredients used in this book may be different from any you may have cooked with before even if you are an experienced gluten-free or special diet cook. They are all healthy natural foods, however, and include vitamin C powder for leavening, non-hydrogenated shortening for a few recipes that require a solid fat, and alternative sweeteners such as fruit sweeteners, agave (from a plant in the cactus family) and the herb stevia which is used in a few recipes for those who can have no caloric sweeteners. See the "Know Your Ingredients" chapter, pages 19 to 33, for more about the ingredients used in this book.

Because those of us on special diets may be cooking most or all of our food from scratch, we might feel that we are already spending plenty of time in the kitchen. Therefore the dessert recipes in this book are simpler to make than those in most cookbooks. The ingredient lists are shorter which saves time on measuring. Most of these recipes are just stirred with a spoon. No need to drag out a heavy mixer and then wash its large bowl by hand! If you are not creaming butter with sugar and eggs, there is no need for a mixer. (However, a very few of the recipes in this book do require a mixer). Other equipment you may already have in your kitchen can also save you time. See the next chapter for more about using kitchen tools and other tricks to make desserts easily and quickly.

Make it Easy: Tricks and Tools of the Dessert Trade

Making desserts for special diets should not be difficult or time consuming. Baking with alternative flours and leavening ingredients *is* different* but not harder than other baking. Because most of the recipes in this book are mixed with a spoon rather than involving creaming of sugar and solid fats, they involve less hand washing of large mixer bowls and special equipment and actually can be easier than making a traditional dessert.

The recipes in this book have simple lists of ingredients. One reason for this is that using fewer ingredients makes a recipe easier to prepare since less measuring is required. Another more important reason to use fewer ingredients is that mixtures of several different flours and a myriad of stabilizing and texture-improving ingredients in each recipe often involves some that are fairly allergenic. If a person with allergic tendencies eats these ingredients often or daily, they are likely to develop an allergy to them. I reserve stabilizers such as eggs, guar gum and xanthum gum for use in recipes where they are really needed such as for yeast bread recipes. Along with fewer ingredients per recipe, the tips given in this chapter will also save you time and effort in the kitchen. Additionally, there are a variety of tools and appliances that can save you time which are discussed at the end of this chapter.

TRICKS

The most important factors for successfully baking special diet desserts are **MEASURING ACCURATELY** and **MIXING CORRECTLY.** When people call me because they are having problems making their baked goods come out well, most commonly the problem is either in measuring or mixing. If you are an experienced baker, the section below on measuring will be review for you, but please take a quick glance at the two paragraphs about mixing on page 14 and refer to them if you encounter problems.

To measure accurately, you must use the right measuring cups for the ingredient you are measuring – nested sets for flour and other solids ingredients or see-through glass or plastic cups with markings for liquids. To measure flour, stir the flour to loosen it. Using

*Note on special diet baking: Do not miss the trick that is the key to the difference between special diet baking and ordinary baking. Be sure to read the "Mixing" section on page 14.

a large spoon, lightly spoon the flour into the cup. Level it off with a straight edged knife or spatula. If you are measuring an amount of flour that you do not have a measuring cup for such as ⅝ cup, use the table of measurements on page 235 to determine how to measure it. In this case it is by using a ½ cup plus ⅛ cup.

To measure liquids, fill a see-through measuring cup with the liquid until the meniscus (the bottom of the curve of the liquid) lines up with the line on the cup that is the amount you want to measure. Get down on your knees so you can read the cup at eye level as it sits on your counter. If your recipe calls for several liquids, you can save yourself time by measuring them all in the same measuring cup and mixing them there before adding them to the dry ingredients. For instance, if you need ½ cup water, ¼ cup thawed apple juice concentrate, and ⅛ cup of oil, do this: Add water to the ½ cup line, add apple juice to the ¾ cup line, and then add oil to the ⅞ cup line. Stir the liquids together in the measuring cup and add them to the dry ingredients. That saves you having to wash an extra bowl used to combine the liquid ingredients.

To measure small amounts of flour, starch, salt, baking powder, spices, and other dry ingredients with measuring spoons, dip the spoon into the container, stir up the ingredient to loosen it, and fill the spoon generously. Pull it out and level it off with a straight edged knife or spatula, or level spices using the straight edge of the hole in the spice container. To measure small amounts of liquids, pour the liquid into the measuring spoon until it is level with the top of the spoon. Do not let it bead up over the top of the spoon.

Proper **MIXING** for allergy and gluten-free recipes is slightly different than for standard baking and it is the technique that is most crucial to success in special diet baking. Because the types of flour used in special diet baking produce a more fragile structure which must trap the gas produced by the leavening, how you mix non-yeast baked goods and how quickly you get them into the oven is very important. Before you begin baking, preheat your oven. Prepare the baking pans ahead of time; oil them or oil and flour them with the same oil and flour used in the recipe. If the recipe directs, also line them with parchment paper or waxed paper. For some recipes, you should also oil or oil and flour the paper as directed in the recipe.

Mix the dry ingredients together in a large bowl and the liquid ingredients together in your measuring cup or another bowl. Working quickly, stir the liquid ingredients into the dry ingredients until they are **just mixed.** It is critical that you do not mix for too long or the leavening will produce most of its gas in the mixing bowl rather than in the baking pan in the oven. Only stir until the dry ingredients are just moistened; a few floury spots in your batter or dough are all right. As soon as you have mixed just enough, quickly put the batter or dough into the prepared baking pan(s) and immediately place them into the preheated oven.

How can you know when your quick bread or cake is ready to come out of the oven? To **TEST FOR DONENESS**, insert a toothpick into the center of the pan. If it comes out dry, it is time to remove the pan from the oven. Most baked goods should be removed from the pan immediately after you take them from the oven, but some fragile cakes and cookies benefit from cooling in the pan for about 10 minutes. The recipe will tell you when to do this. Allow your baked goods to cool on a cooling rack before you slice them or store them in a bag. While plastic bags and containers are great for storing most baked goods, some cookies should be stored in a metal tin to keep them crisp.

A few recipes are in this book (i.e. brownie recipes) where the toothpick test for doneness does not apply, but each of these recipes gives specific information about how to determine when to remove it from the oven.

There are a few other tricks specific to making desserts. Traditionally, chocolate has been melted using a double boiler. Some of the recipes here instruct you to melt it with a double boiler or – to save time and dish-washing – use your microwave oven. **TO MELT CHOCOLATE IN THE MICROWAVE**, place it in a glass bowl and microwave it, checking and stirring it at 30-second intervals, until it is mostly melted with just a few solid parts remaining. Remove it from the microwave and stir it to melt the remaining solid chocolate.

Since most of the recipes in this book do not contain solid fat, you will rarely need to cream the fat. However, a few of the cookie recipes do call for butter or non-hydrogenated shortening. Unlike traditional cookie recipes, they use liquid sweeteners rather than sugar. **CREAMING BUTTER OR SHORTENING WITH A LIQUID SWEETENER** is different from creaming solid fat with sugar. To overcome the tendency of the fat and liquid to separate, cream the fat first, add the sweetener, and beat them together for about a minute at the highest mixer speed. Then use a rubber spatula to scrape the fat clinging to the sides of the bowl and the beater off into the center of the bowl and beat at the highest speed for about a minute again. After repeating this process one more time, the fat and sweetener usually look thoroughly mixed.

TOOLS

Some dessert-specific kitchen equipment is needed to prepare the recipes in this book. The most basic equipment for making desserts is **BAKEWARE.** You will probably need two to three baking sheets, a loaf pan or two, a square cake pan, two round cake pans, and a 13 by 9 inch rectangular pan. I prefer heavy metal bakeware without a non-stick coating. In addition, if you are going to make pies, you will need one or two clear Pyrex™ or glass pie dishes. (Glass or Pyrex™ is ideal for pies because you can see the bottom of the crust while it is baking and tell when it has reached the desired shade of light brown). A 2½ to 3 quart casserole dish is needed for cobblers and similar fruit desserts and can be used for a few of the sweet bread recipes as well.

Because agave tends to make cookies, breads, and other baked goods stick to the baking pans more than some sweeteners, I often use **PARCHMENT PAPER** to line cookie sheets and cake pans. Since many grocery stores now carry parchment paper, it is easy to keep on hand if you plan to bake with agave. Although it is optional in most recipes, using it makes removal of the baked goods much easier.

For some of the recipes where a lining paper is essential (for example, to remove fragile cakes from the pans) an option is given of using waxed paper in case you do not have parchment paper on hand. If parts of the paper will be exposed to oven heat, such as when you line a cookie sheet, waxed paper should not be used because the wax on the exposed areas of the paper will smoke. In recipes where this will be a problem, parchment paper is the only lining option given.

The **COOKWARE** that you will need to prepare the desserts in this book includes saucepans and a double boiler for just a few recipes.

MEASURING EQUIPMENT is essential for making these recipes accurately. You will need a set of nested measuring cups for dry ingredients, a see-through glass or plastic measuring cup for liquids, and a set of measuring spoons. It is helpful to have sets which include a ⅛ teaspoon measure and a ⅛ cup measuring cup or a coffee measure which holds ⅛ cup. For more about measuring, see how to measure and mix on pages 13 to 14 of this chapter and the "Table of Measurements" on page 235.

THERMOMETERS are also needed for a few of the recipes in this book. A yeast thermometer is helpful for the yeast bread recipes if you are making them by hand or using a mixer rather than with a bread machine. A room thermometer or a yeast thermometer can be used to check the temperature of your rising place. A candy thermometer is essential if you plan to make sticky agave for the "Sticky Buns" recipe.

A **ROLLING PIN** is necessary for a few of the cookie recipes in this book and also if you wish to make rolled pie crusts. I prefer a wooden rolling pin with handles and ball bearings that allow the large roller to move. This type of pin works best with the knit rolling pin cover that comes with a pastry cloth.

To make pies most easily, you can simply press the pasty into the pie dish. However, if you want to produce a professional-looking rolled crust, you will need a **PASTRY CLOTH** and knit sock-like **ROLLING PIN COVER.** Flour both generously and you will be able to roll out fragile pie crusts and transfer them to the pie plate with minimal breakage. If you are determined to execute a perfect transfer of the crust to the pie plate, you may wish to purchase a **PIE CRUST SPATULA** (which the wrapping calls a Wilton™ cake layer spatula) from the King Arthur Flour Baker's Catalogue for about $13. (See "Sources," page 231).

A **WIRE STRAINER** is needed for a few of the ice cream and sorbet recipes in this book and also may be needed if you use carob powder. If you make the egg-containing custard base for ice cream on page 224, strain the custard through the strainer after you cook it to remove any particles of egg white that may have found their way into the custard and become cooked into small rubbery pieces. For raspberry sorbet, sherbet, or ice cream, press the raspberry puree through the strainer with the back of a spoon to remove the seeds. If you are using carob powder and it has hard lumps in it, press it through a strainer with the back of a spoon.

A **MICROPLANE™ ZESTER** is wonderful for removing the yellow or orange zest from a lemon or orange without also removing some of the bitter-tasting white pith. After using this zester, I cannot believe I used to try to remove the zest from citrus fruits with a cheese grater! If you cannot find a Microplane™ zester locally, order it from Amazon.com or the King Arthur Flour Baker's Catalogue. (See "Sources," page 231).

A **HAND BLENDER** is an easy-to-store inexpensive gadget that I keep handy next to my stove and use quite often. It certainly beats hauling out a food processor or mixer for most recipes! This versatile little item can overcome lumps in pudding, puree fruits, thoroughly blend methylcellulose into ice cream mixtures, and at times will seem like your best friend in the kitchen. It can be purchased at discount department stores for less than $20 at the time of this writing. On some hand blenders (the more expensive models) the blending blade section detaches from the handle and can be put in the dishwasher. To wash the less expensive models, swish the end with the blending blade in soapy water and then rinse.

A very few of the recipes in this book call for using an electric stand **MIXER** or **FOOD PROCESSOR.** Some of the impressive dessert recipes such as the lemon meringue and lemon chiffon pies and a few of the cookie recipes cannot be made without a mixer. Some of the ice cream and sorbet recipes direct that they be made with an ice cream maker or food processor, but if you do not mind a slightly less creamy texture, you may use the still freezing method for most of them. If you are satisfied with desserts that are delicious without being knock-dead impressive, you can get by with using a hand blender for mixing and you may be able to avoid purchasing and storing a mixer and/or food processor.

An **ICE CREAM MAKER** is another specialized appliance for dessert making that you may wish to have if you plan to make homemade ice cream often and have room to store it. Of course, you may decide to do without one if you rarely make ice cream. Some ice creams, sherbets and sorbets can be made by still freezing or using a hand blender. There are also inexpensive ice cream makers on the market that have a chilling tub that is frozen before use in your freezer and a motor that churns the ice cream.

The recipes in the "Dessert Waffles, Pancakes, and Ice Cream Cones" chapter of this book are made using a **GRIDDLE** or waffle, pizzelle or krumkake **IRON**. If you wish to make pizzelles, the traditional Italian Christmas cookie, you will need a pizelle iron.

The final large piece of kitchen equipment used in the recipes in this book is a **BREAD MACHINE**. Although owning a bread machine may be an extravagance if you might use it only to make pannetone once a year at Christmas time, it can be a wise investment if you make all of your allergy or gluten-free bread at home rather than purchasing bread frozen at the health food store. For more about bread machines, see the "Breads" page of www.food-allergy.org (http://www.food-allergy.org/bread.html) or *Easy Breadmaking for Special Diets* which is described on the last pages of this book.

Some of the equipment discussed above is optional for making great desserts; indeed, you can do without any of the more expensive equipment. Just learn the tricks, read and measure the recipes accurately, mix correctly (don't over-mix!), and supplement your baking equipment with a few inexpensive additions or make do with what you have. You will be producing delicious desserts in no time at all. Enjoy these simple pleasures of life!

Know Your Ingredients

Great desserts come from great ingredients. If you use the right high-quality ingredients, your homemade desserts will taste wonderful – better than anything you could buy – and you will have healthy desserts that are allowed on your special diet.

INGREDIENTS THAT MAKE DESSERTS SPECIAL

My favorite desserts are fruit desserts. To make the most flavorful desserts, whenever possible, take advantage of **IN-SEASON FRUIT**. If you have access to home-grown fruit freshly picked from the tree or vine, it will make a fantastic dessert. Fruit purchased from the farmers' market or a local organic farmer is also likely to be wonderful. The best way to decide what dessert to make during the summer or fall is to see what kind of fruit looks and tastes best when you go shopping and then use a recipe that calls for that fruit.

Winter does not have to mean the end of fruit desserts, however. Many frozen or canned fruits also make delicious desserts. Use frozen blueberries or canned pie cherries to make a homey cobbler when it's chilly outside. If you're pressed for time at any season of the year, consider using water packed canned apples to make an apple pie or "Easy Apple Crisp," page 45.

CHOCOLATE AND CAROB are the basis of ever-popular desserts. Many people have fond childhood memories of chocolate chip cookies. If you can't have chocolate, carob chips also make wonderful cookies. For both chocolate and carob chip cookie recipes, see pages 154 to 159 and 218. Health food stores usually sell a variety of carob and chocolate chips to fit almost any diet. Grain-sweetened chocolate and carob chips are sugar-free but often contain corn, which is an allergy problem for many people, and barley which is a problem for celiacs. Carob chips may contain milk products. If you cannot find a brand of chocolate or carob chips that you tolerate, you can make your own with the recipe on pages 201 to 202.

BAKING CHOCOLATE is used in many recipes in this book such as brownies and fudge sauce. Be sure to purchase high-quality unsweetened baking chocolate to avoid the refined sugar in milk chocolate or bittersweet dark chocolate baking bars.

COCOA is also used in cake, ice cream, and cookie recipes in this book. There are several varieties of cocoa, and which one you use depends on your preference for taste and color. American-style cocoa is more acid and has a stronger flavor but is lighter in color. Dutch process cocoa is darker, alkalized, and some think that it has a more complex flavor. In some recipes, using Dutch process cocoa can affect the leavening, but in this book, the recipes all contain enough of both components necessary for the leavening process, alkaline (baking soda) and acid (usually vitamin C powder), so either type of cocoa may be used.

CAROB POWDER is a bean flour since carob beans are in the legume family. It has a delicious flavor and is usually used as a chocolate substitute in baked goods. This book also contains carob ice cream and sauce recipes. Carob powder is naturally sweet so it does not require as much additional sweetener in most recipes as chocolate does. It tends to form hard lumps when it sits for a while so you may need to press it through a wire mesh strainer with the back of a spoon before using it.

FLAVORINGS are essential to some dessert recipes, but finding flavorings that fit your diet can be problematic. Most flavorings are extracted in alcohol. If grain alcohol is used, the flavorings may be a problem for gluten-intolerant individuals, and all alcohol is a problem for those who are allergic to yeast. Frontier Natural Products™ produces alcohol-free natural flavorings which are made using glycerin instead of alcohol and are widely available in health food stores. Although you may need to order online, The Spicery Shoppe™ produces a wide variety of alcohol-free flavorings. To order either of these brands of flavorings, see "Sources," page 229.

If you are allergic to both alcohol and glycerin and want to make vanilla ice cream, use a **VANILLA BEAN**. The three vanilla ice cream recipes in this book ("Easy Vanilla Ice Cream," page 100, vanilla "Frozen Yogurt," page 106, and "Rich Vanilla Ice Cream," page 224) give the option of using a vanilla bean to flavor the ice cream and instructions on how to extract the vanilla flavor directly from the bean into the ice cream mixture. If you cannot find vanilla beans locally, see "Sources," page 229, for ordering information. For baking, if you are allergic to both alcohol and glycerin, you can omit the flavoring the recipe calls for without any problems arising with the recipe.

CITRUS OILS are pure oils from the rind of citrus fruits and are very strong – a little goes a long way. You can order them from cooking catalogues such as the King Arthur Flour Baker's Catalogue. They are convenient to have on hand as a quick substitute for lemon, orange, or lime zest. For ordering information, see "Sources," page 229.

SWEETENERS

Sweeteners are arguably the most crucial ingredients in this book because these recipes are designed to satisfy the sweet tooth in a healthy way, to be sugar-free yet bring pleasure. (For more about the health implications of sweeteners, see pages 236 to 240). A major problem with desserts purchased at the grocery store or bakery is that they contain a large amount of sugar or high fructose corn sweetener. These sweeteners are highly refined and have been stripped of the vitamins and minerals their plant of origin contained. Sugar and high fructose corn sweetener are high-moderate to high on the glycemic index, and thus may cause blood sugar to rise rapidly and then fall faster and farther. This is bad news for weight watchers and diabetics.

Refined white sugar (sucrose) used to be the sweetener most commonly used in commercially made foods, but now it has been replaced with less-expensive high fructose corn syrup in most processed foods. Avoiding high fructose corn syrup is a strong motivation for making your own desserts! High fructose corn syrup is made from corn by a complex chemical process that removes nutrients (including the chromium our bodies require to metabolize sugars) and may add harmful substances such as mercury. (See page 240 for more about this). It is about 45 percent glucose and 55 percent fructose so its composition is not that much different from sucrose (table sugar), in which each molecule is made of two joined single-sugar units, one of fructose and one of glucose. (Thus sucrose is 50 percent glucose and 50 percent fructose). However, because the single sugars in high fructose corn syrup are free rather than joined as in sucrose, they enter the bloodstream extremely rapidly, so high fructose corn syrup has a very high score on the glycemic index. High fructose corn syrup has been linked to high triglyceride levels in the blood which may contribute to heart disease. In addition, the corn from which high fructose corn syrup is made is usually a genetically modified strain. The increasing prevalence of genetically modified foods in our diets is suspected of having a link to the rising incidence of food allergies.

Sugar is also highly refined. The chromium necessary to metabolize it and other minerals, vitamins, and fiber present in the original sugar beet or sugar cane have been removed. It can cause a major rise in blood sugar levels and also can have a profound effect on intestinal flora which increases problems with *Candida*. Therefore, the recipes in this book avoid sugar.

The sweeteners used in the book are not highly refined and most of them are low to moderate on the glycemic index scale. Fruit sweeteners contain mostly fructose, a single sugar that must be processed by the liver into glucose before we can use it. The necessity for this conversion slows down the rate at which it enters the bloodstream and moderates its impact on blood sugar levels. Of course, large quantities of any simple sugar (i.e. any of the sweeteners used in this book) can stimulate the growth of intestinal *Candida* and affect blood sugar levels. Thus, all of these sweeteners should be used in moderation by diabetics, weight watchers, and those with candidiasis or blood sugar control issues. Be sure to ask your doctor about how much and how often you should eat desserts. Probably none of us should eat dessert – other than fresh fruit – every day! But hopefully very few readers will be told by their doctor that they must avoid a small serving of dessert on their birthday.

AGAVE is the newest among healthy sweeteners and is extremely versatile as well as being delicious in dessert recipes. Its flavor is neutral, without any of the tangy overtones of some fruit sweeteners, so it doesn't overshadow the other flavors in a dessert. Because of its pure sweet flavor, no one will know that you did not use sugar in an agave-sweetened dessert recipe. It is sweeter than sugar so you can use less, thus saving calories. Agave is very low on the glycemic index (11 on a scale where glucose is 100, source: mendosa.com) and about 90% of the sugar in agave is fructose so it does not cause major and rapid swings in blood sugar and insulin levels. It retains the nutrients of the plant in the cactus family from which it is made and therefore contains calcium, iron, magnesium, potassium and other nutrients.

Although it is a liquid sweetener, it will not crystallize with long storage. It is less viscous than honey and thus mixes into other ingredients very easily. Agave becomes sticky when boiled and does not behave like a sugar solution in candy-making, so it cannot be used to make fondant, taffy, caramel, or other candies. However, its stickiness can be an asset in some recipes such as "Sticky Buns," page 138. The color of agave becomes darker when it is baked at a relatively high temperature for a long time. This is not an issue for quick-cooking desserts such as cookies, but if you are making a light colored cake, the color may become brown near the pan or even throughout the cake. Therefore, if you want your lemon cake or other light cake to retain a light color, use the fruit sweetener option given in the recipe. If you don't care about appearances, light-colored cakes are delicious made with agave. In darker cakes, such as spice cakes and chocolate cakes, you will not notice a difference in the color of the cake near the pan.

Agave is available in several different varieties including light, amber, dark, and raw. I have used all of them and they can be used interchangeably in the recipes in this book. The amber and dark varieties have a little more color and flavor, but the flavor level is mild and will not overpower other flavors in most desserts. Agave is becoming very easy to find in grocery stores as well as health food stores in Colorado. I expect that it will soon be common throughout the country because I just learned that the Madhava™ Honey company has successfully marketed their agave to WalMart and the Kroger grocery store chain. If you cannot purchase Madhava™ agave locally, see "Sources," page 233 for ordering information.

Some brands of agave have received bad press recently, so be careful to purchase agave from a reliable source. Several years ago, the FDA found a company guilty of adulterating their agave with corn syrup, and the owners fled the country. More recently, a company which produced agave went out of business because it became public that their production methods involved chemicals.

I use agave produced by Madhava™ Honey. (All of the agave recipes in this book were developed with it). Because I am quite allergic to corn but do not react to Madhava™ agave, I can personally vouch for their agave being corn-free. Madhava™ uses a thermal production method which does not employ any chemicals to break the long chains of sugar units in the juice from the agave plant into single sugar molecules.

LIQUID FRUIT SWEETENERS retain many of the nutrients of whole fruit and make delicious healthy desserts. The least concentrated of these are pureed fruits and fruit juice concentrates. Apple juice concentrate is used in many of the recipes in this book. I routinely keep a can of frozen apple juice concentrate in my refrigerator so I'm ready to bake any time I want.

More concentrated liquid fruit sweeteners include Fruit Sweet™, which is a blend of pear and pineapple juices, Pear Sweet™ and Grape Sweet™. With these sweeteners, you can make desserts which taste very similar to sugar-containing desserts. In most recipes no one will know there is no sugar. These sweeteners are used as the only sweetening option in only a few recipes in this book because the large health food store chains usually do not carry them, but they can be ordered easily. See "Sources," page 233, for information about ordering these sweeteners from Wax Orchards™.

HONEY is given as an alternative sweetener to agave and Fruit Sweet™ in many recipes in this book because it is so readily available. Although it has a more pronounced flavor than the other sweeteners above, it is still delicious in desserts. It has not been stripped of its natural nutrients. It is higher on the glycemic index than agave or fruit sweeteners (honey is 58 on a scale where glucose is 100, or higher for some varieties) so it may be less desirable than agave or fruit sweeteners for diabetics or weight watchers.

MOLASSES comes from sugar cane or sugar beets but is a less refined sweetener than sugar. It adds moistness and flavor to baked goods. Molasses is used in the gingerbread and shoo-fly pie cake recipes in this book. Although it contains sucrose* and is a potent sweetener which may have more effect on blood sugar levels than fruit sweeteners, unlike white sugar, it has not been stripped of its mineral and nutrient content.

RICE SYRUP is a sweetener which may be allowed on gluten-free diets if it is made without barley or other grains. However, most rice syrup is made with barley malt and is therefore not gluten-free, so it is not used in these recipes. It is less sweet than fruit sweeteners. Baked products made with rice syrup do not brown as much as those made with other sweeteners.

MAPLE SUGAR and SYRUP are used in a few recipes in this book. Like white table sugar, they contain sucrose* and thus are higher than fruit sweeteners and agave on the glycemic index. However, they have not been refined and stripped of their natural nutrients.

DATE SUGAR is ground dried dates. It is a concentrated sweetener which is very useful in recipes where more sweetness is desired. The fiber in date sugar helps keep baked goods moist. It is the least refined dry sweetener used in this book and adds potassium, magnesium, iron, B vitamins, and other nutrients as well as fiber to desserts.

SUGAR ALCOHOLS such as sorbitol, maltitol, erythritol, xylitol, etc. are usually made from corn which is a common allergen. Because they are not well absorbed, they can have a laxative effect if eaten in more than small quantities and can affect intestinal flora. They are used only in the chocolate and carob chip recipe in this book. One brand

*****Note about sucrose:** The sucrose molecule is made up of two single sugars joined together. These sugars units must be separated from each other in the intestine before we can absorb them. If this does not happen quickly, unfriendly bacteria and yeast may ferment the sucrose, which can exacerbate candidaiasis or other types of intestinal dysbiosis. For more about this, see pages 236 to 240.

of **XYLITOL**, The Ultimate Sweetener™, is made from birch trees rather than corn. Thus it is an option for those who are allergic to corn and want to make their own carob or chocolate chips. See "Sources," page 234, for ordering information.

STEVIA, a non-nutritive herb useful for sweetening desserts, has been used in Japan, South America, and other parts of the world without problems for hundreds of years. It is approved by the FDA for use as a supplement and as an "additive" in soda pop, but they have ruled against labeling it as a sweetener.

This herb is derived from the plant *Stevia rebaudiana* which is in the composite (lettuce) family. It is available in several forms; the white powder is used in a few recipes in this book because it is the purest form of the sweetening agents found in the plant. Most stevia has a slight licorice-like taste which is most noticeable in bland recipes and almost undetectable in recipes containing strongly flavored ingredients such as cranberries and carob. However, recently a "next generation" white stevia powder has been introduced that is treated during production with an enzyme that reduces the licorice taste. At this time, this type of stevia is available only from health care providers. See page 234 for more information about obtaining pure stevia powder.

Stevia can be a lifesaver for those who would like to have pumpkin pie on Thanksgiving or dessert on other special occasions but cannot have any nutritive sweeteners due to severe *Candidiasis* or diabetes. If you must avoid nutritive sweteners in general, see the pumpkin pie recipe on page 72 and the list of stevia-sweetened desserts on page 257 of the general index.

FLOURS

Alternative flours are the main ingredients in most of the recipes in this book. As you become more familiar with baking with these flours, you will realize that although they may behave differently than wheat in baking, they still are delicious and produce wonderful desserts.

Each of the flour-containing recipes in this book indicates if it is gluten-free in a shaded box at the top of the recipe. Recipes that are made with gluten-free grains or or non-grain alternatives are marked with this symbol:

Gluten-Free

Qualifications on whether the recipe is gluten-free, such as "if made with amaranth," also are included in the shaded box. Recipes thar are gluten-free because they do not contain any flour (such as ice cream recipes) are also marked with this symbol. If this symbol does not appear at the top of a recipe, those with celiac disease should not use it.

Purchase high quality flour and you will save money, time and trouble in the long run. Unlike bulk-bin flour, most high quality alternative flour is consistent from bag to bag. Authentic Foods™, Arrowhead Mills™ and Bob's Red Mill™ are brands that I use and recommend for most types of alternative flour. It is not cost effective to save a few pennies by purchasing an unknown brand from a health food store bulk bin if you end up with a failed dessert that you have to throw away.

If you bake with spelt, always use Purity Food™ brand flour. I have encountered more variability in spelt flour than in other types of flour, even using reputable brands. This is because spelt flour is quite soluble – it literally dissolves in liquid – and this characteristic varies from crop to crop and year to year. (For more about spelt see pages 25 to 26 and 241 to 242). If you use other brands of spelt flour for non-yeast baked goods, you will probably have to add more flour than the recipes call for and have less satisfactory results. If you use other brands for yeast bread, don't be surprised by collapsed loaves.

TRUE GRAIN FLOURS

Many of the flours used in this book are milled from true grains, that is, plants that are members of the cereal family. Those in the same tribe of the grain family as wheat contain gluten. Although it is not in the same tribe, oat contains a gluten-like protein. Some celiac patients are able to tolerate oats, and some cannot. If you have celiac disease, ask your doctor if you can eat oats before trying the oat-containing recipes in this book. Because some celiacs can have oats, I have listed them with the gluten-free grains on page 27 rather than in the section below.

GLUTEN-CONTAINING GRAIN FLOURS

People who are allergic to wheat but are not sensitive to gluten may be able to eat some of the following grains:

KAMUT is a golden yellow grain with excellent flavor. It is very closely related to wheat in its biological classification, being in the same genus but a different species. However, some people who are allergic to wheat can eat kamut without reacting. Kamut seems to be tolerated by fewer wheat-sensitive individuals than spelt however. Kamut makes good yeast breads and very tasty non-yeast baked goods although they are likely to be rather dense.

RYE is a very versatile, tasty grain. It contains a fair amount of gluten and behaves much like whole wheat flour in baking. It has a stronger flavor than some of the other grains but is delicious in breads. Rye is in the same tribe of the grain family as barley, spelt, kamut, and wheat.

SPELT is probably the most versatile non-wheat grain. It is very closely related to wheat in its biological classification, being *Triticum spelta* while wheat is *Triticum aestivum*. (See "About Spelt" on pages 241 to 242 for more about this). In spite of the close relationship, spelt is tolerated by many wheat-sensitive individuals. Cakes made with spelt flour tend to be a little drier than those made with other grains, and so the recipes may contain more oil. Spelt makes excellent yeast bread because it is as high in gluten as wheat although its gluten is more soluble. You may purchase sifted or white spelt flour which has had the bran sifted out but is not processed in any other way. Baked goods made with white spelt often are nearly indistinguishable from standard baked goods. Therefore, if you can eat spelt, have it on the days that you have guests. They will not even know that the dessert or bread you made with white spelt flour is different from what they normally eat.

All of the spelt recipes in this book were developed using Purity Foods™ flour. Purity Foods mills its flour from a European strain of spelt that is higher in protein than most spelt flours. In the years since I first began baking with spelt, several other companies have also begun to produce spelt flour. These other flours do not work as well in the recipes in this book and are unsuitable for yeast breads. If you use them in non-yeast baked goods, you will have to add more flour than the recipes call for and expect less satisfactory results. It is worth the effort to get Purity Foods flour. Many health food stores carry it. If yours doesn't, ask them to get it in or see "Sources," page 230, for ordering information.

BARLEY is a pleasant tasting gluten-containing grain. Although it in the same tribe of the grain family as rye, spelt, kamut, and wheat, it contains considerably less gluten. Therefore, stabilizing ingredients such as guar or xanthum gum are needed to make yeast bread with barley. Baked goods made with barley flour have a delicious flavor but tend to be crumbly. However, its flaky texture makes barley one of my favorite flours for pie crusts.

GLUTEN-FREE GRAIN FLOURS

Several of the flours which can be used on a gluten-free diet are botanically classified as members of the grain family and therefore are true grains. All of the gluten-free grains are more crumbly than wheat in baked goods but have good flavor. The gluten-free true grains used in the recipes in this book are:

RICE is used in a few recipes in this book. Because most commercially available baked goods are based on rice, people who are gluten-intolerant tend to get an overabundance of rice, so this book strives for a counterbalance with non-rice gluten-free recipes. Although rice flour is bland, it is pleasant tasting, but it tends to be gritty in some baked goods unless used with a preponderance of other types of flour or starch. Both brown rice (whole grain) and white rice (refined) flour are widely available in health food stores.

TEFF has been difficult to find in the past, but now Bob's Red Mill™ has made it easily available. If your health food store does not carry it, it is likely that they do carry some of Bob's other products and can easily get it in for you. Teff is a little less bland than the other gluten-free grains but is still delicious. A friend who is a great fan of teff shortbread (recipe on page 174) describes teff as "sweet and less strongly flavored than buckwheat." It does tend to be a little gritty but makes very nice baked products.

MILLET has a delicious flavor. However, it is crumbly and tends to produce very dry baked goods no matter how much oil or pureed fruit you use in the recipe. Millet flour is usually available at health food stores. If your store doesn't carry it, you or your store can order it. For ordering information, see "Sources," page 230.

SORGHUM, which is also called **MILO** or **JOWAR**, is a sweet and delicious non-gluten grain. Like millet, it tends to produce dry baked goods. It is often used to make sorghum molasses and has traditionally been fed to cattle. Formerly very difficult to find, it now is produced by Authentic Foods™ who offer a super-fine grind of sorghum flour that is much less gritty than other brands of sorghum flour that I have used. If your health food store does not carry this super-fine sorghum flour, ask them to get it in for you. For ordering information, see "Sources," page 230.

OATS have recently been allowed on gluten-free diets by some doctors. This grain contains a low level of gluten-like proteins so it is possible that not all celiacs will tolerate it. Oats are delicious and have a familiar flavor but can yield heavy baked products. An occasional batch of oat flour may produce a gummy texture in baked goods. However, oatmeal is a great ingredient for topping fruit desserts and is used in several such recipes in this book. Oat flour and oats also make excellent cookies.

NON-GRAIN FLOURS

The non-grains are not botanically related to wheat. Many of them are the seeds of the plants that they grow on; therefore they are very nutritious and high in protein. In the recipes in this book, the seed flours are often used with small quantities of a starch to help them stick together. The non-grains used in this book include:

AMARANTH is in the same botanical order as quinoa, although it is not in the same food family. Because it is not a grain, it is a welcome dietary addition for those allergic to all grains. It makes very tasty baked goods. Purchase it at a store that refrigerates its flour and refrigerate or freeze it at home since it may develop an unpleasantly strong flavor if stored too long at room temperature. An occasional batch of amaranth flour will yield gummy pancakes or sandwich bread, but the recipes included in this book are not prone to this problem.

QUINOA boasts a high content of high-quality protein. Due to its amino acid balance, it is one of the best protein sources among plant foods. For this reason it is very satisfying to eat; quinoa baked goods really "stick with you." Those allergic to all grains will find quinoa a welcome dietary staple. It has a distinctive but not unpleasant taste so it is best used with other strongly flavored ingredients such as cinnamon, sesame seeds and carob. Quinoa flour is excellent in baked goods of all kinds and makes good yeast bread. Whole grain quinoa has a natural soapy coating on it, so before you cook it, put it in a strainer and rinse it under running water until the water is no longer sudsy. This coating protects the plant from insects. Quinoa is in the same food family as spinach, beets, and Swiss chard.

BUCKWHEAT is an extremely versatile non-grain flour. It is excellent in waffles and pancakes, and a chocolate-eating celiac friend of mine raves about the chocolate buckwheat brownies in this book. In some recipes buckwheat can have a strong flavor which is especially noticeable to those who have never eaten it before. However, in the interest of having desserts that everyone can eat included in this book, some buckwheat recipes are included. If you find the flavor of buckwheat too strong, it may be because commercially produced buckwheat flour is ground from roasted buckwheat groats. You may wish to purchase raw buckwheat groats and grind them into flour in your blender or food processor. Try getting used to buckwheat by making the chocolate brownie recipe on page 169 in which the flavor of the chocolate moderates buckwheat's distinctive taste. Buckwheat is in the same food family as rhubarb.

NUT MEALS such as almond, pecan, and hazelnut meal are great additions to baked goods and are used in some of the cookie recipes in this book. You also can make delicious crunchy waffles from almond meal and a starch. See the recipe on page 117.

Several white, highly refined starches are commonly used in gluten-free cooking. They include **ARROWROOT, TAPIOCA STARCH** (which is the same as tapioca flour), **CORNSTARCH,** and **BEAN STARCH.** These starches serve as binders in gluten-free baking and can also be used as thickeners for sauces and fruit fillings for pies and cobblers. Arrowroot and tapioca starch can be substituted for each other in equal quantities when baking. Sauces thickened with tapioca tend to be a little more ropy than those thickened with arrowroot, and you made need slightly more tapioca than arrowroot. Sauces and desserts thickened with arrowroot may become thinner if overcooked. For this reason, some recipes in this book list tapioca starch as the only option for thickening. Quick-cooking granules of tapioca (Minute™ tapioca) are also used in this book to thicken puddings and pie or cobbler filings.

POTATO FLOUR and **POTATO STARCH** (also called potato starch flour) may also be used in allergy and gluten-free baking. They are not the same thing, however, and cannot be used interchangeably. Potato flour is made from whole potatoes and retains the nutritional value of potatoes including considerable protein. For baking, it must be used with eggs (usually it is folded into beaten egg whites) or the baked product may end up like mashed potatoes on the inside. Potato starch is a highly refined starch, much like the starches in the preceding paragraph, except that it attracts and holds moisture, or is hygroscopic. Both of these ingredients must be used in small amounts in most recipes or their hygroscopic nature may cause a gooey texture in the final product. Potato starch or flour is commonly used as a binder in rice yeast breads. They are used in the rice sweet breads in this book.

FATS

Fat makes our food better tasting and more satisfying. It gives baked desserts a tender and moist crumb. Because fat takes longer to digest, fat-containing foods "stick to the ribs." Of course, we should not eat too much of even good fats or we – and others – may be able to see the fat really sticking to our ribs! A book I recently read categorized fats as "the good, the bad, and the ugly," indicating that there are several types of fats that have a range of effects on our health.

The ugly fats, which are unnatural, chemically hydrogenated oils, are not used in any of the recipes in this book. One of the reasons this book was written was to allow readers to have desserts which do not contain hydrogenated fat. Hydrogenated fats may be completely saturated (hydrogen has been added to all of the double bonds in the fat) or partially saturated (hydrogen has been added to only some of the double bonds). Trans fats are partially hydrogenated fats and are the type of fat which is most detrimental to our health.

Naturally saturated fats are forbidden for some people such as those with heart disease. They include butter, the marbling in meats, and naturally saturated plant oils such as coconut and palm oil. Although a small amount of naturally occurring saturated fat may not be unhealthy for everyone, some have labeled all saturated fats "bad" for everyone regardless of their source.

An intermediate category of fats includes most of the vegetable oils commonly used in commercially made foods such as corn, soy, and safflower oil. Although they are not detrimental to health, these oils are high in omega-6 fatty acids. Excess consumption of these fatty acids creates a problem if they are not balanced by sufficient omega-3 fatty acids in our diets. However we do need some omega-6 fatty acids.

Good fats are vegetable oils which are high in omega-3 fatty acids, such as canola and walnut oil, and those oils high in heart-healthy monounsaturated fats such as olive oil. Our bodies need a few teaspoons per day of omega-3 rich oils for optimal health. I recommend that you do most of your cooking with canola or walnut and olive oil because if you eat commercially prepared foods at all, you are likely to be getting an overabundance of omega-6 fats. Therefore, using omega-3 fat rich oils at home will improve this balance. Olive oil is more heat stable than many oils and thus is ideal for such uses as sautéing foods.

The healthiest fats are oils high in the types of omega-3 fatty acids that we can use as they are without our bodies having to convert them to the biologically active forms needed for essential body functions. Fish oil is the most notable source of these fatty acids. You can promote optimum health by regularly eating fatty fish such as salmon or taking fish oil supplements to get this type of fat.

Most of the baking recipes in this book contain fat; the vast majority of them call for good fats such as vegetable oils. However, the "Cookies" and "Especially for Guests" chapters contain a few recipes made with saturated fat such as butter or Spectrum Naturals™ non-hydrogenated shortening. These are natural fats, not chemically saturated (hydrogenated) unnatural fats but should be used only occasionally for best health.

A few years ago the FDA began requiring that foods be labeled to indicate if they contain trans fats. The response of the food industry was to replace trans fats (partially hydrogenated fats) in many foods with fully hydrogenated fats. These fats are chemically produced, unnatural to our bodies, and are probably almost as bad for our health as trans fats. Do not be fooled by the new shortening cans that say "No Trans Fats." They contain fully hydrogenated fat instead of partially hydrogenated fat. If you want to use shortening to make to-die-for pie crust, use Spectrum Naturals™ non-hydrogenated shortening, which is natural palm oil, and the recipe on page 208.

LEAVENINGS AND BINDERS

Leavenings are the ingredients that make baked products rise. They include baking powder, baking soda combined with an acid ingredient, and yeast. Binders help the leavenings "work" by trapping the gas the leavenings produce. They are not needed when you bake with wheat because the gluten in wheat flour forms sheets that trap the gas. Binders include eggs, starches (discussed on page 28), and fibers such as guar gum and xanthum gum (discussed on the next page).

BAKING POWDER is a combination of acid and basic components that, when moistened, produces gas to make baked goods rise in baking. Some brands of baking powder contain aluminum which should probably be avoided for best health. Most commercial baking powder contains cornstarch. If you are sensitive to corn and need to use baking powder, use Featherweight™ baking powder which contains potato starch instead. Featherweight™ baking powder is also aluminum and sodium-free. Because many people are sensitive to corn starch or potato starch, baking powder is used in only a few recipes in this book. Since most recipes can be leavened just as well with baking soda plus vitamin C, that leavening system is built into most of the recipes in this book because it will rarely make a recipe unacceptable for anyone.

BAKING SODA is pure sodium bicarbonate and is almost universally tolerated by people with severe food allergies. For those on rotation diets, it is usually allowed every day of the rotation cycle. It must be used in conjunction with an acid ingredient to make baked goods rise. The acid ingredients commonly used in normal baking include buttermilk, lemon juice or other fruit juices, and cream of tartar. For the very allergic, **UNBUFFERED VITAMIN C POWDER** is the best way to provide the acid component of the leavening process. Therefore, most of the recipes in this book contain a built-in baking powder made of baking soda and unbuffered vitamin C powder.

When purchasing vitamin C to use for leavening, be sure that the vitamin C powder or crystals that you use are unbuffered i.e., that they do not contain minerals to moderate their acidity. If you are allergic to corn, also make sure they are corn-free. See "Sources," page 232, for information about ordering cassava-source unbuffered vitamin C.

BAKER'S YEAST is what makes most commercially made bread rise and is available in many forms. Active dry yeast is yeast that has been freeze-dried to retain its activity. An expiration date is usually stamped on the package and the yeast should be good until that date if you store it in the refrigerator after opening it. Active dry yeast is available in ¼ ounce (2¼ teaspoon) packets or 4 ounce jars in most grocery stores. In addition, you can purchase it in one pound bags and store the yeast in your freezer. Do not thaw and refreeze this yeast; instead, occasionally take out a small amount to use within a few weeks and keep it in a jar in the refrigerator. Leave the remainder of the yeast frozen. Red Star™ active dry yeast is free of gluten and preservatives and works well in bread machines as well as in the recipes in this book. Instant or quick-rise yeasts leaven bread more rapidly than active dry yeast. They are useful for making bread more quickly. These fast types of yeast are not recommended for gluten-free breads because their structure is more fragile. If quick-rise yeasts are used with gluten-free breads, the bread may over-rise and then collapse during baking. However, if you are baking wheat-containing bread, you may wish to use SAF™ instant yeast, which makes excellent bread. SAF™ also makes a sweetener and acid-resistant yeast called SAF™ Gold which is useful for some sweet breads and sourdough breads.

EGGS and **FRUIT PUREES** are binders that are often used in standard baking. These ingredients help hold your baked goods together while also adding nutritional value and flavor. If you are using eggs in a yeast bread recipe and have forgotten to remove them from the refrigerator early to warm them to room temperature, place them in a bowl of warm water for about five minutes while you are measuring out the other ingredients. Then they should be warm enough to be used in the bread.

GUAR GUM and **XANTHUM GUM** are two types of soluble fiber used as binders in gluten-free baking. Both can be fairly allergenic, so I use them only in yeast breads where they are actually essential. If you do not tolerate one of them, you can substitute the other in the same amount in recipes. Guar gum is made from a legume. Xanthum gum is derived from a type of bacteria, *Xanthomonas compestris,* which may be grown on a corn-containing media. Therefore it is potentially a problem for those who are very sensitive to corn.

INGREDIENT SUBSTITIONS

When you bake for a food allergy or gluten free diet, you might need to purchase many new ingredients. If you are missing an ingredient, you may wonder if you can substitute something else for that new food you do not have on hand. Substitutions are tricky in allergy and gluten-free baking. The recipes in this book should work as written (although an unusual batch of flour from a health food store bulk bin can upset any recipe), but if you substitute, there are no guarantees.

People call me and say, "I've got your recipe made with quinoa flour and I want to make it with oat flour. How can I do this?" I usually can't give them a definite answer although I often try to make suggestions that may or may not work. In my experience, there is no rule or conversion factor for substitutions between any two types of flour that always works predictably.

The bottom line on flour substitutions is this: be prepared to tweak a recipe made with a substitute flour several times before it is right, although some substitutions may never work. If you are looking for a recipe to make, for example, crackers with buckwheat or tortillas with garbanzo flour, see *The Ultimate Food Allergy Cookbook and Survival Guide* as described on the last pages of this book. Because that book is designed to be the ultimate resource for people whose diets may be extremely limited, I attempted to make each type of flour (including rarely eaten foods such as tuber flours, chestnut flour, starch flours, and the less common non-gluten grain flours) into as many types of recipes as possible and only omitted a certain recipe if it really was not possible to make. For example, the only reason the book does not contain a recipe for sorghum yeast bread is because I was unable, after many tries, to make a loaf that did not collapse. However, it does have a sorghum non-yeast bread recipe made with eggs to help hold it together. (This is one of the very few egg-containing recipes in the book). There are also recipes for fruited sorghum non-yeast bread (where the fiber in the fruit keeps it together) and sorghum muffins, crackers, tortillas, pancakes, cake, and cookies. As mentioned earlier in this chapter, buckwheat can be bitter in some recipes, so buckwheat recipes can be hard to find. However, those who eat buckwheat often get used to its flavor. Since there are severely allergic people who can eat only one or two grain alternatives, buckwheat recipes that might be considered marginal on taste by people who can eat more are included in *The Ultimate Food Allergy Cookbook and Survival Guide.* You can save a lot of time and wasted ingredients by getting the recipe you really need rather than experimenting with flour substitutions.

Home ground flour may also behave differently than commercially ground flour, and it can vary from batch to batch of grain. If you use either very finely milled flour or coarsely milled or blender-ground flour you will have to change the amount of liquid used in the recipe. Unless you have time to experiment with each new batch of grain when you grind your own flour, you will get the most predictable baking results if you purchase flour from a reliable commercial source.

Unlike wheat flour, milk is an ingredient where substitutions in baking recipes usually work. In most recipes, you can replace the milk called for with an equal amount of water. Sometimes you can replace milk with fruit juice, but the acidity of the juice can affect the leavening process and result in a collapse of your baked product. Gluten-free yeast breads, in which the protein content contributed by the milk helps strengthen the structure of the bread, can be an exception to the rule that water can be substituted for milk.

In allergy baking, eggs can usually be replaced with an equal volume of water if the recipe is not depending on the egg for structure. However, in a recipe made with a gluten-free or low gluten flour, the egg sometimes is serving to replace part of the structure normally provided by gluten, and replacing the egg with water may lead to a collapse of your bread or cake.

Sometimes sweeteners can be substituted for each other. For instance, agave, Fruit Sweet™ and honey have about the same sweetening power; therefore, many of the recipes in this book give you a choice between these sweeteners. Fruit juice concentrates are less sweet and more acidic, and some, such as pineapple juice concentrate, contain a fair amount of fiber, so they can rarely be used in place of agave, Fruit Sweet™ or honey. (However, there are a few recipes in this book where boiled down fruit juice concentrate is given as a substitute for agave, Fruit Sweet™ or honey). A given fruit juice concentrate often cannot be substituted for another fruit juice concentrate because of differences in their acidity and fiber levels. Obviously, dry sweeteners cannot be substituted for liquid sweeteners without making major (and often unpredictable) adjustments in the level of other liquid ingredients in the recipe and in the leavening ingredients.

The best advice for success with baking recipes is – don't substitute unless you're willing to make a recipe multiple times before it succeeds and are prepared to encounter an occasional recipe that is impossible to convert. With non-wheat flours, the leavening process is easy to upset. If you really have an urge to substitute, make ice cream or a non-baked recipe. For best success, measure accurately, mix correctly (see pages 13 and 14), and then enjoy the desserts you make on the first try.

Simple Fruit Desserts

The most basic and delicious of all desserts are those made from fresh fruit at the peak of its flavor. This chapter contains dessert recipes that are made entirely or mostly from fruit, so they are tops for nutrition as well as for speed and ease of preparation. For other fruit desserts, see pages 45 to 61 and 68 to 73.

Baked Apples or Pears

Gluten-Free

4 large baking apples* or pears
½ cup thawed apple juice concentrate, apple juice, pear juice, or water OR ¼
    cup agave, Fruit Sweet™ or honey plus ¼ cup water
½ teaspoon cinnamon (optional)
¼ cup raisins (optional)

Core the apples or pears and put them in a 2½ quart glass casserole dish with a lid. Pour in the juice, sweetener, and/or water and sprinkle the cinnamon down the centers of the fruit. Stuff the fruit with raisins, if desired. Bake at 350°F for 40 to 50 minutes for the apples or 1 to 1½ hours for the pears or until the fruit is tender when pierced with a fork. Makes 4 servings.

*Note on baking apples: Some varieties of apples hold their shape well when they are baked, such as Rome, Pink Lady, and Granny Smith. If you're planning to make this dessert for guests and will be buying the apples especially for baking, chose a baking apple. However, if you have old apples in your refrigerator that you want to use up, this recipe is a good way to use them.

Baked apples and pears are a delicious addition to an oven meal. Save time by baking a main dish, potatoes or a grain, a non-starchy vegetable, and a dessert such as this or "Quick and Easy Fruit Tapioca" (page 36) together in the oven. This frees the cook to do other things. For more about oven meals, see *Allergy and Celiac Diets With Ease: Money and Time Saving Solutions for Food Allergy and Gluten-Free Diets* as described on the last pages of this book.

Old Fashioned Apple Sauce

Gluten-Free

When I was a child, my mother and I used to spend hours talking and peeling apples from our tree. In addition to making great family memories, we made applesauce that was so flavorful that it bears little resemblance to what comes in a jar nowadays. For that old fashioned flavor, make this recipe in the fall using apples that have just been picked or purchased from a local farmers' market.

4 large apples* weighing about 1½ to 2 pounds
¾ cup apple juice concentrate OR ½ cup apple juice concentrate plus
    ¼ cup water
¼ teaspoon cinnamon
⅛ teaspoon nutmeg (optional)

Peel, quarter, and core the apples. Put them in a saucepan with the apple juice concentrate or concentrate and water. (Use all apple juice concentrate if the apples are tart; use part concentrate and part water if they are sweet). Bring the apples to a boil and then reduce the heat and simmer them, stirring occasionally, for 15 to 20 minutes or until they are tender. Puree them with a blender, food processor, or hand blender.

For an even more delicious old-fashioned taste and texture, cook the apples for 30 to 40 minutes or until they are very soft. Stir them every few minutes and add water if they begin to dry out and are on the verge of sticking to the pan. When they are very soft, use a spoon to cut them up and mash them into a chunky applesauce consistency in the pan. Makes about 3 to 3½ cups of applesauce.

*Note on apples for applesauce: Jonathan apples are my favorite variety to use for a tangy taste in applesauce. However, they have a very short season and do not keep well, so if you put them in your refrigerator for a few weeks and then want to make applesauce, they may be brown and mealy on the inside. For a less tart flavor, mix Jonathans with McIntosh apples. Other good varieties of apples for applesauce include Gala, Fuji, Pink Lady, and Honeycrisp. Try them all and/or use a mixture of different varieties to see which you like best. To get rid of assorted leftover apples in your refrigerator, use them in this recipe. If your applesauce made from older apples lacks flavor, add lemon juice to taste.

Quick and Easy Fruit Tapioca

Gluten-Free

This dessert is very easy to make using canned fruit and is a wonderful treat with an oven meal. Put it in the oven to bake with a main dish, oven grain, and oven vegetable.*

    1 16 to 20-ounce can of fruit, such as juice packed sliced peaches, pears or
        pineapple chunks, not drained, OR water-packed tart pie cherries, drained
    ¼ cup quick-cooking (Minute™) tapioca
    1 cup water, apple, or pineapple juice with the peaches, pears, or pineapple,
        OR 1 cup apple juice concentrate plus ½ cup water or reserved cherry
        juice with the cherries

If you are using the cherries, drain and reserve the juice. Stir together the fruit (peaches, pears, or pineapple with their juice, cherries without), tapioca, and water and/or fruit juice in a 1½-quart casserole dish. Bake at 350°F for 40 to 60 minutes or until the tapioca is clear. Makes 4 servings.

*Note about oven meals: For more about using oven meals to save time and effort, see *Allergy and Celiac Diets With Ease: Money and Time Saving Solutions for Food Allergy and Gluten-Free Diets* as described on the last pages of this book.

Fresh Fruit Tapioca

Gluten-Free

Although this recipe is not quite as quick to make as the previous recipe, if you have in-season fresh fruit in abundance, this is the recipe for you. To use up ripening fruit, double or triple the recipe and freeze the leftover tapioca for a wintertime treat.

    About 2 pounds of apples*, peaches, or nectarines (3½ cups of sliced fruit)
    ½ cup apple juice concentrate, thawed
    1½ tablespoons quick-cooking (Minute™) tapioca
    ¾ teaspoon cinnamon with the apples or ⅛ teaspoon nutmeg with the peaches
        or nectarines

Peel, core, and slice the fruit. To cook this dessert on the stove top, combine ¼ cup of the apple juice concentrate, the fruit, and the spice in a large saucepan. Bring them to a boil over medium heat, reduce the heat, and simmer until the fruit is tender, about 15 to 25 minutes Near the end of the cooking time, combine the tapioca with the remaining ¼ cup apple juice concentrate and allow it to stand for at least 5 minutes. Stir the tapioca mixture into the fruit when it is tender or near-tender. Return the pan to a boil, and simmer for an additional 5 minutes. Let it stand for at least 20 minutes before serving.

To cook this dessert in the oven as part of an oven meal, combine the peeled and sliced fruit, tapioca, juice and spice in a 1½-quart casserole dish. Bake at 350°F for 40 to 60 minutes, or until the tapioca is clear. Makes about 4 servings.

*Note on apples: Jonathan apples are especially good in this recipe as are any of the new sweet-tart varieties such as Pink Ladies.

Easy Applesauce Tapioca

Gluten-Free

1 tablespoon quick-cooking (Minute™) tapioca
⅓ cup apple juice concentrate
1 teaspoon cinnamon
1½ cups of unsweetened applesauce (half of a 25-ounce jar of applesauce)

Combine the tapioca and apple juice concentrate and allow them to stand for at least 5 minutes. Stir in the cinnamon and applesauce and bring the mixture to a boil over low to medium heat, stirring often. When it comes to a boil, cook it while stirring it continuously for two minutes. Allow it to stand for at least 20 minutes before serving. Makes about 4 servings.

Easy Pineapple Sorbet

Gluten-Free

This is so quick and easy to make with canned pineapple that you may want to keep a can of pineapple in your freezer so you can make it at any time.

1 20-ounce can of pineapple packed in its own juice OR 2½ cups fresh
pineapple with juice to cover

Freeze the pineapple in its juice overnight. If you are using the canned pineapple, you can freeze it in the can. When you are ready to make sorbet, run warm water on the can, remove both can ends, and slide the pineapple out. Break the frozen pineapple and juice into chunks and process it until it is smooth in a food processor or in small batches in a blender or using a hand blender. Serve immediately or store the sorbet in your freezer. If it has been frozen for more than a few hours, remove it from the freezer about 20 minutes before serving. Makes about 1½ pints of sorbet.

Easy Banana-Cherry or Berry Sorbet

Gluten-Free

By using frozen berries, you can make this without any advance preparation when you have ripe bananas to use up.

> 2 ripe bananas
> 2 tablespoons agave, honey or Fruit Sweet™ (optional – use if the bananas are
>   underripe)
> 4 to 6 cups frozen dark (Bing) cherries, strawberries, blueberries, or raspberries

Peel the bananas and break them into chunks. Puree the banana chunks and optional sweetener until smooth using a hand blender, food processor or blender. Gradually add the berries, processing after each addition, until the sorbet reaches the desired consistency. Serve immediately or store the sorbet in your freezer. If this has been frozen for more than a few hours, remove it from the freezer about 20 minutes before serving. Makes about 2 pints of sorbet.

Quick Fruit Sorbet

Gluten-Free

Kids love this dessert. It is like an Icee™ but without the high-fructose corn syrup and artificial color.

> ¾ cup or 1 6-ounce can of frozen pineapple, grape, white grape, apple, or
>   orange juice concentrate
> 1 tray of ice cubes (made with about 2 cups of water)

Put the fruit juice concentrate into a food processor with the metal pureeing blade. Process briefly until smooth. Add the ice cubes one or two at a time, processing until the ice is pulverized after each addition. Serve the sorbet immediately or freeze any that is left over. Remove it from the freezer and let it soften at room temperature for 20 to 30 minutes before serving. This sorbet tends to become very hard if frozen for a long time. Makes about 6 servings

Puddings

Pudding is the ultimate comfort food – sweet, creamy, and warm when freshly prepared. While it doesn't require chewing (a comforting plus after dental work!) it does have a texture that is pleasant to experience on the tongue. Tapioca makes homey desserts with an especially interesting texture.

Pudding does not have to be made with cow's milk, eggs, or sugar. The milk-type puddings in this chapter are made with alternative milks and do not contain eggs or sugar. The fruit tapioca pudding recipes totally avoid any kind of milk. I consider these recipes true puddings because they are made with fruit juice and have a smooth texture. For fruit tapioca desserts that contain whole or cut-up fruit, see pages 36 to 37.

The dark fruit juices used in the first four recipes in this chapter not only are convenient because they are pantry-shelf stable until opened, they also are extremely high in antioxidants and phytonutrients. Therefore, these desserts are good for your eyes, joints, and various medical conditions in addition to being comfort foods. They remind me of the Danish Dessert™ junket pudding my mother made for us when we children were under the weather, but these are without the sugar. The grains of tapioca absorb the dark color of the juice making these puddings visually more pleasing than milk-based tapioca pudding. When I am making fruit juice tapioca pudding while working on other projects in the kitchen at the same time, I often combine the tapioca with the fruit juice up to an hour before I plan to add the rest of the ingredients and cook the pudding. This brings out the beauty of the final pudding more quickly after cooking. Use all of your senses to enjoy these puddings!

Best Blueberry Tapioca Pudding

Gluten-Free

If you keep your pantry stocked with concentrated fruit juice and Minute™ tapioca, you can whip up the next few recipes in a jiffy at any time.

    1 cup Knudsen™ blueberry juice concentrate (1 8-ounce bottle)
    ¼ cup agave, Fruit Sweet™ or honey
    1 cup water
    ¼ cup quick-cooking (Minute™) tapioca

Stir together all the ingredients in a saucepan. Allow them to stand for at least five minutes. Bring them to a full boil over medium-high heat, stirring occasionally. Then cook and stir constantly for one minute. Remove the pan from the heat and allow it to stand for at least 20 minutes before serving. If you want to serve this dessert soon, for optimal taste and texture of the tapioca, allow it to stand long enough to reach luke-warm. Refrigerate the tapioca pudding if you prefer to serve it cold. Makes 4 servings.

Delightful Dark Cherry Tapioca Pudding
Gluten-Free

In addition to being delicious, this dessert is a visual delight. The grains of tapioca look like garnet colored jewels in luscious syrup.

⅞ cup Knudsen™ black cherry juice concentrate
¼ cup agave, Fruit Sweet™ or honey
1⅛ cups water
¼ cup quick-cooking (Minute™) tapioca

Stir together all the ingredients in a saucepan. Allow them to stand for at least five minutes. Bring them to a full boil over medium-high heat, stirring occasionally. Then cook and stir constantly for one minute. Remove the pan from the heat and allow it to stand for at least 20 minutes before serving. If you want to serve this dessert soon, for optimal taste and texture of the tapioca, allow it to stand long enough to reach luke-warm. Refrigerate the tapioca pudding if you prefer to serve it cold. Makes 4 servings.

Holiday Special Cranberry Tapioca Pudding
Gluten-Free

This dessert is so easy to make that you can have it in addition to pumpkin pie for guests who prefer a light dessert after a big holiday meal.

⅓ cup Knudsen™ cranberry juice concentrate
½ cup agave, Fruit Sweet™ or honey
1 cup plus 3 tablespoons water
¼ cup quick-cooking (Minute™) tapioca

Stir together all the ingredients in a saucepan. Allow them to stand for at least five minutes. Bring them to a full boil over medium-high heat, stirring occasionally. Then cook and stir constantly for one minute. Remove the pan from the heat and allow it to stand for at least 20 minutes before serving. If you want to serve this dessert soon, for optimal taste and texture of the tapioca, allow it to stand long enough to reach luke-warm. Refrigerate the tapioca pudding if you prefer to serve it cold. Makes 4 servings.

Tangy Pomegranate Tapioca Pudding

Gluten-Free

This is my favorite fruit tapioca pudding because of its deliciously unique tangy flavor. Pomegranate is high in phytonutrients in addition to being tasty.

¼ cup Cortas™ pomegranate molasses* (See "Sources," page 231)
⅓ cup agave, Fruit Sweet™ or honey
1½ cups water
⅓ cup quick-cooking (Minute™) tapioca

Stir together all the ingredients in a saucepan. Allow them to stand for at least five minutes. Bring them to a full boil over medium-high heat, stirring occasionally. Then cook and stir constantly for one minute. Remove the pan from the heat and allow it to stand for at least 20 minutes before serving. If you want to serve this dessert soon, for optimal taste and texture of the tapioca, allow it to stand long enough to reach luke-warm. Refrigerate the tapioca pudding if you prefer to serve it cold. Makes 4 servings.

*Note on pomegranate molasses: Pomegranate molasses is a very thick pomegranate juice concentrate. While some brands of room temperature-stable (canned, although usually in jars) pomegranate juice and pomegranate juice concentrate have a bitter taste, possibly due to the membranes of the fruit being included, Cortas™ pomegranate concentrate is free from this problem. It is available at our local Whole Foods store at the time of this writing.

If you are unable to get Cortas™ pomegranate molasses, you can still have pomegranate tapioca. Use a brand of good-tasting pure pomegranate juice purchased refrigerated (not canned or room-temperature stable) such as Pom Wonderful™ or Earthly Delights™ brand. Combine 2 cups of the juice with ¼ cup minute tapioca, allow it to stand for at least five minutes, and cook and serve as above.

Coconut Tapioca Pudding

Gluten-Free

¼ cup agave, Fruit Sweet™ or honey
2 tablespoons* quick-cooking (Minute™) tapioca
1 14-ounce can coconut milk
1 teaspoon coconut or vanilla flavoring
About 1 tablespoon unsweetened coconut (optional)

Combine the sweetener and tapioca in a saucepan and allow them to stand for 5 minutes. Stir in the coconut milk until well mixed. Cook over medium heat, stirring occasionally, until it comes to a boil. Boil and stir for 1 to 1½ minutes. Remove the pan from the heat and allow it to stand for at least 5 minutes. Stir in the flavoring. For an impressive presentation, pour the pudding into individual serving glasses or dishes and sprinkle it with the optional coconut. Chill the tapioca in the refrigerator if you prefer to serve it cold. Makes about 4 servings.

Note on the amount of tapioca: If you plan to serve this hot and would like to have it thick, use 3 tablespoons of tapioca.

Tapioca Pudding Made with Alternative Milk

Gluten-Free

2¾ cups goat, rice, gluten-free soy or other alternative milk (or cow's milk, if tolerated)
¼ to ⅓ cup agave, Fruit Sweet™ or honey, to taste
¼ cup quick-cooking (Minute™) tapioca
¼ cup tapioca flour
1 teaspoon vanilla extract or other flavoring

Combine the milk, sweetener, and tapioca in a saucepan and allow them to stand for at least 5 minutes. Stir in the tapioca flour and cook the mixture over medium heat, stirring it almost constantly, until it comes to a full boil. Stir in the flavoring. Chill it thoroughly before serving. Makes about 6 servings.

Elegant Tapioca Parfaits

Gluten-Free

1 batch of blueberry tapioca pudding, page 39, or cherry tapioca pudding, page 40
1 batch of coconut tapioca pudding, page 41, or about ⅔ batch of tapioca pudding made with alternative milk, above

Prepare both batches of tapioca pudding. You can save time by cooking them side-by-side in two saucepans. Allow them to cool at room temperature or put them in the refrigerator to cool more quickly, but check them often. When they are about at room temperature and are very thick, put a small amount of blueberry or cherry tapioca in tall glasses. Add a layer of coconut milk or alternative milk tapioca. Continue alternating layers until the glasses are full. Serve at room temperature immediately, or refrigerate them to serve them later. Makes 3 to 6 servings depending on the size of the glasses used.

Rice Pudding

Gluten-Free

3 eggs, slightly beaten
2 cups milk of any kind - goat, rice, gluten-free soy, or coconut (or cow's milk,
    if tolerated)
½ cup agave, Fruit Sweet™ or honey
2 teaspoons vanilla extract (optional)
¼ teaspoon salt
¼ teaspoon cinnamon or 1 teaspoon grated lemon zest (use lemon with the
    cherries)
2 cups cooked rice
½ cup raisins or tart dried cherries

Begin heating your oven to 350°F. In a 3-quart casserole dish, thoroughly combine the eggs, milk, sweetener, vanilla, salt and cinnamon or lemon zest. Add the rice and dried fruit and stir well. Put the casserole dish in the oven and bake it for 30 minutes. Stir it thoroughly. Bake it for another 40 minutes to an hour or until it is set in the middle. Makes 4 to 6 servings.

Quinoa Pudding

Gluten-Free

This is a delicious gluten, egg, milk, and sugar-free takeoff on rice pudding. Because quinoa contains plenty of high quality protein, when sweetened with stevia, this is an excellent dessert for weight watchers, diabetics or those with hypoglycemia.

1 cup whole quinoa, thoroughly rinsed
2 cups water
1 cup apple juice concentrate, thawed, OR ¼ teaspoon pure stevia powder
    plus 1 cup water
1 teaspoon cinnamon
½ cup raisins or other finely chopped dried fruit (optional)

Place the whole quinoa in a strainer and run water over the quinoa until the water is no longer sudsy and all of the natural soapy coating has been removed from the quinoa. Combine the quinoa and 2 cups water in a saucepan, bring it to a boil, and simmer it for 20 minutes or until the quinoa is translucent. (If you wish to, you may use 3 cups cooked quinoa instead of cooking it for this recipe). Add the apple juice concentrate or the stevia and additional 1 cup of water, the cinnamon, and the dried fruit to the pan. Simmer the mixture for 10 to 15 minutes more, or until the liquid is absorbed.

If you would rather bake the pudding for a "for guests" presentation, combine the cooked quinoa, juice or stevia plus 1 cup of water, cinnamon, and dried fruit in a 1½-quart covered casserole and bake it at 350°F for 20 to 30 minutes or until the liquid is absorbed. Sprinkle the top of the pudding with additional cinnamon and serve it warm. Makes 4 to 6 servings.

Chocolate or Carob Pudding

Gluten-Free

¼ cup cocoa or carob powder
5 tablespoons arrowroot or tapioca starch
2 cups coconut milk, goat or other alternative milk (or cow's milk, if tolerated)
½ cup agave, Fruit Sweet™ or honey
2 teaspoons vanilla extract (optional)

Stir together the carob powder or cocoa and starch in a saucepan. Add ½ cup of the milk and stir the mixture until it forms a smooth paste. Stir in the rest of the milk and the sweetener and cook the pudding over medium heat, stirring frequently, until it thickens and comes to a boil. Remove the pudding from the heat and stir in the vanilla. Serve the pudding warm or cold. Makes about 4 servings.

Vanilla Pudding

Gluten-Free

2 cups milk of any kind – goat, rice, gluten-free soy, or coconut (or cow's milk, if tolerated)
⅓ cup agave, Fruit Sweet™ or honey
5 tablespoons arrowroot or tapioca starch
2 teaspoons vanilla extract

In a saucepan stir together about ⅓ cup of the milk and the starch to form a smooth paste. Stir in the rest of the milk and the sweetener. Cook the pudding over medium heat, stirring frequently until it thickens and comes to a boil. Remove the pudding from the heat and stir in the vanilla. Serve the pudding warm or cold. Makes about 4 servings.

Fancy coconut pudding variation: Make the pudding with coconut milk and use 1 teaspoon coconut flavoring instead of the vanilla. Sprinkle the pudding with grated coconut if desired.

Cobblers, Crisps, Crumbles and Other Fruit Desserts

This chapter is a collection of humble, homey desserts that pair fruit with a topping which enhances the fruit. These desserts remind us of pie but require much less work to make, and that simplicity is part of their charm.

The best cobblers, crisps and crumbles begin with ripe flavorful in-season fruit. However, if you crave cobbler in the middle of the winter or when you're short on time for peeling, high quality frozen or canned fruit may be used instead. The fruit is thickened and sweetened in moderation so as to not detract from the fruit itself, topped with a biscuit-like, sweetened oatmeal, cake-like, or crispy nut topping, and baked in the oven. Serve these desserts warm, possibly topped with ice cream for a special treat. Delicious!

Easy Apple Crisp

Ask your doctor about eating oats on a gluten-free diet

You can make this guest-worthy dessert quickly and easily with water-packed canned sliced apples, such as Mussleman's™ brand. In the fall this is delicious made with freshly picked Jonathan apples. For variety, use other fruits such as peaches or blueberries.

Filling ingredients:

2 20-ounce cans of sliced apples canned in water, drained
1 tablespoon plus 1 teaspoon arrowroot or tapioca starch
1½ teaspoons cinnamon
⅓ cup apple juice concentrate, thawed

Topping ingredients:

¾ cup oatmeal, quick cooking or regular (not instant)
¾ cup white spelt or rice* flour (celiacs see the note on the next page)
½ teaspoon baking soda
¼ cup oil
¼ cup agave or Fruit Sweet™ OR 3 tablespoons honey plus 1 tablespoon water
1 teaspoon vanilla extract

Drain the canned apples. Put the slices in a 2½ to 3-quart glass casserole dish. Add the starch and cinnamon and toss them with the apple slices to coat the slices thoroughly. Drizzle the apple juice concentrate over the apple slices.

Preheat your oven to 350°F. In a mixing bowl, stir together the oatmeal, flour, and baking soda. If you are using the honey, warm it slightly and mix it well with the water. In a cup, combine the sweetener, oil, and vanilla. Stir them into the dry ingredients until just mixed. Drop and spread the topping over the apples in the casserole dish. Bake the dish for 25 to 40 minutes or until the apples are tender, the filling is bubbling and the topping is browned. Check the apple crisp at 25 minutes into the baking time. If the topping is already getting quite brown but the fruit is not done, cover it with foil for the rest of the baking time. Makes 4 to 6 servings.

Fresh Peach Crisp Variation: Substitute 10 to 12 peaches weighing about 3 pounds, peeled, cored, and sliced, for the canned apples and increase the amount of apple juice concentrate you use in the filling to ½ cup.

Blueberry Crisp Variation: Substitute 2 pounds of fresh or frozen blueberries for the canned apples and omit the cinnamon.

Fresh Apple Crisp Variation: Substitute 8 large apples weighing about 3 pounds for the canned apples. Peel, core and slice the apples and put them in a saucepan with 1½ cups of water. Cover the pan and bring the apple slices to a boil. Reduce the heat to medium, and simmer them for 5 to 10 minutes or until they just begin to soften. Drain the apple slices and use them in the recipe above.

*Note for celiacs: If your doctor allows oats on your gluten-free diet, you should be able to have this dessert if made with the rice flour. Ask your doctor before eating the oats in this dessert.

Double Cherry-Berry Seed Cake Cobbler

**Gluten-Free IF
made with amaranth**

Combining fresh and dried fruit gives the filling of this cobbler a delightful texture, and the seeds make the topping deliciously interesting. Choose from three fillings and gluten-free or spelt toppings for variety.

Fillings ingredients:

Bing cherry filling:

1 pound (about 3 to 4 cups) fresh pitted or frozen Bing cherries
1 cup total volume of Bing cherry juice and/or apple juice*
¾ cup unsweetened dried cherries, either Bing cherries or tart cherries
3 tablespoons arrowroot or tapioca starch

Tart cherry filling:

1 pound fresh (about 3 to 4 cups) or 2 14.5-ounce cans water-packed tart
    pie cherries, drained
1 cup total volume of Bing cherry juice, reserved canned tart cherry juice,
    apple juice, Fruit Sweet™ and/or agave*
¾ cup unsweetened dried tart cherries
3 tablespoons arrowroot or tapioca starch

Blueberry filling:

1 pound (about 3 to 4 cups) fresh or frozen blueberries
1 cup total volume of blueberry juice and/or apple juice*
¾ cup unsweetened dried blueberries
3 tablespoons arrowroot or tapioca starch

Topping ingredients:

1½ cups amaranth flour or 1¾ cups whole spelt flour
⅓ cup sesame seeds
1 teaspoon baking soda
¼ teaspoon unbuffered vitamin C crystals
½ cup oil
½ cup agave or Fruit Sweet™
½ teaspoon vanilla (optional)

Preheat your oven to 375°F. Choose the filling you wish to make, above. If you are using canned cherries, drain the cherries and reserve the juice.

In a saucepan, combine the fresh, canned, or frozen cherries or blueberries, dried fruit, 1 cup total volume of juice and/or sweetener (see the notes about the liquid below), and starch. Cook over medium heat, stirring frequently, until the mixture comes to a boil and thickens. While the filling is cooking, begin to prepare the topping as directed in the next paragraph. When the filling has thickened, put the fruit mixture into a 9-inch square baking pan or dish.

To prepare the topping, stir together the flour, sesame seeds, baking soda, and vitamin C crystals in a large bowl. In a separate bowl or cup, stir together the oil, agave or Fruit Sweet™, and vanilla. (You can do this while the filling is coming to a boil).

After the filling has finished cooking and has been put into the baking dish, stir the liquid topping ingredients into the dry ingredients until they are just mixed together. Immediately pour the batter over the fruit in the baking dish and put the dish in the oven. Bake for 20 to 30 minutes or until the topping is brown and a toothpick inserted into the cake part of the cobbler only comes out dry. (The spelt topping may fall slightly in the middle after removing it from the oven). Serve the cobbler immediately or cool it on a wire rack. Refrigerate leftovers. Makes 4 to 6 servings.

*Notes about the liquid filling sweetener ingredients: The type(s) and proportions of the juice(s) and/or sweetener used in each filling will depend upon your personal taste and sweetness preference, but the total volume of the combined liquids should be 1 cup in all cases.

If you are making Bing cherry cobbler with dried Bing cherries and you prefer your desserts not-too-sweet, use Bing cherry juice, apple juice, or a combination of the two. If you prefer sweeter desserts, use ½ cup apple juice concentrate (or more to your taste) for part of the 1 cup total liquid with Bing cherry juice making up the rest of the volume.

If you are making Bing cherry cobbler using tart dried cherries, use part cherry juice and part apple juice concentrate. I find ⅔ cup Bing cherry juice and ⅓ cup apple juice concentrate to be an ideal level of sweetness with the tart dried cherries, but you can add more apple juice concentrate, keeping tht total volume at 1 cup, if you like it sweeter.

If you are making tart cherry cobbler, you will need more sweetness. I make this cobbler with ¼ cup tart cherry juice (reserved from draining the canned cherries) plus ¾ cup agave. To use all fruit juice, boil 1½ cups of apple juice concentrate down to 1 cup in volume and allow it to cool before using it to make the filling. If you prefer your filling sweeter, use 1 cup agave, honey, or Fruit Sweet™ or boil 2 cups of apple juice concentrate down to 1 cup and allow it to cool.

If you are making blueberry cobbler, use all apple juice or all blueberry juice if you prefer your desserts not-too-sweet. If you prefer sweeter desserts, use ½ cup apple juice concentrate (or more to your taste) for part of the 1 cup total liquid with blueberry juice making up the rest of the 1 cup volume.

Traditional Fruit Cobbler Topping

Cobblers are the ultimate easy homey dessert and can be made with almost any grain because crumbling is not a problem. Everyone will enjoy a cobbler they tolerate, so many grain choices are included in the list of toppings below. Pair any of these toppings with the fillings on pages 51 to 54 for a quick and delicious dessert.

Amaranth (GF):

    ¾ cup amaranth flour
    ¼ cup arrowroot
    ¾ teaspoon baking soda
    ⅛ teaspoon unbuffered vitamin C powder
    ⅜ cup apple or pineapple juice concentrate, thawed
    ⅛ cup oil

Barley:

    ⅞ cup barley flour
    ¾ teaspoon baking soda
    ⅛ teaspoon unbuffered vitamin C powder
    ⅜ cup apple or pineapple juice concentrate, thawed
    ⅛ cup oil

Buckwheat (GF):

    ¾ cup buckwheat flour
    ¾ teaspoon baking soda
    ⅛ teaspoon unbuffered vitamin C powder
    ⅜ cup apple or white grape juice concentrate, thawed
    ⅛ cup oil

Kamut:

    ¾ cup kamut flour
    ¾ teaspoon baking soda
    ⅛ teaspoon unbuffered vitamin C powder
    ⅜ cup apple or pineapple juice concentrate, thawed
    ⅛ cup oil

Quinoa (GF):

⅝ cup quinoa flour
⅛ cup tapioca starch
¾ teaspoon baking soda
⅛ teaspoon unbuffered vitamin C powder
⅜ cup apple juice concentrate, thawed
⅛ cup oil

Rice (GF):

⅝ cup brown rice flour
½ cup tapioca starch or arrowroot
¾ teaspoon baking soda
⅛ teaspoon unbuffered vitamin C powder
⅜ cup apple or pineapple juice concentrate, thawed
⅛ cup oil

Rye:

¾ cup rye flour
¾ teaspoon baking soda
⅛ teaspoon unbuffered vitamin C powder
⅜ cup apple or white grape juice concentrate, thawed
⅛ cup oil

White Spelt:

1 cup white spelt flour
¾ teaspoon baking soda
⅛ teaspoon unbuffered vitamin C powder
⅜ cup apple juice concentrate, thawed
⅛ cup oil

Whole Spelt:

⅞ cup whole spelt flour
¾ teaspoon baking soda
⅛ teaspoon unbuffered vitamin C powder
⅜ cup apple juice concentrate, thawed
⅛ cup oil

Teff (GF):

> ¾ cup teff flour
> ¾ teaspoon baking soda
> ⅛ teaspoon unbuffered vitamin C powder
> ⅜ cup apple or white grape juice concentrate, thawed
> ⅛ cup oil

Preheat your oven to 350°F. Prepare the fruit filling from any recipe on pages 51 to 54. When the filling is thickened, put it into a 2½ to 3 quart casserole dish.

While the filling is cooking, combine the flour(s), baking soda, and vitamin C powder in a medium bowl. Stir together the juice and oil in another bowl or cup. After the filling has been put in the casserole dish, add the liquid ingredients to the dry ingredients and stir until they are just mixed in. Drop large spoonfuls of the topping onto the prepared fruit filling. Bake for 25 to 35 minutes or until the topping is slightly browned. Makes 4 to 6 servings.

Blueberry Cobbler

**Gluten-Free IF
made with a GF topping**

This is one of my husband's favorite desserts.

> 4 cups fresh blueberries OR a 1 pound bag of unsweetened frozen blueberries
> ½ cup apple or pineapple juice concentrate, thawed
> 5 teaspoons arrowroot or tapioca starch
> One batch of cobbler topping, pages 49 to 51

Preheat your oven to 350°F. If you are using fresh blueberries, wash them and remove any shriveled berries or stems. In a saucepan, stir the starch into the juice. Add the blueberries to the pan and stir. Heat the mixture over medium heat until it thickens and comes to a boil. You do not need to stir it constantly while it is coming to a boil and can begin preparing the topping during this time. As it begins to steam and nears the boiling point, stir it constantly. When it comes to a boil, boil it for one minute. Put the fruit into a 2½ to 3 quart casserole dish. Finish preparing the topping. Drop the topping by spoonfuls onto the fruit in the casserole dish. Bake for 25 to 35 minutes or until the topping begins to brown. Makes 4 to 6 servings.

Apple Cobbler

Gluten-Free IF
made with a GF topping

4 to 5 apples, peeled, cored, and sliced to make 3½ to 4 cups of slices
    OR 1 20-ounce can of sliced apples canned in water such as Mussleman's™
    brand, drained
½ cup apple juice concentrate, thawed
5 teaspoons arrowroot or tapioca starch OR 2 tablespoons quick-cooking
    (minute) tapioca
½ teaspoon cinnamon
One batch of cobbler topping, pages 49 to 51

Preheat your oven to 350°F. Drain the canned apples if you are using them, or peel, core and slice the fresh apples. In a saucepan, stir together the apple juice concentrate, starch or tapioca, and cinnamon in a sauce pan. If you are using the tapioca, allow it to stand in the liquid for at least 5 minutes. Add the apples to the pan and stir. Heat the mixture over medium heat until it thickens and comes to a boil. You do not need to stir it constantly while it is coming to a boil and can begin preparing the topping during this time. As it begins to steam and nears the boiling point, stir it constantly. When it comes to a boil, boil it for one minute. Put the fruit into a 2½ to 3 quart casserole dish. Finish preparing the topping. Drop the topping by spoonfuls onto the fruit in the casserole dish. Bake for 25 to 35 minutes or until the topping begins to brown. Makes 4 to 6 servings.

Tart Cherry Cobbler

Gluten-Free IF
made with a GF topping

2 1-pound cans water-packed tart pie cherries, drained, OR 4 cups fresh
    pitted pie cherries
1½ cups apple juice concentrate or ¾ cup agave or Fruit Sweet™
2 tablespoons arrowroot or tapioca starch OR 3 tablespoons quick-cooking
    (minute) tapioca
One batch of cobbler topping, pages 49 to 51

Preheat your oven to 350°F. If you are using the apple juice, boil it down to ¾ cup in volume and allow it to cool to lukewarm. Thoroughly drain the canned cherries. Stir the starch or tapioca into the juice or sweetener in a saucepan. If you are using the quick-cooking tapioca, allow it to stand in the liquid for at least 5 minutes. Add the drained cherries to the pan and stir. Heat the mixture over medium heat until it thickens and comes to a boil. You do not need to stir it constantly while it is coming to a boil and can begin preparing the topping during this time. As it begins to steam and nears the boiling point, stir it constantly. When it comes to a boil, boil it for one minute. Put the fruit into a 2½ to 3 quart casserole dish. Finish preparing the topping. Drop the topping by spoonfuls onto the fruit in the casserole dish. Bake for 25 to 35 minutes or until the topping begins to brown. Makes 4 to 6 servings.

Bing Cherry Cobbler

Gluten-Free IF
made with a GF topping

4 cups pitted fresh dark (Bing) cherries OR a 1-pound bag frozen
    unsweetened dark cherries
½ cup apple or pineapple juice concentrate, thawed
5 teaspoons arrowroot or tapioca starch
One batch of cobbler topping, pages 49 to 51

Preheat your oven to 350°F. In a saucepan, stir the starch into the juice. Add the cherries to the pan and stir. Heat the mixture over medium heat until it thickens and comes to a boil. You do not need to stir it constantly while it is coming to a boil and can begin preparing the topping during this time. As it begins to steam and nears the boiling point, stir it constantly. When it comes to a boil, boil it for one minute. Put the fruit into a 2½ to 3 quart casserole dish. Finish preparing the topping. Drop the topping by spoonfuls onto the fruit in the casserole dish. Bake for 25 to 35 minutes or until the topping begins to brown. Makes 4 to 6 servings.

Strawberry Cobbler

Gluten-Free IF
made with a GF topping

1 pound of fresh strawberries or a 1-pound bag of unsweetened frozen
    strawberries
½ cup apple juice concentrate, thawed
3 tablespoons arrowroot or tapioca starch
One batch of cobbler topping, pages 49 to 51

Preheat your oven to 350°F. If you are using fresh strawberries, wash them and cut out the stems. Stir the starch into the juice. Add the strawberries to the pan and stir. Heat the mixture over medium heat until it thickens and comes to a boil. You do not need to stir it constantly while it is coming to a boil and can begin preparing the topping during this time. As it begins to steam and nears the boiling point, stir it constantly. When it comes to a boil, boil it for one minute. Put the fruit into a 2½ to 3 quart casserole dish. Finish preparing the topping. Drop the topping by spoonfuls onto the fruit in the casserole dish. Bake for 25 to 35 minutes or until the topping begins to brown. Makes 4 to 6 servings.

Peach Cobbler

Gluten-Free IF
made with a GF topping

4 cups sliced fresh peaches or a 1-pound bag unsweetened frozen peaches
½ cup apple or pineapple juice concentrate, thawed
5 teaspoons arrowroot or tapioca starch OR 3 tablespoons quick-cooking
    (minute) tapioca
One batch of cobbler topping, pages 49 to 51

Preheat your oven to 350°F. In a saucepan, stir the starch or tapioca into the juice. If you are using the quick-cooking tapioca, allow it to stand in the liquid for at least 5 minutes. Add the peaches to the pan and stir. Heat the mixture over medium heat until it thickens and comes to a boil. You do not need to stir it constantly while it is coming to a boil and can begin preparing the topping during this time. As it begins to steam and nears the boiling point, stir it constantly. When it comes to a boil, boil it for one minute. Put the fruit into a 2½ to 3 quart casserole dish. Finish preparing the topping. Drop the topping by spoonfuls onto the fruit in the casserole dish. Bake for 25 to 35 minutes or until the topping begins to brown. Makes 4 to 6 servings.

Rhubarb Cobbler

Gluten-Free IF
made with a GF topping

4 cups sliced rhubarb (about 1 pound) or a 1-pound bag of frozen sliced
    rhubarb
½ cup agave or Fruit Sweet™
5 teaspoons arrowroot or tapioca starch
One batch of cobbler topping, pages 49 to 51

Preheat your oven to 350°F. In a saucepan, stir the starch into the sweetener. Add the rhubarb to the pan and stir. Heat the mixture over medium heat until it thickens and comes to a boil. You do not need to stir it constantly while it is coming to a boil and can begin preparing the topping during this time. As it begins to steam and nears the boiling point, stir it constantly. When it comes to a boil, boil it for one minute. Put the rhubarb into a 2½ to 3 quart casserole dish. Finish preparing the topping. Drop the topping by spoonfuls onto the rhubarb in the casserole dish. Bake for 25 to 35 minutes or until the topping begins to brown. Makes 4 to 6 servings.

Nutty Cherry Cobbler

Gluten-Free

This recipe is free of grains and grain alternatives, so almost anyone can eat it.

Filling ingredients:

2 cans tart pie cherries, drained
¾ cup agave or Fruit Sweet™
2 tablespoons tapioca starch

Topping ingredients:

½ cup chopped pecans
½ cup coconut shredded to medium coarseness
⅓ cup pecan meal
¼ teaspoon cinnamon
1 tablespoon agave or Fruit Sweet™
2 tablespoons oil

Preheat your oven to 375°F. Thoroughly drain the cherries. In a saucepan, stir together the cherries, ¾ cup sweetener, and starch. Heat the mixture over medium heat until it thickens and comes to a boil. Boil it while stirring constantly for one minute. Put the fruit into a 2½- to 3-quart casserole dish.

While the cherry mixture is coming to a boil, combine nuts, coconut, nut meal, and cinnamon in a bowl. Mix the oil and 1 tablespoon of sweetener together and stir them into nut mixture. After the fruit is cooked and in the casserole dish, spoon the nut mixture evenly over the cobbler filling. Bake 15 minutes and then cover the cobbler with foil. Bake another 20 minutes or until the filling is bubbly. Makes 4 to 6 servings.

"Instant" Nutty Cobbler

Gluten-Free

One batch of "Nutty Topping," page 195
One batch of cobbler filling, pages 51 to 54, or make any filling from the
  "Double Cherry-Berry Seed Cake Cobbler" recipe on page 47

Prepare the "Nutty Topping," page 195. This may be made in advanced and stored in a jar with a tight fitting lid. Prepare the cobbler filling. Put the filling in a casserole dish for serving to a group or into individual serving dishes. Sprinkle the topping on the warm or cooled cobbler filling for "instant" cobbler. This makes dessert quickly because no time is required to bake the fruit and topping together. Makes 4 to 6 servings.

Easy Fruit Crumble

**Ask your doctor about
eating oats on a gluten-free diet**

This recipe is as easy to make as it is delicious. Although millet flakes are currently unavailable in the United States, perhaps the rising number of people on gluten-free diets will convince some entrepreneur to produce or begin importing them again. If you can eat oats, this dessert is excellent made with oatmeal.

4 cups fresh blueberries or peeled and sliced apples or peaches
        OR 4 cups drained water-packed canned peaches or apples
        OR 1 pound frozen blueberries
¾ to 1 cup date sugar, divided
¼ cup arrowroot or tapioca starch
2 to 6 tablespoons water, divided
1 cup quinoa* flakes, millet* flakes or oatmeal*, uncooked
1 teaspoon cinnamon
¼ cup oil

Preheat your oven to 325°F. Taste the fruit you are going to use. If it is sweet, use ¼ cup date sugar with the fruit. If it is tart, use ½ cup date sugar with the fruit. Combine the ¼ or ½ cup date sugar and the arrowroot or tapioca starch in an 8 inch square baking dish. Stir the fruit into the date sugar mixture. If you are using fresh fruit, sprinkle 4 tablespoons water over the blueberries or apples. Sprinkle 2 tablespoons water over fresh peaches, canned apples, or frozen blueberries. No water is needed with canned peaches.

In a small bowl, combine the cereal, remaining ½ cup date sugar, and cinnamon. Stir in the oil until the mixture is crumbly. Stir in 2 tablespoons of water. Sprinkle the mixture on top of the fruit. Bake for 30 to 40 minutes or until the topping browns and the fruit is tender when pierced with a fork. To prevent overbrowning, if the topping is brown before the fruit is cooked, cover the crumble with a piece of foil for the final 10 to 20 minutes of baking. Makes 6 to 8 servings.

*Note: Some doctors allow their celiac patients to eat oats and others do not. Ask your doctor before eating the oat variety of this dessert. If you use quinoa or millet flakes to make this dessert, it is gluten-free. Quinoa flakes may be purchased from Purcell Mountain Farms. See page 230 for ordering information.

No-Grain Easy Fruit Crumble

Gluten-Free

This is my favorite dessert with its pairing of sumptuous fruit and a crunchy topping.

4 cups fresh blueberries or peeled and sliced apples or peaches
  OR 4 cups drained water-packed canned peaches or apples
  OR 1 pound frozen blueberries
¼ cup arrowroot or tapioca starch
½ to ¾ cup date sugar, divided
Up to 4 tablespoons water
¼ cup almond meal/flour or pecan meal/flour (See "Sources," page 232 or
  233).
⅔ cup unsweetened coconut
⅓ cup chopped or sliced almonds or chopped pecans
Cinnamon – 1¼ teaspoon with the apples, divided, or ¼ teaspoon with the
  other fruit
¼ cup oil

Preheat your oven to 375°F. Combine the fruit, arrowroot or tapioca starch, 1 teaspoon cinnamon (with the apples only), and ¼ to ½ cup of date sugar (depending on how sweet the fruit is) in a deep 8 or 9 inch square baking dish or 2 to 3-quart casserole dish. Add just enough water to barely moisten the starch and date sugar. The starch-liquid mixture should be like a thick paste. How much water you will need to add will depend on how juicy your fruit is; with canned peaches you will not need to add any water.

In a bowl, stir together the remaining ¼ cup date sugar, nut meal, coconut, nuts, and ¼ teaspoon cinnamon. Pour the oil over the mixture and stir until it is evenly distributed. Sprinkle the nut mixture over the fruit in the baking dish. Bake for 10 minutes. Then cover it with foil to prevent excessive browning. Bake for another 35 to 45 minutes or until the filling is bubbly throughout. Makes about 6 servings.

One Layer "Shortcake"

Traditionally, a shortcake is a sturdy biscuit-like pastry that is split and filled with fruit. Since baked goods made with many alternative grains are often less than sturdy, here is a non-traditional shortcake made with many choices of grains or grain alternatives. Serve it from the pan, and don't try to split it into layers. It tastes great topped with fresh fruit and sugar-free whipped cream, page 196, or "Nutty Whipped Cream," page 196.

Amaranth (GF):

1½ cups amaranth flour
½ cup arrowroot
1½ teaspoons baking soda
¼ teaspoon unbuffered vitamin C powder
¾ cup apple or pineapple juice concentrate, thawed
¼ cup oil

Barley:

1¾ cups barley flour
1½ teaspoons baking soda
¼ teaspoon unbuffered vitamin C powder
¾ cup apple or pineapple juice concentrate, thawed
¼ cup oil

Buckwheat (GF):

1½ cups buckwheat flour
1½ teaspoons baking soda
¼ teaspoon unbuffered vitamin C powder
¾ cup apple or white grape juice concentrate, thawed
¼ cup oil

Kamut:

1½ cups kamut flour
1½ teaspoons baking soda
¼ teaspoon unbuffered vitamin C powder
¾ cup apple or pineapple juice concentrate, thawed
¼ cup oil

Quinoa (GF):

1¼ cups quinoa flour
¼ cup tapioca flour
1½ teaspoons baking soda
¼ teaspoon unbuffered vitamin C powder
¾ cup apple juice concentrate, thawed
¼ cup oil

Rice (GF):

1¼ cups brown rice flour
1 cup tapioca starch or arrowroot
1½ teaspoons baking soda
¼ teaspoon unbuffered vitamin C powder
¾ cup apple or pineapple juice concentrate, thawed
¼ cup oil

Rye:

1½ cups rye flour
1½ teaspoons baking soda
¼ teaspoon unbuffered vitamin C powder
¾ cup apple or white grape juice concentrate, thawed
¼ cup oil

White Spelt:

2 cups white spelt flour
1½ teaspoons baking soda
¼ teaspoon unbuffered vitamin C powder
¾ cup apple juice concentrate, thawed
¼ cup oil

Whole Spelt:

1¾ cups whole spelt flour
1½ teaspoons baking soda
¼ teaspoon unbuffered vitamin C powder
¾ cup apple juice concentrate, thawed
¼ cup oil

Teff (GF):

> 1½ cups teff flour
> 1½ teaspoons baking soda
> ¼ teaspoon unbuffered vitamin C powder
> ¾ cup apple or white grape juice concentrate, thawed
> ¼ cup oil

Preheat your oven to 350°F. Oil and flour an 8 inch round or square cake pan. Use the pan bottom to trace a circle or square on waxed or parchment paper, cut the shape out, and lay the circle or square of paper in the pan.

In a large bowl, mix together the flour(s), baking soda, and vitamin C. In a small bowl or cup stir together the juice and oil. Pour them into the dry ingredients and stir until just barely combined. Quickly spread the batter in the prepared pan. Bake for 25 to 30 minutes or until it is lightly browned and a toothpick inserted in the center comes out dry. Cool it in the pan. Cut it into wedges or squares. Serve it with fresh, thawed frozen, or canned fruit and, if tolerated, sugar-free whipped cream, page 196, or "Nutty Whipped Cream," page 196. Makes 6 servings.

Traditional Strawberry Shortcake

Made with spelt flour and an egg, this cake-type shortcake is sturdy enough to be sliced into two layers. For a biscuit-type strawberry shortcake recipe, see page 206.

> 2¼ cups white spelt flour
> 2 teaspoons baking powder*
> ½ teaspoon baking soda
> ½ teaspoon salt
> ¾ cup apple juice concentrate, thawed
> ⅓ cup oil
> 1 large egg, slightly beaten
> 4 cups sliced strawberries (or use sliced peaches or other fruit)

Preheat your oven to 375°F. Oil and flour an 8 or 9 inch square or round cake pan. Line the bottom of the pan with waxed or parchment paper. In a large bowl, stir together the flour, baking powder, baking soda, and salt. In a cup, thoroughly stir together the juice, oil, and egg. Pour the liquid ingredients into the dry ingredients and stir until just mixed.

Put the batter into the prepared pan and bake for 30 to 35 or until nicely browned and a toothpick stuck into the center comes out dry. Cool in the pan on a wire rack for about 10 minutes. Then remove it from the pan, place it on a serving dish, and allow it to cool completely. Cut it into 6 pieces. Using a serrated knife, carefully slice each piece horizontally. Serve with fruit and sugar-free whipped cream (page 196) or "Nutty Whipped Cream" (page 196) between the layers and on the top of the shortcake. Makes 6 servings.

* **Note on baking powder:** Use Featherweight™ brand baking powder if you are allergic to corn. It contains potato starch instead of cornstarch.

Blueberry Squares

This easy recipe saves washing dishes because you mix the crust ingredients right in the baking pan.

Crust ingredients

> 1¼ cups white spelt flour
> 1½ cups oatmeal, regular or quick-cooking (not instant)
> ½ teaspoon baking soda
> Dash of salt
> ¼ cup agave, Fruit Sweet™, or slightly warmed honey
> ⅜ cup oil
> 2 teaspoons vanilla extract

Blueberry filling ingredients

> 3 cups (about ¾ pound) fresh or frozen blueberries
> ¼ cup agave, Fruit Sweet™ or honey
> 2 tablespoons arrowroot or tapioca flour

Preheat your oven to 350°F. In an 8 inch square cake pan, stir together the flour, oatmeal, baking soda, and salt. Mix together the oil, sweetener, and vanilla in a cup or bowl. Stir the liquids into the flour mixture in the pan. Remove about one third of the crumbs from the pan. Press the remaining crumbs into a thin layer of dough which covers the whole bottom of the pan. Bake for 5 to 10 minutes or until it is just beginning to brown. Let the dough cool on a wire rack until it is at least lukewarm; cooler is all right also.

While the crust is baking and/or cooling, combine the blueberries, sweetener, and starch in a small saucepan. Cook them over medium heat, stirring often, until they come to a boil. Then simmer, stirring constantly, for another three to five minutes until the mixture is thickened and clear. Remove the pan from the heat and allow the filling to cool for at least five minutes.

Spread the blueberry mixture on top of the crust in the pan. Crumble the remaining dough over the blueberry mixture. Bake for 20 to 25 minutes or until lightly browned. Put the pan on a wire rack to cool. Cut into squares to serve. Makes 9 servings.

Pies

Pie is the food of memories. Many of us associate our favorite pie with a certain mellow and loving person. For some people, the memory is of Mom's apple pie. My memory is of my Aunt Louise's spicy brown sugar pumpkin pie, and of her teaching me how to make a fluted edge on a pie crust. Good pie makers tend to have laid-back personalities, and I've read that they also have cool hands. My husband tells me I make good pie crust because I'm not a perfectionist who would over-work the dough trying to get it just right. Although making a traditional pie with wheat flour and shortening is different from making the pies in this chapter, I urge you to take a calm approach and not be a perfectionist. Your homemade pie will taste delicious even if it doesn't look like something from a bakery store window. Making pie really can be "as easy as pie" if you approach it in a relaxed way.

Pie crusts made with alternative flours and oil break easily if you roll the dough out. In fact, some types of pie crusts cannot be rolled. There is a way around this problem, however. Just press the dough into the pie plate and, if you wish to use a top crust, sprinkle crumbs of the dough over the top of the filling. If you want to make a rolled crust, spelt, rye, kamut, and barley pie crusts can be rolled out, with spelt and rye pastry being the easiest to work with.

To roll a pie crust made with alternative flours, use a well-floured pastry cloth and a cloth-covered and floured rolling pin. The next step is to transfer the crust to the pie dish. One way to meet this challenge is to invest about $13 in a pie crust spatula. (See "Sources," page 231). If you make pie crust infrequently, you probably can make do with just your pastry cloth. Roll out the bottom crust. Then set the pie dish on the edge of the pastry cloth next to the rolled crust, pick up the edge of the cloth farthest away from the dish, and flip the crust and cloth over the pie dish. Peel off the pastry cloth from the crust and patch and trim the crust as needed. If you are making a two-crust pie, fill the bottom crust with the filling, repeat the rolling process with the top crust, and flip the crust over the filling. Patch and trim the top crust, prick it gently with a fork, and crimp the edges of the top and bottom crusts together.

At the beginning of this chapter you will find a very easy recipe for quick-mix no-roll pie crust. The amaranth version of this crust is so tasty that I always use this recipe when I want an amaranth crust. Also included is a recipe for oil pastry made with your choice of ten different grains or grain alternatives, coconut crust, and "graham" cracker pie crust. The sugar-free pie filling recipes range from such old favorites as apple and cherry to novel pie fillings such as grape and no-bake pumpkin. If you can eat spelt and want a traditional pie crust, see page 208 for such a recipe made with white spelt flour and non-hydrogenated natural shortening.

Making a great pie for a special diet is not difficult. With these recipes, you can do it, and family and friends will love your pies!

Quick-Mix No-Roll Pie Crust

**Gluten-Free IF
made with a GF grain**

Are the holidays coming? With this recipe you can easily make a special diet treat. Here are three varieties of a quick-to-make pie crust to go with the fillings on pages 68 to 73. The amaranth crust has a delicious nutty taste. If you are allergic to wheat rather than gluten-intolerant, the spelt crust is near normal and will be enjoyed by guests. The rice crust is bland-tasting, but is included for celiacs who are not used to amaranth.

Amaranth (GF):

1½ cups amaranth flour
¾ cup arrowroot
½ teaspoon salt
½ teaspoon baking powder*
⅝ cup oil
¼ cup cold water

Rice (GF):

3 cups rice flour
½ teaspoon salt
½ teaspoon baking powder*
¼ teaspoon cinnamon (optional)
⅔ cup oil
⅓ cup cold water or apple juice

White Spelt:

2¾ cups white spelt flour
½ teaspoon salt
½ teaspoon baking powder*
½ cup oil
¼ cup cold water

Chose one set of ingredients above. In a large bowl, stir together the flour(s), salt, baking powder, and optional cinnamon. Measure the water or juice and oil and stir them together thoroughly. Before they have a chance to separate, pour them into the bowl with the flour. Stir the ingredients together quickly; if the flour does not all incorporate into the dough readily, cut the mixture with the side of the spoon to help it come into a crumbly mixture. Do not stir or cut the dough for very long; you should not over-work the dough.

For two one-crust pies, press half of the dough on to the bottom and sides of each of two pie plates. Preheat your oven to 400°F. Bake for 10 to 15 minutes or until the pie crust is lightly browned.

For a two-crust pie, press half of the dough on to the bottom and sides of pie plate, add the filling, and crumble the other half of the dough over the filling. Bake as directed in the filling recipe. Makes two single pie crusts or enough pastry for a two-crust pie.

*Note on baking powder: Use Featherweight™ brand baking powder if you are allergic to corn. It contains potato starch instead of cornstarch.

Oil Pastry

**Gluten-Free IF
made with a GF grain**

This pastry is a little more difficult to handle than pastry made with shortening but is more healthy because it avoids saturated fat. Use a pasty cloth to roll your pastry out, or just press half of the dough into the pie plate for the bottom crust and crumble the remaining half of the dough over your fruit filling.

Amaranth (GF):

1½ cups amaranth flour
¾ cup arrowroot
½ teaspoon salt
½ cup oil
4 to 5 tablespoons water

Barley:

3 cups barley flour
½ teaspoon salt
½ cup oil
6 to 7 tablespoons water

Buckwheat (GF):

3 cups buckwheat flour
½ teaspoon salt
¾ cup oil
6 to 8 tablespoons water

Kamut:

3 cups kamut flour
½ teaspoon salt
⅔ cup oil
4 to 5 tablespoons water

Oat:

3 cups oat flour
½ teaspoon salt
½ cup oil
4 to 5 tablespoons water

Quinoa (GF):

2 cups quinoa flour
1 teaspoon baking soda
¼ teaspoon unbuffered vitamin C powder
½ teaspoon cinnamon (optional)
½ cup oil
4 to 7 tablespoons water

Rice (GF):

3 cups brown or white rice flour
½ teaspoon salt
½ cup oil
6 to 8 tablespoons water

Rye:

2½ cups rye flour
½ teaspoon salt
⅔ cup oil
4 to 5 tablespoons water

White Spelt:

2½ cups white spelt flour
½ teaspoon salt
⅜ cup oil
5 to 6 tablespoons water

Whole Spelt:

3 cups whole spelt flour
½ teaspoon salt
½ cup oil
5 to 6 tablespoons water

Teff (GF):

3 cups teff flour
½ teaspoon salt
½ cup oil
5 to 6 tablespoons water

Choose one set of ingredients above or from the previous pages. If you are making a one-crust pie, preheat your oven to 350°F for the quinoa crust or to 400°F for any other type crust.

In a large bowl, combine the flour(s) with the salt, or for the quinoa crust, with the baking soda, vitamin C crystals, and cinnamon. Add the oil and blend it in thoroughly with a pastry cutter. Add the smallest amount of water listed and mix the dough with a large fork or spoon until it begins to stick together, adding more water if needed. Divide the dough in half.

For one-crust pies, press each half of the dough into a glass pie dish, gently prick it with a fork, and bake it until the bottom of the crust begins to brown. The baking temperatures and times for each kind of crust are as follows:

Amaranth: 15 to 18 minutes at 400°F
Barley: 15 to 18 minutes at 400°F
Buckwheat: 15 to 18 minutes at 400°F
Kamut: 13 to 18 minutes at 400°F
Oat: 15 to 20 minutes at 400°F
Quinoa: 20 to 25 minutes at 350°F
Rice: 15 to 18 minutes at 400°F
Rye: 15 to 20 minutes at 400°F
White Spelt: 13 to 17 minutes at 400°F
Whole Spelt: 18 to 22 minutes at 400°F
Teff: 15 to 18 minutes at 400°F

For a two-crust pie, make the pie filling (or have the fruit prepared and cooking) before you make the crust. Preheat your oven to the temperature given in the filling recipe. Press half of the dough into the bottom of a glass pie dish. Fill the crust with the filling. To top the pie, crumble the second half of the dough and sprinkle it over the filling. Bake as directed in the pie recipe.

White spelt is the best grain for a rolled pie crust, but if you do not mind a little patching if necessary, you can also roll whole spelt, barley or rye crust using a pastry cloth. Flour the pastry cloth and cloth-covered rolling pin well. Roll half of the dough to about ⅛ inch thick. Use the pastry cloth to fold the crust in half, transfer it to the pie dish and unfold it, or flip the crust into the pie dish as described on page 62, or use a pie spatula to transfer it. Gently ease the crust into the pie dish without stretching it. Cut the excess dough off about ½ outside the edge of the dish and fold it under. Crimp the edge of the crust. If you have pie weights, place them in the crust to help prevent it from shrinking. Bake the crust for the time directed above or until it is golden brown.

For a two crust pie, place the bottom crust in the pie dish as above. Trim the pastry even with the edge of the dish. Preheat your oven to the temperature directed in the filling recipe. Put the pie filling in the bottom crust. Roll out the top crust. Use the pastry cloth to fold the top crust in half, transfer it to the pie dish and unfold it over the filling, or use a pie crust spatula, or flip the top crust over the filling as described on page 62. Cut the edge of the pastry so it overlaps the bottom crust by about ½ inch. Fold the edge of the top crust under the bottom crust and press the three-layer edge together with a fork. Pierce the top crust with the fork to allow steam to escape. Bake as directed in the filling recipe. Makes two single pie crusts or enough pastry for a two-crust pie.

Coconut Pie Crust

Gluten-Free

This grain-free pie crust makes a delicious pumpkin or cherry pie. It is best made with very finely shredded coconut.

> 2 cups very finely shredded or shredded unsweetened coconut (See "Sources," page 233 for very finely shredded coconut).
> Melted coconut oil – ⅜ cup with very finely shredded coconut OR ¼ cup with regular shredded coconut

Preheat your oven to 300°F. Melt a little more coconut oil than you expect to use in a saucepan or microwave oven. Measure the coconut into a glass pie dish. Measure and add the coconut oil to the pie dish. Thoroughly mix the coconut with the melted coconut oil in the dish. Firmly press them onto the bottom and sides of the pie dish. Bake the crust for 12 to 15 minutes, or until it begins to brown. Cool the crust completely before filling it with the slightly-cooled pie filling of your choice. Makes a single pie crust.

"Graham" Cracker Pie Crust

Gluten-Free IF
made with GF crackers

1 cup graham cracker crumbs made from "Spelt 'Graham' Crackers," page
203, or commercially made gluten-free graham crackers such as
Out of the Breadbox™ brand (See "Sources," page 231).
2 tablespoons date sugar (optional)
¼ cup (½ stick) butter, Earth Balance™ non-hydrogenated margarine, or
Spectrum Naturals™ non-hydrogenated shortening,

Pulse the graham crackers in a food processor to make crumbs, or put the graham crackers in a plastic bag and roll it with a rolling pin or drinking glass to make fine crumbs. Melt the butter, margarine, or shortening. In a 9 inch or 10 inch pie plate, stir together the graham cracker crumbs, date sugar, and melted butter, margarine or shortening. Press the crumbs firmly into the bottom and up the sides of the pie dish. If you have another pie plate of the same size, put it into the first pie plate and press it down to make a nice, firm crust; then remove the second pie plate. Bake the crust for 15 minutes or until it is nicely browned. Cool the crust completely before filling it.

Apple Pie

Gluten-Free IF
made with a GF crust

You will never miss the sugar in this all time favorite pie.

6 to 7 apples, peeled, cored and sliced to make about 5 cups of slices or
1½ 20-ounce cans of water-packed apple slices such as Mussleman's™
brand, drained
⅜ cup apple juice concentrate, thawed
1 teaspoon cinnamon
An additional ¼ cup of apple juice concentrate, thawed
2 tablespoons arrowroot or tapioca starch OR 3 tablespoons quick cooking
(Minute™) tapioca
Pastry for a two crust pie, recipes on pages 63 to 67

Combine the apple slices, ⅝ cup apple juice concentrate, and cinnamon in a saucepan. Bring them to a boil and reduce the heat to a simmer. For fresh apples, simmer for about 10 minutes. If you are using canned apples, simmer for a minute or two to heat them. While they are cooking, stir together the additional ¼ cup apple juice concentrate with the starch or tapioca. If you are using the quick-cooking tapioca, let it stand for at least five minutes in the juice. Stir the mixture into the saucepan at the end of the simmering time for the apples. Continue to cook on medium heat until the fruit mixture returns to a boil and thickens.

While the fruit is simmering, preheat your oven to 400°F. When the filling is cooked, put it into the unbaked bottom pie crust. Cover the filling with the top crust. Bake the pie at 400°F for 10 minutes; then reduce the heat to 350°F and continue to bake it for another 40 to 50 minutes or until the top and bottom crusts are golden brown. Makes 6 servings.

Blueberry Pie

**Gluten-Free IF
made with a GF crust**

This pie is quick, easy, and convenient to make using frozen blueberries.

1½ pounds fresh or frozen unsweetened blueberries
1 cup of apple juice concentrate, thawed
3 tablespoons arrowroot or tapioca starch OR 5 tablespoons quick cooking
  (Minute™) tapioca
1 baked single pie crust OR 1 batch of pastry for a two-crust pie, recipes on
  pages 63 to 68

Combine the apple juice concentrate and thickener in a saucepan. If you are using the quick cooking tapioca, let it stand in the juice for at least 5 minutes. Add the blueberries to the pan and stir. Heat the fruit mixture over low to medium heat, stirring frequently, until it comes to a boil and thickens.

For a one-crust pie, cool the filling for 10 minutes before putting it into a baked and cooled crust. Refrigerate the pie.

For a two-crust pie, while the fruit is cooking, preheat your oven to 400°F. Put the filling into the unbaked bottom pie crust. Cover the filling with the top crust. Bake the pie at 400°F for 10 minutes; then reduce the heat to 350°F and continue to bake it for another 40 to 50 minutes or until the top and bottom crusts are golden brown. Makes 6 servings.

Peach Pie

Gluten-Free IF
made with a GF crust

This is delicious made with fresh peaches in the summer, but you can make it year-round using canned or frozen peaches.

> 5 cups of peeled, pitted, and sliced fresh peaches OR 5 cups of canned water packed peaches, drained, OR 1½ 16-ounce bags of unsweetened frozen peaches
> ⅞ cup apple or pineapple juice concentrate, divided
> ¼ teaspoon cinnamon (optional)
> 3 tablespoons tapioca starch or arrowroot
> 1 baked single pie crust OR 1 batch of pastry for a two-crust pie, recipes on pages 63 to 68

If you are using fresh or frozen peaches, simmer the peaches and cinnamon with ⅝ cup of the juice until the peaches are just tender. If you are using canned peaches, combine the peaches and ⅝ cup of juice and bring to a boil. Mix the remaining ¼ cup juice with the tapioca starch or arrowroot, stir it into the peaches, and cook the mixture over medium heat until it has thickened. For a one-crust pie, cool the peaches for 10 minutes, then pour the filling into a baked and cooled pie crust and refrigerate the pie.

For a two-crust pie, you do not need to simmer the peaches until they are tender. Just bring the peaches plus ⅝ cup juice to a boil, stir in the tapioca flour or arrowroot mixture, and simmer the mixture until it is thickened before putting the filling into the crust.

Preheat your oven to 400°F. Put the filling into the prepared bottom pie crust of a two-crust pie. Cover it with the top crust and crimp the edges together. Prick the top crust to allow steam to escape. Bake the pie at 400°F for 10 minutes; then reduce the heat to 350°F and continue to bake it for another 40 to 50 minutes or until the top and bottom crusts are golden brown. Makes 6 servings.

Cherry Pie

Gluten-Free IF
made with a GF crust

> 2 16 ounce cans water-packed tart pie cherries, drained
> ¾ cup Fruit Sweet™ or ⅝ cup agave or honey plus ⅛ cup water or cherry juice
> 3 tablespoons arrowroot or tapioca starch OR ¼ cup quick-cooking (Minute™) tapioca
> Pastry for a two crust pie, recipes on pages 63 to 67

Thoroughly drain the liquid from the cherries in the can. Combine the Fruit Sweet™ or agave or honey plus cherry juice or water with the thickener in a saucepan. If you are using the quick cooking tapioca, let it stand in the liquid for at least five minutes before you begin cooking the filling. Add the cherries and stir. Heat the fruit mixture over low to medium heat, stirring frequently, until it comes to a boil and thickens.

Preheat your oven to 400°F. Put the filling into the prepared bottom pie crust. Cover it with the top crust and crimp the edges together. Prick the top crust to allow steam to escape. Bake the pie at 400°F for 10 minutes; then reduce the heat to 350°F and continue to bake it for another 40 to 50 minutes or until the top and bottom crusts are golden brown. Makes 8 servings.

Grape Pie

**Gluten-Free IF
made with a GF crust**

You will be surprised at how flavorful this unusual fruit-sweetened pie is.

4 cups seedless red grapes
⅜ cup unsweetened purple grape juice concentrate, thawed
2½ tablespoons quick-cooking (Minute™) tapioca
1 batch of pastry for a two-crust pie, recipes on pages 63 to 67

Prepare the pastry. Roll out half of the pastry and put it into a glass pie dish as described on page 62 or pat half of it into the dish. Combine the grapes, juice, and tapioca in a saucepan and allow them to stand for five minutes. Bring them to a boil and then pour them into the bottom crust.

Preheat your oven to 350°F. Roll out the top crust and cover the filling with it, or sprinkle the filling with crumbs of the other half of the dough. Bake the pie for 50 to 60 minutes, or until the top and bottom crusts are golden brown. Makes 1 pie, or about 6 servings.

No Bake Pumpkin Pie

Gluten-Free IF
made with a GF crust

This pie is too delicious to serve only on holidays. Those who have severe diabetes or Candidiasis might be able to indulge in dessert if you make this pie with stevia.

1 envelope unflavored gelatin OR 1 tablespoon coarse agar flakes OR
    2 teaspoons fine agar powder
1 cup water
1 16-ounce can pumpkin
1 cup date sugar OR ¼ teaspoon pure stevia powder
1 teaspoon cinnamon
1 teaspoon nutmeg
¼ teaspoon ground cloves
¼ teaspoon allspice
¼ teaspoon ginger
1 baked pie crust, recipes on pages 63 to 68

Prepare and bake the pie shell. Put the water in a saucepan and sprinkle the gelatin or agar over the surface of the water. Heat the water over medium heat, stirring occasionally, until it comes to a boil and the gelatin or agar dissolves. If you are using the stevia, stir it in and make sure it completely dissolves, using a spoon to press any lumps against the side of the pan until they are totally dissipated. Stir in the rest of the ingredients. Put the pumpkin mixture into the pie shell and refrigerate it for several hours until it is thoroughly chilled. Serve with sugar-free whipped cream if tolerated, page 196, or "Nutty Whipped Cream," page 196. Makes 6 servings.

No-Bake Strawberry Pie

Gluten-Free IF
made with a GF crust

6 cups (about 1½ quarts) fresh strawberries
½ cup agave, Fruit Sweet™ or honey
4 tablespoons tapioca starch
1 baked pie crust, recipes on pages 63 to 68

Wash and hull the strawberries. If they are very large, cut them in half. Set aside about 4½ cups of the strawberries. Mash the remaining 1½ cups thoroughly with a fork to yield 1 cup of mashed strawberries. If the yield is less than 1 cup, add some more whole strawberries and mash them to bring the volume of mashed strawberries up to 1 cup. Combine the mashed strawberries, sweetener, and tapioca starch in a saucepan. Cook the mixture over medium heat, stirring it frequently at first and then constantly as it gets quite warm, until it thickens and boils. Then cook it another minute or two until the color becomes darker and clearer. Remove the pan from the heat and allow the strawberry mixture to cool until it is just warm. Then stir in the whole or halved strawberries and put the filling into the pie shell. Chill the pie at least three hours or until it is set before you serve it. Makes 6 servings.

Cream Pies

**Gluten-Free IF
made with a GF crust**

Use this recipe to make chocolate, carob, vanilla, or coconut cream pie.

    1 baked pie crust, recipes on pages 63 to 68
    1 batch of pudding, recipes on page 44

Prepare and bake a single pie crust. Allow it to cool thoroughly. Make the pudding according to the recipe. Cover the surface of the pudding with waxed or parchment paper or with plastic wrap to prevent a skin from forming and allow it to cool to lukewarm. Put the pudding into the pie shell and refrigerate it for several hours or until it is thoroughly chilled. Serve with sugar-free whipped cream, page 196, if tolerated. Makes 6 servings.

Cakes and Frostings

Cakes are a significant part of most of our lives. They remind us of special occasions and past celebrations. What is a birthday or graduation party without a cake? A cake made by a family member or friend for a special event says, "Your accomplishment is important to me." I have spent hours planning what kind of cake to bake and sometimes even developing a new recipe for significant events in the lives of my children and other loved ones. Baking a cake connects me to the process of finishing a dissertation, getting a new job, or other special milestones in a way that nothing else can.

Those of us on special diets usually cannot eat a typical bakery cake piled high with decorator's icing made from shortening and powdered sugar. Although our cakes may not be as pretty as what the bakery produces, they taste better because they are made from wholesome ingredients and are not overwhelmingly sweet.

This chapter provides recipes for cakes rich with fruits and vegetables, spice cakes and gingerbread, chocolate, carob, lemon and vanilla cakes, and many more. Most are sweetened with fruit, fruit sweeteners or agave; a few are sweetened with molasses. The cake toppings and frostings are unique and delicious. Because this book avoids white sugar and corn (the two ingredients in powdered sugar), there is no decorator icing recipe here. Yet you will find coconut frosting, broiled nut toppings, fruit-based toppings, and cream cheese frostings that are much more flavorful than typical bakery icing. Try one of the carrot cake recipes with lemon cream cheese frosting and you will wonder why anyone prefers bakery-type cakes.

Cakes made with alternative flours are not as light or as sturdy as cakes made with refined wheat flour, but they make up in flavor for what they lack in lightness. There are ways to deal with the fragility of these cakes. The simplest solution is to serve the cake from the pan instead of trying to remove it in one piece. Cakes kept in the pan are good candidates for broiled nut topping and are also easy to store.

When making a layer cake for a special occasion, you will be able to remove the layers from the pans more easily if you line the bottom of the pans with parchment paper. (Waxed paper can be substituted if you do not have parchment paper). Lay one of the pans on a piece of parchment paper and trace around it. Then cut the paper to yield as many pieces of paper as you have layers and which are nearly the same size and shape as the pans. Oil and flour the pans using the same kind of oil and flour that are in the cake. Place a piece of cut parchment paper in each pan; then oil and flour the paper. Add the cake batter and bake the cake as directed in the recipe. Cool it in the pans for ten to fifteen minutes after removing it from the oven. Run a knife around the sides of the cake in each pan. Place a wire rack on top of the cake, invert it, and lift off the pan. Remove the paper and hold a serving plate or another wire rack against the bottom of the cake and invert it again. Cool the cake completely before frosting it. Some of these cakes have rough tops; if you are making a two-layer cake, put one layer upside-down on the plate and top it with the second layer right-side up. For a three layer cake, use a serrated knife to level the top of the middle layer as needed.

Don't worry if some alternative frostings do not produce a cake that looks like a picture from a magazine, complete with swirls on the top and sides. Rather than being cosmetically perfect, these cakes and frostings are delicious and can be enjoyed without an allergic reaction or other health consequences. Frostings that are more challenging to spread, such as dairy-free chocolate frosting, should be appreciated for their flavor and the concern for health they represent rather than for strictly cosmetic reasons. Similarly, although agave can cause the color of vanilla, lemon, and other light cakes to be darker than expected, the flavor is superior. If you are concerned with the darker color of these cakes, use the fruit sweetener option which is given in the recipes instead of agave.

Every oven bakes a little differently, so you need to exercise special care when baking chocolate or carob cakes. Be sure you do not over-bake them because this can lead to dryness. The first time you make a chocolate or carob cake recipe, at the minimum baking time given in the recipe (or even a few minutes before this time if your oven bakes hot) test the cake by inserting a toothpick in the center of the pan. If the toothpick comes out dry, remove the cake from the oven immediately. If not, re-test the cake with a toothpick every two minutes until the toothpick comes out dry. Record your actual baking time in the margin of the recipe so you will know what to expect the next time you make that cake.

Celebrate your creativity and your pride in special accomplishments and occasions by baking a cake. You and your cake will likely be the recipient of many "oohs" and "aahs." Then when it is time for the party, cut the cake and watch everyone enjoy it and the special occasion!

Barley Pineapple Upside-Down Cake

The fruit topping eliminates the need for frosting on this easy, flavorful cake.

> 6 slices of fresh pineapple or pineapple canned in its own juice, drained (about ⅔ of a 20-ounce can)
> A few seedless red grapes or cherries (optional)
> 1 cup pineapple canned in its own juice or fresh pineapple with enough juice to cover it
> 1 cup pineapple juice concentrate, thawed
> ¼ cup oil
> 3 cups barley flour
> 1½ teaspoons baking soda
> ½ teaspoon unbuffered vitamin C powder

Preheat your oven to 375°F. Oil a 9 inch square cake pan. Arrange the pineapple slices in the pan, cutting them to fit as needed, and place a grape or pitted cherry in the center of each slice. Puree the 1 cup pineapple together with its juice with a hand blender or in a blender or food processor. Add the pineapple juice concentrate and oil to the puree and blend again briefly. Combine the flour, baking soda, and vitamin C powder in a large bowl. Add the pureed pineapple mixture and stir just until the liquid ingredients are mixed into the dry ingredients. Put the batter into the prepared pan and bake the cake for 30 to 40 minutes or until it is golden brown. Cool the cake in the pan for 10 minutes; then run a knife around the edges of the pan and invert it onto a serving dish. Makes one 9 inch square cake, about 9 servings.

Shoo Fly Pie Cake

Gluten-Free

This cake, based on the traditional Pennsylvania Dutch pie, is sweet, spicy, and grain and gluten-free.

> 2 cups amaranth flour
> ⅔ cup arrowroot
> 1 teaspoon baking soda
> ½ teaspoon unbuffered vitamin C powder
> 1½ teaspoons cinnamon
> ½ teaspoon nutmeg
> ½ teaspoon cloves
> ¾ cup molasses
> ½ cup water
> ¼ cup oil

Preheat your oven to 350°F. Oil and flour a 9 inch square baking pan. Combine the amaranth flour, arrowroot, baking soda, vitamin C powder, and spices in a large bowl. Mix together the molasses, water, and oil thoroughly and stir them into the dry ingredients until they are just mixed in. Put the batter into the prepared pan. Bake the cake for 25 to 30 minutes, or until a toothpick inserted in its center comes out dry. Makes one 9 inch cake, or about 9 servings.

Date-Nut Bundt Cake

Your non-allergic guests will ask for second helpings when this rich cake is served.

1½ cups quick rolled oats (uncooked)
1½ cups boiling water
¾ cup oil
¾ cup cool water
1½ cups oat flour
1 cup date sugar
1¼ teaspoons baking soda
½ teaspoon unbuffered vitamin C powder
1 teaspoon salt (optional)
2 teaspoons cinnamon
½ teaspoon ground cloves
1 cup chopped pitted dates
½ cup finely chopped nuts

Combine the oats and boiling water in a large bowl. Allow them to cool for 5 to 10 minutes. Stir in the oil and cool water and beat the mixture with a spoon until all the lumps are gone. While the oatmeal mixture is cooling, oil and flour a 12-cup bundt pan or an 8 or 9 inch square cake pan. Preheat your oven to 375°F. In another bowl, stir together the flour, date sugar, baking soda, vitamin C powder, salt, spices, dates and nuts. Add them to the oatmeal mixture and stir until they are just mixed in. Put the batter into the prepared pan. Bake the cake for 55 to 60 minutes. Cool the bundt cake in the pan for 30 minutes, then invert it onto a serving dish. The square cake may be served from the pan. If you want to frost this cake, drizzle the bundt cake with "Date Glaze," page 91, or frost the square cake with ⅔ of a batch of "Date Frosting," page 91. Makes 9 to 12 servings.

Rye Carrot Cake

This flavorful, moist cake is a favorite at our house.

2½ cups rye flour
2 teaspoons baking soda
½ teaspoon unbuffered vitamin C powder (Omit if using the pineapple juice).
1½ teaspoons cinnamon
¼ teaspoon cloves
1 cup raisins (optional)
1½ cups grated carrots
2 cups apple or white grape juice OR 1 cup thawed pineapple juice
    concentrate plus 1 cup water
¼ cup oil

Preheat your oven to 350°F. Grate and measure the carrots. Oil and flour a 9 inch square cake pan. In a large bowl, combine the flour, baking soda, vitamin C powder (if you are using it), spices, and raisins. In a small bowl, combine the carrots, juice, water (if you are using it), and oil. Stir the liquid ingredients into the dry ingredients until they are just mixed in. Put the batter into the prepared pan. Bake the cake for 45 to 55 minutes, or until it is lightly browned and a toothpick inserted into its center comes out dry. Makes one 9 inch square cake, or about 9 servings.

White Spelt Carrot Cake

This is especially delicious with lemon cream cheese frosting, page 93.

2¼ cups white spelt flour
¾ cup date sugar
1½ teaspoons baking soda
⅜ teaspoon unbuffered vitamin C powder
1¼ teaspoons cinnamon
¼ teaspoon cloves
¼ teaspoon salt
¾ cup raisins (optional)
1 cup grated carrots
⅜ cup oil
⅞ cup water

Preheat your oven to 350°F. Grate and measure the carrots. Oil and flour a 9 inch square cake pan. In a large bowl, combine the flour, date sugar, baking soda, vitamin C powder, salt, spices, and raisins. In a small bowl, combine the carrots, water, and oil. Stir the liquid ingredients into the dry ingredients until they are just mixed in. Put the batter into the prepared pan. Bake the cake for 30 to 40 minutes, or until it is lightly browned and a toothpick inserted into its center comes out dry. Makes one 9 inch square cake, or about 9 servings.

Quinoa Carrot Cake

Gluten-Free

Don't be alarmed if this grain and gluten-free cake falls a little in the middle. It will still be delicious.

1 cup raisins (optional)
1 teaspoon cinnamon
¼ teaspoon nutmeg
¼ teaspoon cloves
1½ cups apple juice concentrate
⅜ cup oil
1 cup grated carrots
1½ cups quinoa flour
½ cups tapioca flour
1½ teaspoons baking soda

Combine the raisins, spices, juice and oil in a saucepan. Bring them to a boil and simmer them, covered, for 5 minutes. Allow the mixture to cool to room temperature or just a little above room temperature. Preheat your oven to 325°F. Grate and measure the carrots and add them to the juice mixture. Oil and flour two 8 by 4 inch loaf pans. In a large bowl, combine the quinoa flour, tapioca flour, and baking soda. Stir the liquid ingredients into the dry ingredients until they are just mixed in. Put the batter into the prepared loaf pans. Bake the cakes for 40 to 50 minutes, or until they are lightly browned and a toothpick inserted into their centers comes out dry. This cake may appear to rise and then fall slightly during baking, but the texture will still be good. Makes two 8 by 4 inch cakes which freeze well.

Gingerbread

Gluten-Free IF
made with amaranth or quinoa

This is wonderful served from the baking pan with whipped topping. See the sugar-free whipped cream and "Nutty Whipped Cream" recipes on page 196.

Amaranth (GF):

1½ cups amaranth flour
½ cup arrowroot
1 teaspoon baking soda
¼ teaspoon unbuffered vitamin C powder
¾ teaspoon ginger
1 teaspoon cinnamon
¾ cup molasses
¼ cup water
¼ cup oil

Quinoa (GF):

1¼ cups quinoa flour
½ cup tapioca starch
1 teaspoon baking soda
¼ teaspoon unbuffered vitamin C powder
¾ teaspoon ginger
1 teaspoon cinnamon
¾ cup molasses
¼ cup water
¼ cup oil

Spelt:

2 cups whole spelt flour
1 teaspoon baking soda
¼ teaspoon unbuffered vitamin C powder
¾ teaspoon ginger
1 teaspoon cinnamon
¾ cup molasses
¼ cup water
¼ cup oil

Choose one set of ingredients above. Preheat your oven to 350°F. Oil and flour an 8 or 9 inch square cake pan. Combine the flour(s), baking soda. vitamin C, and spices in a large bowl. Mix the molasses with the water until the molasses is dissolved. Then add the oil and mix thoroughly. Stir the liquid ingredients into the dry ingredients until they are just combined. Put the batter into the prepared baking pan. Bake the cake for 30 to 35 minutes, or until a toothpick inserted in its center comes out dry. Makes about 9 servings.

Banana Spice Cake

**Gluten-Free IF
made with sorghum**

This sugar-free cake is moist and tasty. It is good plain or frosted with "Date Frosting," page 91.

> 4 cups oat, sorghum (milo), or barley flour
> 1 cup date sugar, pressed through a strainer to remove lumps if needed
> 2 teaspoons baking soda
> ½ teaspoon unbuffered vitamin C powder
> 2 teaspoons cinnamon
> ¾ teaspoon cloves
> ½ teaspoon allspice
> Pureed or thoroughly mashed bananas - 3 cups with oat or sorghum (milo)
>   flour OR 4 cups with barley flour
> ¾ cup oil
> 1 teaspoon vanilla extract (optional)

Preheat your oven to 375°F. Oil and flour a 13 by 9 inch cake pan, two 8 or 9 inch round cake pans, or muffin pans containing 24 to 28 wells. (For the best results with removing cupcakes from the pan, line the muffin cups with paper liners). In a large bowl, combine the flour, date sugar, baking soda, vitamin C powder, and spices. In a small bowl, combine the bananas, oil, and optional vanilla. Stir the liquid ingredients into the dry ingredients until they are just mixed. The batter will be thick. Scrape the batter into the prepared pan(s) and level it with a spatula or spoon. Bake the cake for 25 to 30 minutes or the cupcakes for 20 to 25 minutes or until lightly browned and a toothpick inserted in the center comes out dry. If you are making a layer cake, cool the layers in the pans for 15 minutes and then remove them carefully because they are very fragile. (See the tips on page 74 about lining the pans and removing layer cakes from their pans). Makes one 9 by 13 inch cake, two 8 or 9 inch cake layers, or 24 to 28 cupcakes.

Rice Banana Spice Cake

Gluten-Free

Although this spice cake is good made with rice, you may find yourself eating mostly rice if you are on a gluten-free diet. For more variety, try the other gluten-free spice cake recipes such as the cake on the previous page with made with sorghum (milo) flour or the amaranth cake which follows this recipe.

2¼ cups brown rice flour
½ cup tapioca starch
½ cup date sugar
2 teaspoons baking soda
½ teaspoon unbuffered vitamin C powder
1½ teaspoons cinnamon
¼ teaspoon cloves
¼ teaspoon allspice
¼ cup oil
2¼ cups pureed or thoroughly mashed bananas
½ teaspoons vanilla (optional)

Preheat your oven to 375°F. Oil and flour two loaf pan or an 8 or 9 inch round or square cake pan. In a large bowl, combine the flour, tapioca starch, date sugar, baking soda, vitamin C powder, and spices. In a small bowl, combine the bananas, oil, and optional vanilla. Stir the liquid ingredients into the dry ingredients until they are just mixed. The batter will be thick. Put the batter into the prepared pan. Bake for 25 to 40 minutes or until the cake is lightly browned and a toothpick inserted in the center comes out dry. If you are doubling this recipe to make a layer cake, cool the layers in the pans for 15 minutes and then remove them carefully because they are fragile. Makes one 8 or 9 inch round or square cake or two loaf cakes.

Note on layer cakes: This cake is sturdy enough to make an impressive layer cake. Double the recipe for a 3-layer cake. To easily remove the cake from the pans, line the bottoms of three round cake pan with parchment paper and oil and flour the paper as directed on page 74. Bake as above. Frost with 1½ batches of cream cheese frosting, page 93, or date frosting, page 91.

Amaranth Spice Cake

This cake is a real treat for those who must avoid all grains. Sweet spices and amaranth go together well.

2¼ cups amaranth flour
¾ cup arrowroot
2 teaspoons baking soda
½ teaspoon unbuffered vitamin C powder
1 teaspoon cinnamon
¼ teaspoon cloves
⅛ teaspoon allspice
½ cup agave or Fruit Sweet™
½ cup water
¼ cup oil

Preheat your oven to 350°F. Oil and flour a 8 by 4 inch loaf pan. In a large bowl, combine the amaranth flour, arrowroot, baking soda, vitamin C powder, and spices (and also the stevia if you are using it; see below). Mix together the agave or Fruit Sweet™, water and oil, and stir them into the dry ingredients until they are just mixed in. (The batter will be stiff). Put the batter into the prepared pan and bake it for 30 to 40 minutes. Cool the cake in the pan for 10 minutes, and then remove it if you wish to. Makes one 8 by 4 inch cake, or about 6 servings.

Stevia-sweetened spice cake variation: To sweeten this cake with stevia, omit the agave or Fruit Sweet™ and increase the water to 1 cup. Add ¼ to ½ teaspoon pure stevia powder, to taste, to the dry ingredients. If you are just getting used to stevia, start with the smaller amount.

Barley Vanilla Cake

3 cups barley flour
1 teaspoon salt
1½ teaspoons baking soda
½ teaspoon unbuffered vitamin C powder
1½ cups agave or Fruit Sweet™
½ cup water
⅜ cup oil
1 teaspoon vanilla

Preheat your oven to 350°F. Oil and flour two 8 by 4 inch loaf pans or a round or square cake pan. In a large bowl, combine the flour, baking soda, vitamin C powder, and salt. Mix together the sweetener, water, oil, and vanilla and stir them into the dry ingredients until they are just mixed in. Put the batter into the prepared pan(s) and bake for 45 to 50 minutes. Cool the cake in the pan for 10 minutes, and then remove it if you wish to. However, this cake is fragile so you may want to serve it from the pan. Makes about 9 to 10 servings.

***Note on the color of this cake:** When agave is baked with light-colored flour for a long time, the cake darkens in color. This cake will appear golden-brown on the inside, not white like you might expect from a vanilla cake. However, the flavor is delicious. The neutral flavor of agave allows the vanilla to shine. If the dark color concerns you, make this cake with Fruit Sweet™ instead of agave.

Rice Vanilla Cake

Gluten-Free

2¼ cups brown rice flour
1 cup tapioca starch
1 teaspoon salt
4 teaspoons guar gum
1½ teaspoons baking soda
¼ teaspoon unbuffered vitamin C powder
1½ cups agave or Fruit Sweet™
¼ cup oil
2 eggs, slightly beaten
1 teaspoon vanilla

Preheat your oven to 350°F. Oil and flour two 8 by 4 inch loaf pans or a round or square cake pan. In a large bowl, combine the flour, tapioca starch, baking soda, vitamin C powder, and salt. Mix together the sweetener, oil, eggs, and vanilla and stir them into the dry ingredients until they are just mixed in. Put the batter into the prepared pan(s) and bake for 45 to 50 minutes. Cool the cake in the pan for 10 minutes, and then remove it if you wish to. However, this cake is fragile so you may want to serve it from the pan. Makes about 9 to 10 servings.

*Note on the color of this cake: When agave is baked with light-colored flour for a long time, the cake darkens in color. This cake will appear golden-brown on the inside, not white like you might expect from a vanilla cake. However, the flavor is delicious. The neutral flavor of agave allows the vanilla to shine. If the dark color concerns you, make this cake with Fruit Sweet™ instead of agave.

Dark Carob Cake

Gluten-Free

This cake is intensely carob flavored and delicious. It makes a nice layer cake for special occasions.

2¼ cups quinoa flour
¾ cup tapioca starch
1½ cups carob powder pressed through a strainer to remove lumps if necessary
1 tablespoon baking soda
2 cups apple juice concentrate, thawed
1 cup oil

Preheat your oven to 350°F. Oil and flour two 8 or 9 inch round cake pans. Stir together the quinoa flour, tapioca starch, carob powder, and baking soda in a large bowl. Mix the apple juice and oil and stir them into the dry ingredients until they are just mixed in. Put the batter into the prepared pans and bake the cake for 30 to 35 minutes, or until a toothpick inserted into its center comes out dry. Do not overbake carob cakes since extra baking time tends to make them dry. Cool the cake in the pans for 10 minutes and then remove it from the pans. This cake is great frosted with "Banana Carob Frosting", page 90 or a double batch of "Coconut Frosting," page 92. Makes one 2-layer cake, or about 12 servings.

Carob Cake

**Gluten-Free IF
made with quinoa**

This cake is lighter than the cake above in both flavor and color and thus is good for "German carob cake." It can be made with either a gluten-free non-grain or a grain flour.

1½ cups quinoa flour plus ¾ cup tapioca starch OR 2¼ cups rye flour
⅓ cup carob powder
1½ teaspoons baking soda
1 cup apple juice concentrate, thawed
½ cup oil

Preheat your oven to 350°F. Oil and flour a round or square cake pan. Combine the flour(s), carob powder, and baking soda in a large bowl. Mix the juice and oil and stir them into the dry ingredients until they are just mixed in. Put the batter into the prepared pan and bake the cake for 25 to 30 minutes, or until a toothpick inserted in its center comes out dry. Do not overbake carob cakes since extra baking time tends to make them dry. Cool the cake in the pan for 10 minutes and then remove it from the pan if you wish to. This cake is not as fragile as some, and the recipe may be doubled to make a 2-layer cake. If you wish to frost this cake, use a half batch of "Banana Carob Frosting," page 92, or a full batch of "German Chocolate Frosting," page 95, or "Coconut Frosting," page 90. Makes one 8 inch or 9 inch cake, about 8 servings. For a two-layer cake, double the amounts of all the ingredients and the amount of frosting.

Stevia-sweetened carob cake variation: To sweeten this cake with stevia, omit the apple juice concentrate and replace it with 1 cup of water. Add ½ teaspoon unbuffered vitamin C powder and ¼ to ½ teaspoon pure stevia powder, to taste, to the dry ingredients. If you are just getting used to stevia, start with the smaller amount.

White Spelt Carob or Chocolate Cake

This is great served with cherry fruit sauce, page 115, instead of frosting, or make a double batch in round pans to use in "German Chocolate or Carob Cake," page 88.

2⅓ cups white spelt flour
¼ cup cocoa or carob powder
1¼ teaspoons baking soda
¼ teaspoon unbuffered vitamin C powder

½ teaspoon salt
1 cup plus 3 tablespoons apple juice concentrate, thawed
3 tablespoons oil
1 teaspoon vanilla extract (optional)

Preheat your oven to 350°F. Oil and flour an 8 inch square or round cake pan. In a large bowl, stir together the flour, cocoa or carob powder, baking soda, vitamin C powder, and salt. In a cup combine the apple juice concentrate, oil and vanilla. Stir the liquid mixture into the flour mixture until they are just combined. Put the batter into the prepared pan and bake the cake for 25 to 40 minutes or until a toothpick inserted into the center of the pan comes out dry. Do not overbake chocolate or carob cakes since extra baking time tends to make them dry. When the cake is done, place it on a cooling rack and allow it to cool completely. If desired, top it with cherry sauce, page 115, or frost it with coconut frosting, page 90, or chocolate cream cheese frosting, page 94. Cut it into squares and serve it from the pan. Makes about 9 servings.

Amaranth Chocolate Cake

Gluten-Free

This fudgey cake is a delicious treat for those who cannot have grains or gluten.

2 cups amaranth flour
¾ cup tapioca starch or arrowroot
⅓ cup cocoa
2 teaspoons baking soda
½ teaspoon unbuffered vitamin C powder
¾ cup agave or Fruit Sweet™
½ cup oil
1 teaspoon vanilla extract (optional)

Preheat your oven to 350°F. Oil and flour an 8 by 4 inch loaf pan. In a large bowl, stir together the flour, starch, cocoa, baking soda, and vitamin C powder. In a small bowl or cup combine the sweetener, oil and vanilla. Stir the liquid mixture into the flour mixture until they are just combined. (The batter will be stiff). Put the batter into the prepared pan and bake the cake for 30 to 40 minutes or until a toothpick inserted into the center of the pan comes out dry. Do not overbake chocolate cakes since extra baking time tends to make them dry. Place the pan on a cooling rack and allow it to cool completely. If desired, top it with cherry sauce, page 115, or frost it with coconut frosting, page 90, chocolate cream cheese frosting, page 94, or dairy-free chocolate frosting, page 94. Cut it into thick slices and serve it from the pan. Makes about 6 to 8 servings.

Rice Chocolate Cake

1¼ cups brown rice flour
⅓ cup tapioca starch
⅓ cup potato flour
⅓ cup cocoa
2¾ teaspoons guar gum (optional)
1½ teaspoons baking powder
⅜ teaspoon baking soda
¼ teaspoon salt
2 tablespoons oil
2 extra large eggs or enough smaller eggs to yield ½ cup slightly beaten egg
¾ cup agave or Fruit Sweet™
⅝ cup applesauce
1 teaspoon vanilla extract (optional)

Preheat your oven to 350°F. Oil and flour two 8 by 4 inch loaf pans or an 8 or 9 inch round or square cake pan. In a large bowl, stir together the flours, starch, cocoa, guar gum, baking soda, vitamin C powder, and salt. In a small bowl or cup combine the sweetener, oil, eggs, applesauce, and vanilla. Stir the liquid mixture into the flour mixture until they are just combined. (The batter will be stiff). Put the batter into the prepared pan and bake the cake for 35 to 45 minutes or until a toothpick inserted into the center of the pan comes out dry. Do not overbake chocolate cakes since extra baking time tends to make them dry. Place the pan on a cooling rack and allow it to cool completely. If desired, top it with cherry sauce, page 115, or frost it with coconut frosting, page 90, chocolate cream cheese frosting, page 94, or dairy-free chocolate frosting, page 94. Cut it into squares and serve it from the pan. Makes about 9 servings.

German Chocolate or Carob Cake

Two layers of carob or chocolate cake, recipes on pages 85 to 88 or 214
Frosting of your choice from this list:
    Dairy-Free German Chocolate Cake Frosting, page 95
    German Chocolate Frosting, page 215

If the cake recipe you have chosen makes only one layer of cake, double it to make two layers. For the amaranth chocolate cake recipe, page 87, make a triple batch of cake batter and bake it in two round cake pans. You will need to remove the cake layers from the pans, so as with all layer cakes made with alternative flour, oil and flour the cake pans, line the bottoms of the pans with parchment paper cut to fit, and then oil and flour the paper. (See page 74 for details). Bake the cake, remove the layers from the pans, and allow them to cool completely. Put one layer of the cake on a serving dish top side down. Prepare the frosting. Immediately spread the first layer with half of the frosting. Place the second layer on top of the first layer with the smooth bottom side down. Frost the top of the cake with the second half of the frosting. Makes about 12 servings.

Barley Lemon Cake

This lemon cake is delicious! If you can eat spelt and want to impress guests with a lemon layer cake, also try "Luscious Lemon Cake," page 212.

    3 cups barley flour
    1 teaspoon salt
    1½ teaspoons baking soda
    ½ teaspoon unbuffered vitamin C powder
    1½ cups agave or Fruit Sweet™
    ½ cup water
    ⅜ cup oil
    1 teaspoon lemon zest or ⅛ teaspoon lemon oil (See "Sources," page 229)

Preheat your oven to 350°F. Oil and flour two 8 by 4 inch loaf pans or a round or square cake pan. If you are using lemon zest, remove it from a lemon being careful to take only the yellow outer layer. (The white layer is bitter). In a large bowl, combine the flour, baking soda, vitamin C powder, and salt. Mix together the sweetener, water, oil, and lemon zest or oil and stir them into the dry ingredients until they are just mixed in. Put the batter into the prepared pan(s) and bake for 45 to 50 minutes. Cool the cake in the pan for 10 minutes, and then remove it if you wish to. However, this cake is fragile so you may want to serve it from the pan. If desired, frost the cake with a half batch of lemon cream cheese frosting, page 93, or coconut frosting, page 90. Makes about 8 to 10 servings.

*Note on the color of this cake: When agave is baked with light-colored flour for a long time, the cake darkens in color. This cake will appear golden-brown on the inside, not yellow like you might expect from a lemon cake. However, the flavor is delicious. If the dark color concerns you, make this cake with Fruit Sweet™ instead of agave.

Rice Lemon Cake

Top this gluten-free cake with lemon cream cheese frosting (page 93) for a real treat!

2¼ cups brown rice flour
1 cup tapioca starch
1 teaspoon salt
4 teaspoons guar gum
1½ teaspoons baking soda
¼ teaspoon unbuffered vitamin C powder
1½ cups agave or Fruit Sweet™
¼ cup oil
2 eggs, slightly beaten
1 teaspoon lemon zest or ⅛ teaspoon lemon oil (See "Sources," page 229)

Preheat your oven to 350°F. Oil and flour two 8 by 4 inch loaf pans or a round or square cake pan. If you are using lemon zest, remove it from a lemon being careful to take only the yellow outer layer. (The white layer is bitter). In a large bowl, combine the flour, tapioca starch, guar gum, baking soda, vitamin C powder, and salt. Mix together the sweetener, oil, eggs, and lemon zest or oil and stir them into the dry ingredients until they are just mixed in. Put the batter into the prepared pan(s) and bake it for 45 to 50 minutes. Cool the cake in the pan for 10 minutes, and then remove it if you wish to. However, this cake is fragile so you may want to serve it from the pan. If desired, frost the cake with a half batch of lemon cream cheese frosting, page 93, or coconut frosting, below. Makes about 8 to 10 servings.

***Note on the color of this cake:** When agave is baked with light-colored flour for a long time, the cake darkens in color. This cake will appear golden-brown on the inside, not yellow like you might expect from a lemon cake. However, the flavor is delicious. If the dark color is a problem for you, make this cake with Fruit Sweet™ instead of agave.

Coconut Frosting

This frosting can be used on any kind of cake, but it is especially good on chocolate or carob cakes.

½ cup agave, Fruit Sweet™ or honey
½ cup water
2½ tablespoons of tapioca starch OR 3 tablespoons arrowroot
2 to 3 cups of unsweetened coconut – 2 cups if it is very finely shredded or
up to 3 cups for regular shredded unsweetened coconut

Combine the sweetener, water, and starch in a saucepan. Cook it over medium heat, stirring frequently, until it thickens and boils. Immediately stir in enough of the coconut to make a thick, yet spreadable, paste. Spread it on the cake immediately before it cools. This recipe makes enough frosting for one 8 or 9 inch cake.

#

Gluten-Free IF
made with sorghum or rice

This is especially good on the barley or rice vanilla cakes, page 84, any of the spice cake recipes on pages 81 to 83, or a square date-nut cake, page 77.

1⅓ cups water
3 tablespoons spelt, rye, sorghum (milo), kamut, oat, rice, or barley flour
2 cups date sugar

Remove any lumps in the date sugar by pressing it through a wire mesh strainer with the back of a spoon. Mix the water and flour in a small saucepan. Cook the mixture over medium heat until it is thick, smooth, and bubbly, stirring frequently. Remove the pan from the heat, add the date sugar, and beat the frosting until it is smooth. Frost the cake immediately. Makes enough frosting for one 9 by 13 inch cake or two 8 or 9 inch layers.

#

Gluten-Free IF
made with sorghum or rice

Drizzle this on "Date-Nut Bundt Cake," page 77.

⅔ cup water
2 tablespoons spelt, rye, sorghum (milo), kamut, oat, rice, or barley flour
⅔ cup date sugar

Remove any lumps in the date sugar by pressing it through a wire mesh strainer with the back of a spoon. Mix the flour and water in a small saucepan. Cook the mixture over medium heat until it is thick, smooth, and bubbly, stirring it frequently. Remove it from the heat and add the date sugar. Beat it until it is smooth and drizzle it on the cake.

Broiled Nut-Coconut Cake Topping

Gluten-Free

Use this on a chocolate or carob cake for a dessert that's quick and easy to make yet much like German chocolate cake.

⅜ cup agave, Fruit Sweet™, or honey
2 tablespoons butter or Spectrum Naturals™ non-hydrogenated shortening
½ cup finely shredded unsweetened coconut
½ cup finely chopped nuts

Turn on your broiler to 450°F. Put the sweetener and butter or shortening in a sauce pan, bring it to a boil, and boil for about one minute. Add the coconut and nuts while the liquid mixture is still hot, mix it well, and spread it on a cake which is still in its baking pan. Put the cake under the broiler about 5 inches from the element. Watch it carefully while it is broiling; broil it for about 3 to 6 minutes, or until the nuts and coconut are golden brown. This recipe makes enough frosting for one loaf cake, generously topped, or a round cake thinly spread with the topping. Double the recipe to frost a 13-inch by 9-inch cake.

Banana Carob Frosting

Gluten-Free

This not-too-sweet frosting was developed for "Dark Carob Cake," page 85, but is good with other carob cakes too.

2 cups thoroughly mashed bananas
¼ cup tapioca flour or arrowroot
1¾ cups carob powder

Beat all of the ingredients together with an electric mixer for about 2 minutes on high speed, or until the frosting is smooth. Frost the cake immediately. This recipe makes enough frosting for the tops and sides of two cake layers.

Cream Cheese Glaze

Gluten-Free

This is good drizzled over almost any cake.

> 3 ounces of cream or Neufatchel cheese
> ¼ cup (½ stick) butter
> ¼ cup agave, Fruit Sweet™, or honey
> ½ teaspoon vanilla, lemon, or other flavoring (optional)

Allow the cream cheese and butter to come to room temperature. The butter will soften more quickly if you cut it into 4 or 5 slices. Combine all of the ingredients with a hand blender. Drizzle cake, rolls or doughnuts with this glaze and refrigerate them until serving time, or refrigerate the glaze and frost the cake, rolls or doughnuts right before serving. Makes a scant cup of glaze.

Cream Cheese Frosting

Gluten-Free

This is an alternative frosting that looks beautiful! It also tastes divine – full of flavor that shines through because it is not too sweet.

> 1 8-ounce package cream cheese at room temperature
> ½ cup (1 stick) butter at room temperature
> 4 to 6 tablespoons agave, Fruit Sweet™, or honey, to taste
> 1 teaspoon vanilla extract, 2 teaspoons lemon or orange zest, or ¼ teaspoon
>   lemon or orange oil (See "Sources," page 229)

If you are using lemon or orange zest, remove the zest from the fruit being careful to take only the colored outer layer. (The white layer is bitter) Using an electric mixer, blender, food processor, or hand blender, mix together the cream cheese and butter, beating until fluffy. Mix in the vanilla extract, citrus zest, or citrus oil. Add the agave, Fruit Sweet™ or honey one tablespoon at a time, tasting it as you add the sweetener until you get it to your preferred level of sweetness. If you add enough sweetener to make the frosting too thin to spread easily, refrigerate it for 15 minutes or more until it is a good spreading consistency. Frost the cake. This frosting will be very soft but it gets firmer when chilled. Store any cake frosted with this frosting in the refrigerator. Makes about 1¾ cups of frosting, or enough to frost a two-layer cake.

Chocolate Cream Cheese Frosting

Gluten-Free

This is the ideal chocolate frosting for those who tolerate dairy products — smooth, fluffy, and delicious.

>1 8-ounce package cream cheese at room temperature
>½ cup (1 stick) butter at room temperature
>⅜ cup cocoa
>⅝ to ⅞ cup agave, Fruit Sweet™, or honey, to taste

Using an electric mixer, blender, food processor, or hand blender, mix together the cream cheese, butter, and cocoa, beating until fluffy. Mix in ⅝ cup of the agave, Fruit Sweet™, or honey. Then add the rest of the sweetener one tablespoon at a time, to taste. (How much sweetener you use will depend on what kind of cocoa and sweetener you used and how sweet you like your frosting). If you add enough sweetener to make the frosting too thin to spread easily, refrigerate it for 15 minutes or more until it is good spreading consistency. Frost the cake. This is an alternative frosting that looks beautiful. This frosting will be very soft but it gets firmer when chilled. Store any cake frosted with this frosting in the refrigerator. Makes about 2 cups of frosting, or enough to frost a two-layer cake.

Dairy-Free Chocolate Frosting

Gluten-Free

If you can have chocolate but not dairy products, try this frosting. It is very flavorful and tastes much better than the additive-laden frosting that comes in a plastic tub although it is not as easy to spread.

>3 ounces unsweetened baking chocolate
>3 tablespoons Spectrum Naturals™ non-hydrogenated shortening
>¼ cup water just under the boiling point
>2 cups very finely ground* maple sugar, such as India Tree™ maple sugar
>   (See "Sources," page 233)
>2 tablespoons agave

Bring some water to a simmer in the bottom of a double boiler, making sure that the water level is below, not touching, the bottom of the upper insert. Put the chocolate and shortening in the top of the boiler. While they are melting, bring some water to a boil and then remove it from the heat. When the chocolate and shortening are melted, remove the pan from the heat and add ¼ cup of the just-boiled water, stirring while you add it. The chocolate will thicken. Keep stirring it until the consistency is uniform. Return the pan to the heat and add the maple sugar a little at a time, beating with a spoon or wire whisk after each addition, over about 2 minutes of time. Then continue cooking the frosting over simmering water for another 4 to 5 minutes, beating nearly constantly, until it becomes thicker and the graininess of the sugar has diminished. Remove the upper insert of the double boiler from the pan. Continue to beat the frosting for a minute or two; it will become somewhat crumbly. Then beat in the agave to make the frosting a spreadable consistency. Immediately frost the cake. This makes about 1½ cups of frosting, or enough for a two-layer cake.

This frosting is not especially easy to spread. Don't be hesitant to use your fingers to make the frosting go where you want it. Also, don't expect cosmetic perfection. Although this frosting isn't gorgeous and fluffy, it is fudgey and delicious and will keep those on dairy-free diets from being deprived of chocolate-frosted cake.

***Note on maple sugar:** If the maple sugar you are using is not very finely ground, almost to the point of being powder, you can make it finer by blending it in a food processor.

Dairy-Free German Chocolate Frosting

Gluten-Free

This is a low-allergen frosting for German chocolate or carob cake. If you tolerate dairy products and eggs, see the more traditional German chocolate frosting recipe on page 215.

> ½ cup agave, Fruit Sweet™ or honey
> ½ cup water
> 2½ tablespoons of tapioca starch OR 3 tablespoons arrowroot
> 1 to 1¼ cups of chopped pecans or almonds
> 1 to 1½ cups of unsweetened coconut – about 1 cup if it is very finely
>   shredded or up to 1½ cups for "regular" shredded unsweetened coconut

Combine the sweetener, water, and starch in a saucepan. Cook over medium heat, stirring frequently, until the mixture thickens and boils. Immediately stir in 1 cup of the nuts and 1 cup of the coconut. If the frosting is not totally saturated with nuts and coconut, stir in the rest of the nuts and enough of the coconut to make a thick, yet spreadable, paste. Spread it on the cake immediately before it cools. This recipe makes enough frosting for one 8 or 9 inch cake. Double the amounts for a layer cake.

Creamy Cake Topping

Gluten-Free

This topping is not thick enough to put between two layers of cake when freshly made, but it is wonderful on a one-layer cake. If you refrigerate the cake, it will firm up to the consistency of creamy frosting.

½ cup cashew or almond butter
⅓ cup water
⅓ cup agave, or to taste
¼ cup oil
1 teaspoon vanilla

Combine the nut butter, water, and agave using a hand blender, blender, or food processor. Slowly add the oil while processing until the topping becomes thicker and creamy. Briefly blend in the vanilla. Use it to top the cake immediately or refrigerate the topping for later use. It will thicken as it chills. If you find that the topping is not sweet enough or too sweet for your taste preference, adjust the amount of agave used by a tablespoon the next time you make this topping. Makes about 1½ cups of topping.

Ice Cream, Sherbet and Sorbet

Sweet and creamy, cold and luscious, there is nothing like ice cream on a hot summer day. Freshly homemade ice cream is always the best you have ever eaten, and you do not need an ice cream maker or a lot of time to make it at home. See pages 98 to 99 for two easy methods of making ice cream, sherbet, and sorbet without an ice cream maker.

High quality ingredients are the basis of delicious frozen desserts. If you can have cow's milk dairy products and an occasional splurge on fat, use cream or half-and-half to make great ice cream. If you are allergic to cow's milk or lactose intolerant, other types of milk, such as goat, soy, rice, nut, and coconut milk, also make delicious ice cream. Coconut milk can be purchased in either full-fat or reduced-fat varieties. Full-fat coconut milk makes exceptionally creamy ice cream that can be still frozen with great results. See page 98 for this easy method of making ice cream.

The sweeteners used in the ice cream, sherbet, and sorbet recipes in this chapter include agave, honey, Fruit Sweet™, and fruit juice concentrates. Agave has the most neutral, pure sweet flavor and therefore allows the flavor of the vanilla to shine through in vanilla ice cream, although honey is also delicious with vanilla. Both agave and honey make great chocolate or carob ice cream. Fruit Sweet™ has a trace of fruity tang in its flavor and is delicious used in fruit-flavored frozen desserts, as are fruit juice concentrates.

Fruit and flavorings give each frozen dessert its distinctive taste. For vanilla ice cream be sure to use high-quality *real* vanilla – made from vanilla beans – rather than artificial vanilla. My favorite vanilla extract is Frontier™ organic alcohol free natural vanilla. See "Sources," page 229, for ordering information if you cannot get it at your health food store. To make lemon or orange sorbet, sherbet or ice cream in a jiffy or on the spur of the moment, keep some lemon oil or orange oil. This will save you the need to have fresh citrus fruit on hand and also saves the time spent zesting it. See "Sources," page 229, for information about purchasing citrus oils from the King Arthur Flour Baker's Catalogue or website.

Fresh in-season fruit makes wonderful frozen desserts. However, if the fruit you want to use isn't in-season, good frozen fruit will work well in these recipes. The amount of sweetener needed in fruit ice creams, sherbets and sorbet will vary with the sweetness of the fruit. Taste the mixture before freezing it and adjust the amount of sweetener if needed. It should taste just a little on the sweet side because the sweetness will be less apparent when it is frozen.

There are several ingredients that can be used to stabilize frozen desserts and keep them from developing a rock-hard consistency or ice crystals if they are stored in the freezer for a long time. Using milk with a high fat content such as full-fat coconut milk or cream is one way to retain good texture in ice cream when it is frozen for a while. A traditional ingredient added to promote creaminess and good freezing qualities in ice cream is eggs. Those who tolerate eggs may wish to try the ice cream recipes on pages 224 to 227 of the "Especially for Guests" chapter which use an egg-containing cooked custard as the basic component of the ice cream. For those who are allergic to eggs or avoid high fat foods, methylcellulose imparts a creamy texture to any kind of ice cream or sherbet. Methylcellulose is simply refined fiber from plant sources. It must be thoroughly blended into the ice cream mixture before freezing. To order it, see "Sources," page 232.

Homemade ice cream, sherbet, or sorbet is best eaten shortly after you make it rather than after it has been stored in the freezer for days or weeks because it does not contain the chemical stabilizers that commercial ice cream usually contains. However, if you do not eat it all right away, take the leftover frozen dessert out of the freezer about 20 minutes before serving and hold it at room temperature. It will then soften up and be delicious and easy to serve. If you plan to make homemade ice cream for guests, one or two hours in the freezer will firm your ice cream but not produce a hard texture. Make it an hour or two before you expect to serve it, put it in the freezer, and the consistency will be great. The added bonus is that you will be able to spend time with your guests rather than in the kitchen making dessert. If you make the custard-base ice creams in the "Especially for Guests" chapter and they have been frozen overnight, remove them from the freezer and allow them to stand at room temperature for about 10 minutes or in the refrigerator for about 20 minutes before serving for an ideal texture.

Methods for Freezing Ice Cream, Sherbet, and Sorbet

STILL FREEZING METHOD

The still freezing method is best suited to high-fat ice creams, such as those made with cream, half-and-half, or full-fat coconut milk, or to ice cream, sherbet or sorbet that contains a good quantity of fiber from fruit. The fat or fiber helps promote a creamy texture. The recipes in this chapter indicate if they are suitable for the still freezing method.

To still freeze ice cream, sherbet, or sorbet, mix the ingredients and put them in a shallow metal cake pan, loaf pan(s) or old-fashioned ice cube tray(s) without the dividers. Put the pan(s) or tray(s) in the freezer and allow them to freeze until the mixture is firm around the edges and slushy in the middle, about 20 to 45 minutes. Remove the pan from the freezer and stir it until the consistency is uniform throughout. Put the pan back in the freezer and freeze it until the mixture becomes firm around the edges again. Remove it from the freezer and stir it again. Repeat this one or two more times until the stirred mixture is the consistency you prefer. Serve the frozen dessert immediately, or scoop it into a container and freeze it. If it has been frozen for more than a few hours before serving time, allow it to stand at room temperature for about 20 minutes to soften before serving.

FOOD PROCESSOR OR BLENDER METHOD

To make ice cream, sherbet, or sorbet using a food processor or blender, start the day before you wish to serve the frozen dessert. Mix the ingredients, put them into ice cube trays, and freeze overnight.

The next day, at least a half hour to forty five minutes or more before you wish to serve the ice cream, sherbet, or sorbet, remove the frozen cubes from the freezer. Allow them to stand at room temperature for 10 to 20 minutes or until they are just barely beginning to soften. Add about three cubes to the blender or food processor and process until the mixture is smooth. Add cubes two at a time and process until all of the dessert mixture has been processed. (If you are using a blender, you may have to do this in several small batches rather than processing it all together). Serve immediately or transfer it to a container and freeze the ice cream, sherbet, or sorbet a few hours until serving time. If it has been frozen for more than a few hours, allow it to stand at room temperature for about 20 minutes to soften before serving.

ICE CREAM MAKER METHOD

There are many kinds of ice cream makers, from those that you add rock salt and ice to and crank by hand to those that contain a built-in freezing unit. The most common ice cream makers for home use have a tub that you put in your freezer until it is thoroughly chilled (usually overnight). Then the tub attaches to a motorized unit that stirs the ice cream mixture while it freezes.

To make the ice cream, sherbet, or sorbet recipes in this book with an ice cream maker, combine all the ingredients and chill them thoroughly before adding them to the machine. This is especially important if you are using the custard base found in the "Especially for Guests" chapter because the custard will be very hot right after you make it! Add the chilled mixture to your machine and process as the machine's instruction book directs.

ICE CREAM

Easy Vanilla Ice Cream

"Plain vanilla" ice cream is not plain if it is made with good quality natural vanilla. It is the most classic of all ice creams, delightful either alone or paired perfectly with another dessert.

> 2½ cups cream, half-and-half, milk of any kind (cow, goat, gluten-free soy, etc.), or coconut milk (about 1½ 14-ounce cans)
> ⅜ cup agave, Fruit Sweet™ or honey
> 1 tablespoon vanilla extract OR a 2-inch piece of vanilla bean, cut open
> 1 tablespoon methylcellulose (optional)

Combine the milk, sweetener, and vanilla. If you are using a vanilla bean rather than vanilla extract for flavoring, add it to the milk mixture and let the mixture sit overnight in the refrigerator. In the morning scrape the seeds out of the bean into the milk mixture and discard the bean pod. Add the methylcellulose and blend the mixture thoroughly with a hand blender, blender, or food processor. Freeze as directed in your ice cream machine's instruction booklet, use the food processor method on page 99, or if you made it with cream or full-fat coconut milk, you can use the still freezing method on page 98. Serve immediately or store the ice cream in your freezer. If it has been frozen for more than a few hours, remove it from the freezer about 20 minutes before serving. Makes about 1½ pints of ice cream.

Easy Chocolate Ice Cream

> 2¼ cups cream, half-and-half, milk of any kind (cow, goat, gluten-free soy, etc.), or coconut milk (about 1⅓ 14-ounce cans)
> ⅜ cup agave, Fruit Sweet™ or honey
> 3 tablespoons cocoa
> 1 tablespoon methylcellulose (optional)

Blend the milk, sweetener, cocoa and methylcellulose with a hand blender, blender, or food processor until the cocoa and fiber are evenly dispersed in the milk mixture. Freeze as directed in your ice cream machine's instruction booklet or use the food processor method on page 99. Serve immediately or store the ice cream in your freezer. If it has been frozen for more than a few hours, remove it from the freezer about 20 minutes before serving. Makes about 1½ pints of ice cream.

Easy Carob Ice Cream

Gluten-Free

2½ cups cream, half-and-half, milk of any kind (cow, goat, gluten-free soy,
    etc.), or coconut milk (about 1½ 14-ounce cans)
⅜ cup agave, Fruit Sweet™ or honey
2 tablespoons carob powder
1 tablespoon methylcellulose (optional)

Blend the milk, sweetener, carob powder and methylcellulose with a hand blender, blender, or food processor until the carob and fiber are evenly dispersed in the milk mixture. Freeze as directed in your ice cream machine's instruction booklet or use the food processor method on page 99. Serve immediately or store the ice cream in your freezer. If it has been frozen for more than a few hours, remove it from the freezer about 20 minutes before serving. Makes about 1½ pints of ice cream.

Easy Strawberry Ice Cream

Gluten-Free

This ice cream has a good consistency without methylcellulose because the strawberries add fiber that keeps it creamy.

A little more than 1 pint of ripe strawberries
1 cup cream, half-and-half, milk of any kind (cow, goat, gluten-free soy, etc.),
    or coconut milk
⅜ cup agave, Fruit Sweet™ or honey OR ¾ cup apple juice concentrate

Wash and stem the strawberries. Puree them with a hand blender, blender, or food processor. Measure out 1 cup of puree. Combine the cream or milk, sweetener, and strawberry puree. Freeze as directed in your ice cream machine's instruction booklet, use the food processor method on page 99, or use the still freezing method on page 98. Serve immediately or store the ice cream in your freezer. If it has been frozen for more than a few hours, remove it from the freezer about 20 minutes before serving. Makes about 1½ pints of ice cream.

Chocolate Chip Ice Cream

**Gluten-Free IF
made with GF chips**

1 batch of vanilla ice cream, recipes on pages 100 or 224
¼ cup chocolate chips or mini-chips (preferably sugar-free* if purchased)
    OR 1 batch of "Chocolate Chips for Ice Cream," page 202,
    OR ¼ cup milk-free chocolate or carob chips, page 201

Freeze the ice cream mixture from the recipe you are using as directed in your ice cream machine's instruction booklet, use the food processor method on page 99, or if you made it with cream or full-fat coconut milk, you can use the still freezing method on page 98. Stir in the chocolate chips. If you are using "Chocolate Chips for Ice Cream," use them directly from the freezer. Serve immediately or store the ice cream in your freezer. If it has been frozen for more than a few hours, remove it from the freezer about 20 minutes before serving. Makes about 1½ pints of ice cream.

***Note on chocolate chips:** This recipe contains sugar in commercially-made chocolate chips unless sugar-free chips are used. Grain-sweetened chips are usually not gluten-free however. See "Sources," page 228, to purchase maltitol sweetened chocolate chips.

Mint Chocolate Chip Ice Cream

**Gluten-Free IF
made with GF chips**

Make "Chocolate Chip Ice Cream," above, except when you prepare the ice cream mixture, omit the vanilla flavoring from the ice cream and substitute ½ teaspoon peppermint extract. If you must have your ice cream green, add 3 to 4 drops of food coloring to the mixture before freezing.

Butter Pecan Ice Cream

Gluten-Free

1 batch of vanilla ice cream, page 100 or 224
⅓ cup chopped pecans
¾ cup butterscotch sauce, page 190, thoroughly chilled

Freeze the ice cream mixture from the recipe you are using as directed in your ice cream machine's instruction booklet, use the food processor method on page 99, or if you made it with cream or full-fat coconut milk, you can use the still freezing method on page 98. If the ice cream is not frozen fairly firm (as it may not be if made by the food processor method), put it into your freezer for an hour or two until it is quite firm. Stir together the pecans and sauce. In a shallow freezer container, layer about one fourth of the ice cream. Spread it with about one third of the nut-sauce mixture. Put another layer of about one fourth of the ice cream on top of this. Spread it with a second third of the nut-sauce mixture. Put another layer of about one fourth of the ice cream on top of this. Spread with the remaining nut sauce mixture. Fill the freezer container with the remaining ice cream and put it in the freezer for at least an hour. Serve when it is frozen fairly solid. Store leftovers in your freezer. If it has been frozen for more than a few hours, remove it from the freezer about 20 minutes before serving. Makes about 2 pints of ice cream.

Cherry Vanilla Ice Cream

Gluten-Free

1 batch of any vanilla ice cream or frozen yogurt, pages 100, 106 or 224
1 cup halved and pitted fresh Bing cherries or halved frozen Bing cherries

Freeze the ice cream mixture from the recipe you are using as directed in your ice cream machine's instruction booklet, use the food processor method on page 99, or if you made it with cream or full-fat coconut milk, you can use the still freezing method on page 98. Stir in the cherries. Serve immediately or store the ice cream in your freezer. If it has been frozen for more than a few hours, remove it from the freezer about 20 minutes before serving. Makes about 1½ pints of ice cream.

Café au Lait Ice Cream

Gluten-Free

Because different brands of instant coffee vary in their potency or level of bitterness, taste this mixture before freezing it and adjust the amount of sweetener if necessary.

1¾ cups cream, half-and-half or milk of any kind (cow, goat, gluten-free soy, etc.) or 1 14-ounce can of coconut milk
⅜ to ½ cup agave, Fruit Sweet™ or honey
½ teaspoon vanilla (optional)
2 tablespoons instant coffee, preferably decaffeinated
1 tablespoon methylcellulose (optional)

Combine the milk, sweetener, vanilla, and instant coffee. If you are using the methylcellulose, mix it into the mixture with a hand blender, blender, or food processor until thoroughly combined. Freeze as directed in your ice cream machine's instruction booklet, use the food processor method on page 99, or if you made it with cream or full-fat coconut milk, you can use the still freezing method on page 98. Serve immediately or store the ice cream in your freezer. If it has been frozen for more than a few hours, remove it from the freezer about 20 minutes before serving. Makes a little over 1 pint of ice cream.

Peach Ice Cream

Gluten-Free

This is best when made with fresh ripe peaches in the summertime, but in the winter you can use frozen or canned peaches.

> 1 cup cream, half-and-half, milk of any kind (cow, goat, gluten-free soy, etc.), or coconut milk
> ⅜ cup agave, Fruit Sweet™ or honey OR ¾ cup apple juice concentrate, thawed
> ¾ cup fresh sliced peaches, unsweetened frozen peaches, or drained juice- or water-packed canned peaches

Puree the peaches with a hand blender, blender, or food processor to yield about ½ cup of puree. Stir in the cream or milk and sweetener. Freeze as directed in your ice cream machine's instruction booklet, use the food processor method on page 99, or use the still freezing method on page 98. Serve immediately or store the ice cream in your freezer. If it has been frozen for more than a few hours, remove it from the freezer about 20 minutes before serving. Makes about 1½ pints of ice cream.

Pina Colada Ice Cream

Gluten-Free

> 1¾ cups coconut milk (1 14-ounce can)
> ½ cup pineapple juice concentrate, thawed
> 1 tablespoon methylcellulose (optional)

Combine the coconut milk, pineapple juice concentrate and methylcellulose with a hand blender until the fiber is evenly dispersed in the milk mixture. Freeze as directed in your ice cream machine's instruction booklet or use the food processor method on page 99. Serve immediately or store the ice cream in your freezer. If it has been frozen for more than a few hours, remove it from the freezer about 20 minutes before serving. Makes about 1½ pints of ice cream.

Spice Cream

1¾ cups coconut milk (1 14-ounce can)
1 teaspoon cinnamon
Dash of nutmeg
Dash of cloves
⅜ cup agave

Stir together all the ingredients thoroughly. Freeze as directed in your ice cream machine's instruction booklet, use the food processor method on page 99, or if you made this with full-fat coconut milk, you can use the still freezing method on page 98. Serve immediately or store the ice cream in your freezer. If it has been frozen for more than a few hours, remove it from the freezer about 20 minutes before serving. Makes about 1½ pints of ice cream.

Orange Ice Cream

This tangy ice cream will remind you of "Creamsicles™."

1½ cups cream, half-and-half or milk of any kind (cow, goat, gluten-free soy, etc.) or 1 14-ounce can of coconut milk
¾ cup orange juice concentrate, thawed
1 teaspoon orange zest or ⅛ teaspoon orange oil
1 tablespoon methylcellulose (optional)

If you are using the orange zest, remove it from an orange being careful to remove only the outer orange part of the peel, not the inner white part which can be bitter.

Using a hand blender, mix together the milk, orange juice concentrate, orange zest or oil, and methylcellulose until the fiber is completely mixed in. Freeze as directed in your ice cream machine's instruction booklet or use the food processor method on page 99. Serve immediately or store the ice cream in your freezer. If it has been frozen for more than a few hours, remove it from the freezer about 20 minutes before serving. Makes about 1½ pints of ice cream.

FROZEN YOGURT

Frozen Yogurt

Gluten-Free

2 cups of plain yogurt of any kind (regular, low-fat, fat-free, goat, sheep,
    gluten-free soy, etc.)
⅜ to ½ cup agave, Fruit Sweet™ or honey
One flavoring ingredient of your choice from the following list:
    1 tablespoon vanilla extract or a 2-inch piece of vanilla bean
    2 tablespoons cocoa or carob powder
    ½ cup pureed fruit (strawberries, peaches, or other fruit)

Combine the yogurt, ⅜ cup of the sweetener, and the flavoring ingredient. If you
use the carob or cocoa, use a hand blender, blender, food processor, or electric mixer to
mix it in thoroughly. If you use the vanilla bean, combine it with the yogurt and sweetener and refrigerate it overnight. The next morning scrape the seeds out of the bean into
the yogurt and discard the bean pod. Taste the mixture before freezing it. It should taste
a little on the sweet side; if does not, add an additional 1 to 2 tablespoons of sweetener.
(You will need the extra sweetener if the yogurt or fruit you are using is tart). Freeze
as directed in your ice cream machine's instruction booklet or use the food processor
method on page 99. Serve immediately or store the ice cream in your freezer. If it has
been frozen for more than a few hours, remove it from the freezer about 20 minutes
before serving. Makes about 1½ pints of frozen yogurt.

SHERBET

Orange Sherbet

Gluten-Free

¾ cup orange juice concentrate, thawed
⅜ cup agave, Fruit Sweet™ or honey
1½ cups milk of any kind (cow, goat, gluten-free soy, etc.) or 1 14-ounce can
    of coconut milk*
1½ teaspoons orange zest or ⅛ teaspoon orange oil

Combine the orange juice concentrate, sweetener, milk, and orange zest or oil. Freeze
as directed in your ice cream machine's instruction booklet or use the food processor
method on page 99. Serve immediately or store the sherbet in your freezer. If it has been

frozen for more than a few hours, remove it from the freezer about 20 minutes before serving. Makes about 1½ pints of sherbet.

*Note on coconut milk: If you prefer a less-filling traditional sherbet, use light coconut milk. However, if you don't mind the fat and would like to use the still-freezing method for this sherbet, use full fat coconut milk.

Lemon Sherbet

Gluten-Free

¼ cup lemon juice, freshly squeezed if possible
⅜ cup agave, Fruit Sweet™ or honey
2 cups milk of any kind (cow, goat, gluten-free soy, etc.) or 1 14-ounce can of coconut milk*
1½ teaspoons lemon zest or ⅛ teaspoon lemon oil

If you are using the lemon zest, remove it from a lemon being careful to remove only the outer yellow layer, not the bitter white layer.

Combine the lemon juice, sweetener, milk, and lemon zest or oil. Freeze as directed in your ice cream machine's instruction booklet or use the food processor method on page 99. Serve immediately or store the sherbet in your freezer. If it has been frozen for more than a few hours, remove it from the freezer about 20 minutes before serving. Makes about 1½ pints of sherbet.

*Note on coconut milk: If you prefer a less-filling traditional sherbet, use light coconut milk. However, if you don't mind the fat and would like to use the still-freezing method for this sherbet, use full fat coconut milk.

Banana Sherbet

Gluten-Free

¾ cup puree of very ripe bananas (about 4 bananas)
⅜ cup agave, Fruit Sweet™ or honey
1½ cups milk of any kind (cow, goat, gluten-free soy, etc.) or 1 14-ounce can of coconut* milk

Combine the banana puree, sweetener, and milk. Freeze as directed in your ice cream machine's instruction booklet or use the food processor method on page 99. Serve immediately or store the sherbet in your freezer. If it has been frozen for more than a few hours, remove it from the freezer about 20 minutes before serving. Makes about 1½ pints of sherbet.

*Note on coconut milk: If you prefer a less-filling traditional sherbet, use light coconut milk. However, if you don't mind the fat and would like to use the still-freezing method for this sherbet, use full fat coconut milk.

Raspberry Sherbet

Gluten-Free

The fruit used determines the flavor of this sherbet. Taste the mixture before freezing it. If it needs a little more zip, add the lemon juice.

> About 6 ounces fresh raspberries or frozen raspberries, thawed
> 1½ cups milk of any kind (cow, goat, gluten-free soy, etc.) or 1 14-ounce can
> of coconut milk*
> ½ cup agave, Fruit Sweet™ or honey
> 1 tablespoon lemon juice, if needed especially with the agave or honey (optional)

Puree the raspberries with a food processor, blender, or hand blender. Press the puree through a wire mesh strainer with the back of a spoon to remove the seeds. This should yield about ½ cup of seedless puree. Combine the seedless raspberry puree, sweetener, and milk. Taste it, and if desired, add the lemon juice. The mixture should taste just a little on the sweet side before freezing. Freeze as directed in your ice cream machine's instruction booklet or use the food processor method on page 99. Serve immediately or store the sherbet in your freezer. If it has been frozen for more than a few hours, remove it from the freezer about 20 minutes before serving. Makes about 1½ pints of sherbet.

*Note on coconut milk: If you prefer a less-filling traditional sherbet, use light coconut milk. However, if you don't mind the fat and would like to use the still-freezing method for this sherbet, use full fat coconut milk.

Strawberry Sherbet

Gluten-Free

> ¾ to 1 pint of ripe strawberries
> ⅜ cup agave, Fruit Sweet™ or honey
> 1½ cups milk of any kind (cow, goat, gluten-free soy, etc.) or 1 14-ounce can
> of coconut milk*

Wash and stem the strawberries. Puree them with a hand blender, blender, or food processor. Measure out ¾ cup of puree. Combine the milk, sweetener, and strawberry puree. Freeze as directed in your ice cream machine's instruction booklet or use the food processor method on page 99. Serve immediately or store the sherbet in your freezer. If it has been frozen for more than a few hours, remove it from the freezer about 20 minutes before serving. Makes about 1½ pints of sherbet.

*Note on coconut milk: If you prefer a less-filling traditional sherbet, use light coconut milk. However, if you don't mind the fat and would like to use the still-freezing method for this sherbet, use full fat coconut milk.

SORBET

For very easy sorbet recipes that can be made with little or no advance preparation, see "Easy Pineapple Sorbet," page 37, "Easy Banana-Cherry or Berry Sorbet," page 38, and "Quick Fruit Sorbet," page 38.

Gluten-Free

4 to 5 kiwi fruits to make 1½ cups of puree
½ cup apple or pineapple juice concentrate, thawed, OR ¼ cup water plus
    ¼ cup agave, Fruit Sweet™ or honey

Peel the kiwis and cut them into chunks. Puree them using a hand blender, food processor or blender, and measure out 1½ cups of the puree. Add the juice or the water and sweetener to the puree and blend the mixture again briefly. Chill the mixture thoroughly. Freeze as directed in your ice cream machine's instruction booklet or use the food processor method on page 99. Serve immediately or store the sorbet in your freezer. If it has been frozen for more than a few hours, remove it from the freezer about 20 minutes before serving. Makes about 1 pint of sorbet.

Stevia-sweetened kiwi sorbet variation: Omit the fruit juice concentrate or sweetener plus water. Instead, stir $1/16$ teaspoon of pure stevia powder into ½ cup of water very thoroughly until it is completely dissolved and add this to the pureed kiwis. If you are making this by the food processor method, you may need to let the frozen mixture cubes soften longer than usual before you can process them.

Peach Sorbet

Gluten-Free

2 to 2¼ pounds fresh or frozen peaches or 1 16- to 20-ounce can of juice
   packed peaches.
½ cup agave, Fruit Sweet™ or honey

Puree the peaches with a hand blender, blender, or food processor. Measure out 2 cups of puree. Combine the peach puree with the sweetener. Chill the mixture thoroughly before freezing it as directed in your ice cream machine's instruction booklet. You may also use the still freezing method on page 98 or the food processor method on page 99 without chilling the mixture first. Serve immediately or store the sorbet in your freezer. If it has been frozen for more than a few hours, remove it from the freezer about 20 minutes before serving. Makes about 1½ pints of sorbet.

Cranberry Sorbet

Gluten-Free

This tart and tangy dessert is a perfect light ending to a big holiday meal.

12 ounces fresh cranberries (about 4 cups)
1½ cups apple or pineapple juice concentrate, thawed, OR ¾ cup water
   plus ¾ cup agave, Fruit Sweet™ or honey

Combine the cranberries with the juice or sweetener and water in a saucepan. Bring the mixture to a boil, reduce the heat, and simmer, stirring occasionally, for about 20 minutes, or until the cranberries have popped and lost their shape. If you wish to remove the cranberry skins which may be bitter, put the mixture through a food mill or press it through a strainer at this point. Chill the mixture thoroughly and freeze it according to the instructions for your ice cream maker or use the food processor method on page 99. Serve immediately or store the sorbet in your freezer. If it has been frozen for more than a few hours, remove it from the freezer about 20 minutes before serving. Makes about 1½ pints of sorbet.

Stevia-sweetened cranberry sorbet variation: Omit the fruit juice concentrate or sweetener plus water. Instead, stir ¼ teaspoon of pure stevia powder into 1½ cups of water in the saucepan very thoroughly until the stevia is completely dissolved. Then add the cranberries, bring the cranberry mixture to a boil, and proceed with the recipe as above. If you are making this by the food processor method, you may need to let the frozen mixture cubes soften longer than usual before you can process them.

Raspberry Sorbet

This is our favorite sorbet and very much worth the time spent removing the seeds from the raspberries.

About 10 to 12 ounces fresh raspberries or frozen raspberries, thawed
½ cup agave, Fruit Sweet™ or honey plus 1 cup water OR 1 cup thawed apple
    juice concentrate plus ½ cup water

Puree the raspberries with a food processor, blender, or hand blender. Press the puree through a wire mesh strainer with the back of a spoon to remove the seeds. Measure out ¾ cup of seedless puree. Combine the apple juice or sweetener and water with the raspberry puree. Chill the mixture thoroughly before freezing it as directed in your ice cream machine's instruction booklet. You may also use the still freezing method on page 98 or the food processor method on page 99 without chilling the mixture first. Serve immediately or store the sorbet in your freezer. If it has been frozen for more than a few hours, remove it from the freezer about 20 minutes before serving. Makes about 1½ pints of sorbet.

Strawberry Sorbet

About 1½ pints of ripe strawberries
¾ cup apple juice concentrate OR ⅜ cup agave, Fruit Sweet™ or honey
    plus ¼ cup water

Wash and stem the strawberries. Puree them with a hand blender, blender, or food processor. Measure out 2 cups of puree. Combine the apple juice or sweetener plus water with the strawberry puree. Chill the mixture thoroughly before freezing it as directed in your ice cream machine's instruction booklet. You may also use the still freezing method on page 98 or the food processor method on page 99 without chilling the mixture first. Serve immediately or store the sorbet in your freezer. If it has been frozen for more than a few hours, remove it from the freezer about 20 minutes before serving. Makes about 1½ pints of sorbet.

Banana Sorbet

4 large very ripe bananas
⅜ cup agave, Fruit Sweet™ or honey

Peel the bananas, break them into chunks, and puree them using a hand blender, blender, or food processor. Combine the banana puree and sweetener. Chill the mixture thoroughly before freezing it as directed in your ice cream machine's instruction booklet. You may also use the still freezing method on page 98 or the food processor method on page 99 without chilling the mixture first. Serve immediately or store the sorbet in your freezer. If it has been frozen for more than a few hours, remove it from the freezer about 20 minutes before serving. Makes about 2 pints of sorbet.

Cantaloupe Sorbet

This is a cool and delicious treat when the cantaloupes are at their peak flavor in the late summer.

2 medium-size sweet ripe cantaloupes

Peel the cantaloupes, cut them into chunks, and puree them in a food processor or blender. Chill the mixture thoroughly. Freeze as directed in your ice cream machine's instruction booklet or, to make the sorbet with a food processor or blender, measure out 1 cup of the puree and chill it in the refrigerator. Freeze the rest of the puree in ice cube trays. Put the chilled puree in your food processor and then add the frozen cantaloupe cubes and process as in the food processor method on page 99. Serve immediately or store the sorbet in your freezer. If it has been frozen for more than a few hours, remove it from the freezer about 20 minutes before serving. Makes about 2 pints of sorbet.

Mango Sorbet

The natural fiber in the mangoes makes this sorbet very smooth.

3 ripe mangoes
2 to 4 tablespoons agave, Fruit Sweet™ or honey (optional, to taste)

Peel the mangoes and cut the flesh off the pits. Cut the fruit into chunks. Puree the chunks with a hand blender or a blender or food processor until smooth. Taste and add the sweetener if desired to bring the fruit to the slightly-sweet level. Chill the mixture thoroughly. Freeze as directed in your ice cream machine's instruction booklet or use the food processor method on page 99 or the still freezing method on page 98. Serve immediately or store the sorbet in your freezer. If it has been frozen for more than a few hours, remove it from the freezer about 20 minutes before serving. Makes about 1½ pints of sorbet.

Quick Lemon Sorbet

Gluten-Free

If you want a frosty dessert but don't want to make a trip to the grocery store, this tangy sorbet can be put together from ingredients you have in your pantry. Use bottled lemon juice and lemon oil to save time.

    1 cup freshly squeezed or bottled lemon juice
    1 cup agave
    1½ cups water
    Grated zest of one lemon or ¼ teaspoon lemon oil

Combine the lemon juice, agave, water and lemon zest or oil. Chill the mixture thoroughly. Freeze as directed in your ice cream machine's instruction booklet or use the food processor method on page 99. Serve immediately or store the sorbet in your freezer. If it has been frozen for more than a few hours, remove it from the freezer about 20 minutes before serving. Makes about 1½ pints of sorbet.

Dessert Waffles, Pancakes and Cones

What is every child's favorite breakfast? Pancakes! I used to love pancakes so much that at about age ten or twelve I learned to make them myself. My mother enjoyed a break from cooking when I made them for dinner on Sunday nights.

Breakfast foods are not only for breakfast and dinner; they also can be for dessert. Top these freshly-made pancakes or waffles with a sauce or fresh fruit and whipped topping or ice cream, and you will have a delicious dessert that will be thoroughly enjoyed by young and old alike. For sauce and topping recipes, see pages 189 to 196. Ice cream, sherbets, and sorbet recipes can be found on pages 100 to 113.

While you are cooking with a waffle iron, if you have a pizzelle or krumkake iron, get it out and make some scrumptious ice cream cones as well. This chapter features a recipe for several kinds of cones on pages 118 and 119.

Dessert Pancakes

Gluten-Free

Try these delicious gluten-free pancakes for breakfast with any of the fruit sauces on pages 191 to 194.

  2¼ cups sorghum (milo) flour
  1 cup arrowroot or tapioca starch
  1 teaspoon baking soda
  ½ teaspoon unbuffered vitamin C powder
  ½ teaspoon salt
  ¼ cup oil plus additional oil for the griddle
  1 cup water
  ¾ cup agave, Fruit Sweet™ or honey
  1 teaspoon vanilla extract

Lightly oil your griddle by rubbing it with a piece of paper towel moistened with a little oil. Begin heating your griddle on medium heat or heat an electric pancake griddle to 350°F or the "pancake" setting.

In a large bowl combine the flour, starch, baking soda, vitamin C powder, and salt. In a separate bowl or cup, stir together the oil, water, vanilla, and sweetener. Pour the liquid ingredients into the flour mixture and mix with a wire whisk until the batter is combined and most of the lumps are gone.

Pour 3 to 4 tablespoons of batter onto the heated griddle to form each pancake. Cook the pancakes until they are dry around the edges on the top and light brown on the bottom. Turn them with a spatula and cook them until the other side is also light brown. If the pancakes break, are difficult to turn, or stick to the griddle, re-oil the griddle with the paper towel between cooking successive batches. This pancake batter tends to thicken as it stands. You may need to add an additional 1 to 4 tablespoons of water to the batter as you cook successive batches to keep the right consistency.

If you will not be eating the pancakes immediately, cool them on a wire rack to keep them from getting soggy. Makes 3 to 4 dozen 3-inch pancakes

Dessert Waffles

2½ cups whole grain spelt flour OR 2¾ cups white spelt flour
1 teaspoon baking soda
¼ teaspoon unbuffered vitamin C powder
½ teaspoon salt
1⅔ cups water
⅓ cup agave or Fruit Sweet™
¼ cup oil plus additional oil for the iron
1 teaspoon vanilla extract

Brush your iron with the oil. If you have trouble with the waffles sticking to the iron, melted coconut oil, goat butter, or ghee are good choices to use to brush the iron and also to use in the recipe. Heat the iron on medium-high heat or on the waffle setting for 15 minutes before you begin cooking waffles. If the iron is not hot enough, you may have difficulty removing the waffles from the iron.

In a large bowl, mix the flour, baking soda, vitamin C powder, and salt. In a separate bowl or cup, combine the oil, water, and sweetener. Stir the liquid ingredients together in another bowl or cup. Then stir them into the flour mixture until thoroughly mixed. Allow the batter to stand for about 10 minutes while the iron is heating before you begin cooking the waffles.

Put enough batter into the iron for it to reach to about 1 inch from the edge of the iron (about 1 cup for a large iron that makes four square waffles). Overfilling the iron may make the waffles difficult to remove. Close the iron and cook the waffles until the steaming lessens and the waffles are brown, about 10 to 15 minutes depending on your iron. After you have made these waffles once, make a note in the margin of this recipe about the length of time it takes them to be cooked in your iron. If you peek into the iron before the waffles are done, you may split your waffles down the middle, so it is good to have a note on how long they take to cook with your iron for future reference.

Remove the waffles from the iron when they are browned. Reheat your waffle iron until the light goes off before cooking more waffles. If you do not eat the waffles immediately, cool them on a wire rack. These waffles freeze well and are good reheated in the toaster. Makes 10 to 15 4-inch square waffles.

Nutty Waffles

Gluten-Free

These gluten and grain-free waffles can be made "plain" or sweetened with the herb stevia. Using this non-nutritive natural and healthy sweetener makes them taste sweet without the sweetener causing them to stick to the iron.

1 cup walnuts, pecans, cashews, blanched almonds or almonds, filberts,
    pumpkin seeds, or sunflower seeds
1¾ cups arrowroot or tapioca starch
⅛ teaspoon salt
1¾ cups water
1 tablespoon oil (optional but good to use) plus additional oil for the iron
⅛ teaspoon pure stevia powder (optional)

Brush your iron with the oil you will be using in your waffles. Heat the iron on "high" for 15 minutes before you begin cooking waffles. If the iron is not hot enough, you may have difficulty removing the waffles from the iron.

Put the nuts or seeds and ½ cup of the starch or flour in a food processor bowl and process until the nuts or seeds are finely ground. (You can also do this in a blender in small batches). Add the rest of the starch, salt, and optional stevia and process for a few seconds. With the processor running, add the water and oil and process briefly. The batter will be thin. Allow the batter to stand for about 15 minutes while the iron is heating before you begin cooking the waffles. Process the batter again for a few seconds before you put it into the iron.

Put enough batter into the iron for it to reach to about 1 inch from the edge of the iron (about 1½ cups for a large iron that makes four square waffles). Overfilling the iron may make the waffles difficult to remove. Close the iron and cook the waffles for about 15 minutes or longer or until they are brown and crisp. Do not peek into the iron until the waffles should be done and the iron is no longer steaming, or you may split the waffles down the middle.

Remove the waffles from the iron when they are lightly browned. Reheat your waffle iron until the light goes off before cooking more waffles. Process the batter again for a few seconds before putting more batter into the iron. If you do not eat the waffles immediately, cool them on a wire rack. These waffles freeze well and are good reheated in the toaster. Makes 8 4-inch square waffles.

Easy Almond Waffles

Gluten-Free

These waffles are a simpler version of the previous recipe which can be made with a hand blender. They are great for snacks as well as dessert. Omit the stevia to use them with savory foods.

1⅜ cups almond meal/flour
1¾ cups arrowroot or tapioca starch
⅛ teaspoon salt
1¾ cups water
1 tablespoon oil plus additional oil for the iron
⅛ teaspoon pure stevia powder (optional)

Brush your waffle iron with oil. Heat the iron on "high" for 15 minutes before you begin cooking waffles. (If the iron is not hot enough, you may have difficulty removing the waffles from the iron).

While the iron is heating, measure the ingredients and mix the batter. First, stir the almond meal before measuring it because it tends to become packed together in the bag. Measure the almond meal, starch, and salt into a deep mixing bowl or 4-cup measuring cup if you will be using a hand blender or into the bowl of a blender or food processor with the "puree" blade in place. Add the water and oil. Blend with a hand blender, food processor or blender. Let the batter stand 5 minutes before beginning to cook the waffles.

Then, for the first waffle and each waffle you make, re-blend right before putting batter in the iron. Put enough batter into the iron for it to reach to about ½ to 1 inch from the edge of the iron (about 1½ cups for a large iron that makes four square waffles). Overfilling the iron may make the waffles difficult to remove. Cook on high for 15 to 18 minutes or until golden brown and crisp. Do not peek into the iron until the waffles should be done and the iron is no longer steaming or you may split the waffles down the middle. Reheat your waffle iron until the light goes off before cooking more waffles.

If you do not eat the waffles immediately, cool them on a wire rack. If these waffles soften after they are cool, cook them longer the next time. Makes 8 to 12 4-inch square waffles.

Ice Cream Cones

Gluten-Free IF
made with amaranth or quinoa

You can make ice cream cones with a special ice cream cone iron or with a krumkake or pizzelle iron. This is one of the rare recipes in which what kind of oil you use makes a difference. The cones are less likely to stick to the iron if you use coconut oil, although you can use other kinds of oil if necessary for any of the cones except the fragile oat cones. If you can tolerate butter, ghee, or goat butter occasionally, substitute melted butter for the oil, and the cones will be easy to remove from the iron.

Amaranth (GF):

> 1 cup amaranth flour
> 1 cup arrowroot
> 1 teaspoon baking soda
> ⅛ teaspoon unbuffered vitamin C powder
> ¼ cup melted coconut oil, butter, or other oil
> ¼ cup honey
> ⅝ cup water

Quinoa (GF):

> 1½ cups quinoa flour
> ½ cup tapioca starch
> ½ teaspoon baking soda
> ½ cup melted coconut oil, butter, or other oil
> ½ cup apple juice concentrate, thawed

Carob-Quinoa (GF):

> 1 cup quinoa flour
> ½ cup carob powder
> ½ cup tapioca starch
> ½ teaspoon baking soda
> ½ cup melted coconut oil, butter, or other oil
> 1 cup apple juice concentrate, thawed

"Sugar" Cones:

2 cups rye flour OR 3 cups whole spelt flour
½ cup melted coconut oil, butter, or other oil
1¼ cups apple juice concentrate, thawed OR ½ cup water plus ¾ cup apple
   juice concentrate, thawed, depending on the amount of sweetness desired

Carob-Rye:

1½ cups rye flour
½ cup carob powder
½ cup melted coconut oil, butter, or other oil
¾ cup grape juice concentrate, thawed
½ cup water

Oat:

1 cup oat flour
1 cup arrowroot
½ cup melted coconut oil, butter, or other oil
¾ cup pineapple juice concentrate, thawed

Choose one set of ingredients above. Begin heating the iron. Combine the flour(s), carob powder (if it is used in the set of ingredients you have chosen), baking soda (if used), and vitamin C powder (if used) in a large electric mixer bowl. In a small bowl, stir together the oil, juice or honey, and water (if used), and pour them into the dry ingredients. Beat the dough on low speed until the flour is all moistened, then beat it on medium speed for one minute.

Spray or brush both the top and the bottom of the iron with oil before you begin coooking the cones. If they stick (more likely if you are using a kind of oil other than coconut oil) re-oil both plates before cooking each cone. Put one heaping tablespoon of dough in the iron. (You may need more – this is a starting point as you determine how much dough you should put in to fill the iron when you close it). Cook each cone for 20 to 30 seconds, or until it is golden brown, and remove it from the iron using two forks. You may have to experiment to determine what cooking time makes the cones easiest to remove. If the cones stick at all, brush the iron with melted coconut oil before cooking the next cone.

Immediately after removing each cone from the iron, roll it into a cone shape. If you wish to have perfectly shaped cones, roll them around metal cone-shaped forms and allow them to cool before removing the forms. Makes 1 to 1½ dozen cones.

Sweet Breads, Coffee Cakes, Buns and Doughnuts

I love making bread. My grandmother taught me to make it completely by hand using cake yeast when I was about 16, and I've had my hands in bread dough multiple times almost every week for most of the 40 years since then. I love making bread so much that being unable to eat any grains myself does not stop me from making it for other people. When bread machines came out in the early 90s, a friend loaned me her Zojirushi BBCC-S-15, the first programmable machine made, with the request that I develop allergy bread recipes for her, and I got hooked on bread machines. If you've never made bread, I urge you to try at least one yeast bread recipe in this chapter and see if you find it to be a relaxing and enjoyable experience.

The most enticing aroma that comes from the kitchen may be the smell of yeast bread baking, and dessert breads smell the best. They are not difficult to make and you will impress and delight everyone who eats your bread. If you have a bread machine, you can just measure ingredients into the machine and it does the rest of the work. With a mixer you can reduce or eliminate kneading. Using the directions on pages 121 to 123 you will find that making yeast dough or bread entirely by hand is not difficult; I find it good for the soul to bake bread in this way. While hand-made yeast breads require intermittent attention over a few hours time, the actual time you spend working on them is not that great. This chapter also contains quickly made recipes for baking-powder leavened doughnuts, date nut bread, and banana bread.

Success in making yeast bread depends on two conditions: activating and stimulating the yeast so it will produce gas, and trapping the gas in the dough so the dough will rise properly. The most important factor to promote yeast activity is temperature, both of the liquid used to dissolve the yeast and of the place the dough is set to rise. A yeast thermometer is a very useful tool for determining the temperature of both the liquid and the rising place. The second factor is the provision of food, usually some type of sugar, to support the yeast's metabolism. The yeast bread recipes in this book contain fruit sweeteners, agave, or honey. Although fruit sweeteners provide food for yeast, they also add acid to the yeast's environment. If they are used in small amounts, this is not a problem. However, when you try to make yeast dough very sweet using any of these sweeteners, the larger amount of sweetener can increase osmotic pressure in addition to making the dough more acid, thus inhibiting the growth of the yeast and causing long rising times. Sometimes you can just wait longer for your dough to rise. Another option is using SAF Gold™ yeast, a strain of yeast specially bred to be resistant to acid and high concentrations of sweeteners. (See "Sources" page 232).

The dough must also trap and hold the gas made by the yeast in order to have yeast bread rise properly. If you use flour that is high in gluten and knead the dough sufficiently, this will happen easily. Wheat and spelt flour are naturally high in gluten, the protein found in grains that helps bread to rise. When you beat or knead wheat or spelt dough, the gluten molecules join together to make long strands of gluten which trap the gas that the yeast produces. Kamut and rye flours contain less gluten than wheat and spelt but still have enough to allow the bread to rise. Adequate beating and/or kneading is vital to developing the gluten in bread made with these flours so that it will rise properly.

Spelt flour is the most "normal" and versatile flour for making non-wheat yeast breads, but its behavior in yeast bread and dough can be variable. Because spelt proteins dissolve more readily in liquids that wheat, the gluten may break down as the dough is kneaded. Although this is usually not a problem in kneading by hand where the consistency of the dough is easily corrected, it can be a problem with bread machine spelt bread or dough. Watch the dough as it kneads, and add more flour if it becomes softer or sticky before the kneading part of the cycle is finished. The type of spelt flour I recommend for bread baking is Purity Foods flour but even their flour can vary from batch to batch and year to year. Therefore, the amount of spelt flour in these recipes is not absolute. Be prepared to add more if needed.

Other flours, such as barley, oats, rice, and quinoa, contain no gluten or not enough gluten to trap the gas from the yeast on their own. However, although bread made with these flours will not be as light as wheat or spelt bread, you can overcome this problem by adding guar or xanthum gum to the dough to trap the gas. Do not allow xanthum or guar-gum-containing dough to rise to more than double its original volume during the final rising period or it may collapse during baking. To purchase guar or xanthum gum, see "Sources," page 232.

To make yeast bread or dough with high-gluten flour by hand or by using a mixer, begin by putting one-half to two-thirds of the flour, the yeast, the salt, and the other dry ingredients in a bowl. Mix on low speed for about 30 seconds, or stir to combine the dry ingredients by hand. Warm the liquid ingredients, excluding eggs, to 115 to 120°F. With the mixer running on low speed, add the liquids to the dry ingredients in a slow stream, or stir them into the dry ingredients by hand. Have eggs at room temperature (or warm them quickly as described on page 31) and add them after the other liquids. Continue mixing until the dry and liquid ingredients are thoroughly mixed.

To complete making the bread by hand, stir in as much of the remaining flour as you can, and then turn the dough out onto a floured board to knead it. Knead it by pushing on it with the heels of your hands, folding it over, turning it 90 degrees, and then repeating the process over and over for about ten minutes, gradually adding more flour, until the dough is smooth and elastic. The feel of the bread will tell you when enough flour has been added; it will no longer be sticky and will be very resilient. Hand-kneaded bread will absorb a little more flour than called for in most of the recipes in this book. If it becomes softer while kneading it, as spelt may, knead in more flour. Other ingredients, such as nuts and raisins, may be added and kneaded in near the end of the kneading time.

To complete making the bread with a mixer that is not a heavy-duty mixer, beat the dough for 5 to 10 minutes with just the initial two-thirds of the flour added. With some types of bread you will be able to tell that the gluten is developing because the dough will begin to climb up the beaters. Then stir and knead the rest of the flour in by hand as above, kneading for about 10 minutes, or until the dough is very smooth and elastic. If you wish to add raisins or nuts to the dough, do it during this hand kneading period.

To complete making the bread with a heavy-duty mixer, after the liquids are thoroughly mixed with the first two-thirds of the flour and with the mixer still running, begin adding the rest of the flour around the edges of the bowl ½ cup at a time. Mix well after each addition before adding more flour until the dough forms a ball and cleans the sides of the bowl. Knead the dough on the speed directed in your mixer manual for 5 to 10 minutes, or until the dough is very elastic and smooth. If spelt dough begins to soften during the kneading time, add more flour. Turn the dough out onto a floured board and knead it briefly to check the consistency of the dough, kneading in a little more flour if necessary. Raisins or nuts should be added to the dough by hand after the mixer is finished kneading it.

Put the dough into an oiled bowl and turn it once so that the top of the ball is also oiled. Cover it with plastic wrap or a towel and let it rise in a warm (85°F to 90°F) place until it has doubled in volume, about 45 minutes to 1 hour.

Your oven can become an ideal place for your yeast bread to rise. If you have an electric oven, heat the oven to 350°F for five minutes, turn it off, and leave the door open for seven to ten minutes or until it cools to about 90°F. (A yeast thermometer or room thermometer is an essential tool for checking the temperature of your rising place). Then close the door and you will have a warm, draft-free rising place for your bread. Or if you have a gas oven, I have heard that the pilot light should keep the inside of the oven at the right temperature for bread dough to rise. Be sure to use your thermometer, however, to check the temperature.

Near the end of the rising time, prepare the pan(s) you will need for your yeast bread or rolls. For loaves, use 8 by 4 inch or 9 by 5 inch loaf pans. Rub the inside of the pans with oil. If you are making spelt bread, cut a piece of waxed or parchment paper to the length of the pans. Line the bottom and long sides of the pans with the paper and also oil the paper. If you are making buns, oil the baking sheets. Although you can usually use a spatula to remove spelt bread or buns from a baking sheet, you may also prefer to line them with parchment paper.

After the dough has doubled in volume, punch it down and shape it into loaves or rolls as desired. Place it into the prepared pan(s) and allow it to rise until double again, about 45 to 60 minutes. To tell if gluten-containing dough is ready to bake, touch it gently with your finger. If it does not spring back, it is ready.

If your bread has been rising in your oven, remove it. Preheat the oven to 350°F for loaf breads or 375°F for rolls unless directed otherwise in the recipe. Bake rolls or buns for 15 to 25 minutes. Light, fluffy, gluten-containing breads will take 45 minutes to an hour to bake. Dense whole grain, low-gluten, or non-gluten breads can take over an hour to bake. The bread is done when it is brown and pulls away from the sides of the pan. To keep the crust from getting soggy, remove the bread from the pan immediately after baking. For light, fluffy, gluten-containing breads, if you tap the bottom of the loaf and it sounds hollow, it is done. The more dense breads may not sound hollow but should be well browned. If sweet breads brown too rapidly during baking, cover them with a piece of foil partway through the baking time. Try to allow breads to cool completely before cutting them with a serrated knife.

Making gluten-free and low-gluten breads is quite different from making high-gluten breads. These must be made with a mixer or bread machine. Instead of the machine developing the gluten, it develops the guar or xanthum gum structure of the bread. Because low-gluten and gluten-free bread dough is much softer, ranging in consistency from a heavy batter to a soft dough, all of the kneading can be done by your mixer even if it is not a heavy duty mixer. The beating times are shorter (about 3 minutes) for gluten-free and low-gluten breads than for gluten-containing mixer breads. In addition, you beat the dough twice, once initially and once after the first rising period.

The method used for low-gluten or gluten-free bread and dough is as follows: Combine the flour(s), yeast, guar or xanthum gum, vitamin C crystals, salt, spices, and other dry ingredients in your mixer bowl and mix for about 30 seconds. Combine the water, sweetener, oil and other liquid ingredients and heat them to 115 to 120°F. With the mixer running on low speed, add the liquids to the dry ingredients in a slow stream, or stir them into the dry ingredients by hand. Have eggs at room temperature (or warm them quickly as described on page 31) and add them after the other liquids. When the ingredients are completely combined, beat the dough for three minutes at medium speed. Scrape the dough from the beaters and the sides of the bowl into the bottom of the bowl. Cover the bowl, put it in a warm (85°F to 90°F) place, and let the dough rise for one hour. See the fourth paragraph on page 122 for a good way to create a warm draft-free rising place.

After it has risen the first time, beat the dough again for three minutes at medium speed. Mix in raisins or nuts with a spoon at the end of this second beating time. Oil an 8-inch by 4-inch loaf pan and coat the inside of it generously with the type of flour used in the recipe. Put the dough in the pan and allow it to rise in a warm place until it is not quite doubled, about 30 to 40 minutes. If you are making rolls, shape them as directed in the recipe and let them rise until barely doubled.

Remove the bread from the oven if it is rising there before it has doubled. Begin to preheat your oven at least five minutes before you expect the dough to be ready to bake. Let the bread rise until it is a bit under doubled. DO NOT let gluten-free or low gluten bread over-rise in the pan or it will collapse during baking. Bake low-gluten bread and rolls a little longer than the times given above or as directed in the recipe.

To make the breads, dough, or buns in this chapter using a bread machine, choose the ingredient list that matches the size of your bread machine. If you have a 2-pound machine, double the ingredient amounts given for a 1-pound loaf unless the recipe indicates otherwise. Add the ingredients to the machine in the order listed in the recipe. Start the cycle indicated in the recipe. If you are making buns, doughnuts, or a hand-formed loaf of bread, use the dough cycle. After it is completed, shape and bake your goodies as directed in the recipe.

When the yeast bread or rolls are done, remove them from the pan immediately and allow them to cool on a wire rack. Store them in plastic bags. Freshness is maintained best if they are stored at room temperature.

Although some of these recipes are written in bread machine style, any of the recipes in this chapter can be made by hand or mixer using the directions on pages 121 to 124. To learn more about making yeast breads by any method or about bread machines, see *Easy Breadmaking for Special Diets* as described on the last pages of this book. For further information about the operation of and cycles on your bread machine, refer to the instruction booklet for the machine.

For delicious sweet bread in a hurry, use the non-yeast recipes at the end of this chapter (pages 146 to 152) to make cake doughnuts, banana bread and date nut bread. Store the doughnuts in a plastic bag at room temperature. If you live in a warm, humid climate, to prevent mold growth you should store moist quick breads such as banana bread or date-nut bread in the refrigerator, or slice and freeze them if you are going to be eating the bread slowly over several days time. If you place plastic wrap between the slices, you can easily remove one slice at a time from the freezer.

Whether you make yeast or non-yeast sweet breads, you will find them delicious and well worth the time you spent making them. There is nothing as wonderful as freshly made bread!

Quinoa Cinnamon Raisin Bread

Gluten-Free

This bread has an amazingly wheat-like texture for a gluten-free loaf. Try it toasted for breakfast.

¼ cup water
⅓ cup apple juice concentrate
About 4 large or 3 extra large eggs*, or enough to measure ¾ cup in volume,
    at room temperature
2 tablespoons oil
¾ teaspoon salt
1 teaspoon cinnamon
4 teaspoons guar or xanthum gum

2½ cups quinoa flour
¾ cup tapioca starch
2¼ teaspoons active dry yeast
½ cup raisins

To make this bread with a programmable bread machine, add the ingredients except for the raisins to the pan in the order listed. Program your machine to have rise 1 set to the lowest time possible, rise 2 be 30 to 40 minutes (use 30 minutes the first time you make this and adjust the time up in 5 minute increments each time you make it to as much as 60 minutes if it needs to raise more in the future), and set the bake time to 50 minutes. Add the raisins at the "beep" or 5 to 8 minutes before the end of the last kneading time. Allow the cycle to run to completion and remove the bread from the machine.

With some machines you may need to reserve ¼ cup of the quinoa flour and add it as the dough mixes, using a spatula to assist mixing. Also, if your bread over-rises in the machine (i.e. doubles or more than doubles in volume) and collapses during baking, the rise 2 time may need to be decreased. Adjust it downwards in 5 minute increments each time you make the bread. Another solution for this problem is to make the dough using the bread machine but have the second rise happen in a baking pan where you are in total control and can bake the bread in the oven at exactly the right time as directed in the paragraph below.

If your bread machine is not programmable, use the dough cycle to make the dough. Add the raisins at the "beep" or 5 to 8 minutes before the end of the last kneading time After the dough from the machine has risen the first time, re-start the cycle and allow it to mix for three minutes. Then remove the dough from the machine, put it in a prepared loaf pan, allow it to rise the second time, and bake it as below.

To make this bread with a mixer, heat the water and apple juice concentrate to about 115 to 120°F. Have the eggs and room temperature and beat them lightly. Stir together the dry ingredients in a large electric mixer bowl. With the mixer running at low speed, gradually add the liquid mixture, eggs, and oil. Beat the dough for three minutes at medium speed. Scrape the dough from the beaters and the sides of the bowl into the bottom of the bowl. Oil the top of the dough and the sides of the bowl, and cover the bowl with a towel. Put the bowl in a warm (85°F to 90°F) place and let the dough rise for 1 to 1½ hours. Beat the dough again for three minutes at medium speed. Stir in the raisins by hand. Oil and flour an 8 by 4 inch loaf pan. Put the dough in the pan and allow it to rise in a warm place for about 20 to 30 minutes, or until it barely doubles. Watch it carefully to prevent over-rising which will lead to a collapse during baking. Preheat the oven to 375°F. Bake the loaf for about 50 to 70 minutes, loosely covering it with foil after the first 15 minutes to prevent excessive browning. Makes one loaf.

*Note on eggs: If you are allergic to eggs, use ¾ cup warm water in their place.

White Spelt Cinnamon Raisin Bread

Ingredients:	1½ pound loaf	1 pound loaf
Water	1¼ cups	¾ cup + 1 tablespoon
Oil	2 tablespoons	1 tablespoon + 1 teaspoon
Date sugar	⅓ cup	¼ cup
Salt	1 teaspoon	¾ teaspoon
Cinnamon	1½ teaspoons	1 teaspoon
White spelt flour	3¾ cups	2⅝ cups
Active dry yeast	2¼ teaspoons	1¼ teaspoons
Raisins	½ cup	⅓ cup

To make this bread by hand or with a mixer, use the ingredients for a 1½ pound loaf and the directions on pages 121 to 124. To keep this bread from sticking to the pan, oil a loaf pan, line it with parchment paper or waxed paper, and oil the paper before adding the dough to the pan for the last rise.

To use a bread machine, use the ingredient list that is the correct size for your machine. If you have a bread machine that makes 2-pound loaves of bread, double the amounts of the ingredients in the "1 pound loaf" column. Add the ingredients except for the raisins to the pan in the order listed. Start the raisin bread or basic yeast bread cycle. Watch the dough while it is kneading and if it begins to soften, add more spelt flour. Do not be surprised if you have to add up to ½ cup of additional flour. When the "beep" to add raisins sounds, or 5 to 8 minutes before the end of the last kneading time, add the raisins to the machine. Allow the cycle to run to completion and remove the bread from the machine.

Rice Cinnamon Raisin Bread

Gluten-Free

Ingredients:	1½ pound loaf	1 pound loaf
Water	¾ cup	½ cup
Oil	2 tablespoons	1½ tablespoons
Eggs OR egg substitute	3 eggs OR ¾ cup egg substitute	2 eggs OR ½ cup egg substitute
Salt	1 teaspoon	¾ teaspoon
Vitamin C crystals	⅛ teaspoon	Scant ⅛ teaspoon
Guar gum	4 teaspoons	3 teaspoons
Cinnamon	1½ teaspoons	1 teaspoon

Brown rice flour	2 cups	1⅓ cups
Potato flour	⅓ cup	¼ cup
Tapioca flour	⅓ cup	¼ cup
Date sugar	⅓ cup	¼ cup
Active dry yeast	2¼ teaspoons	1½ teaspoons
Raisins	½ cup	⅓ cup

To make this bread by hand or with a mixer, use the ingredients for a 1½ pound loaf and the directions on pages 123 to 124.

To use a bread machine, use the ingredient list that is the correct size for your machine. If you have a bread machine that makes 2-pound loaves of bread, double the amounts of the ingredients in the "1 pound loaf" column. Add the ingredients except for the raisins to the pan in the order listed. Start the raisin bread or basic yeast bread cycle. When the "beep" to add raisins sounds, or 5 to 8 minutes before the end of the last kneading time, add the raisins to the machine. Allow the cycle to run to completion and remove the bread from the machine.

Whole Spelt Cinnamon Raisin Bread

Ingredients:	1½ pound loaf	1 pound loaf
Water	1¼ cups	¾ cup + 1 tablespoon
Oil	2 tablespoons	1 tablespoon + 1 teaspoon
Date sugar	⅓ cup	¼ cup
Salt	1 teaspoon	¾ teaspoon
Cinnamon	1½ teaspoons	1 teaspoon
Whole spelt flour	3¾ cups	2⅝ cups
Active dry yeast	2¼ teaspoons	1¼ teaspoons
Raisins	½ cup	⅓ cup

To make this bread by hand or with a mixer, use the ingredients for a 1½ pound loaf and the directions on pages 121 to 124. To keep this bread from sticking to the pan, oil a loaf pan, line it with parchment paper or waxed paper, and oil the paper before adding the dough to the pan for the last rise.

To use a bread machine, use the ingredient list that is the correct size for your machine. If you have a bread machine that makes 2-pound loaves of bread, double the amounts of the ingredients in the "1 pound loaf" column. Add the ingredients except for the raisins to the pan in the order listed. Start the raisin bread or basic yeast bread cycle. Watch the dough while it is kneading and if it begins to soften, add more spelt flour. Do not be surprised if you have to add up to ½ cup of additional flour. When the "beep" to add raisins sounds, or 5 to 8 minutes before the end of the last kneading time, add the raisins to the machine. Allow the cycle to run to completion and remove the bread from the machine.

Cranberry Orange Bread

**Gluten-Free IF
made with rice**

Try this recipe for Thanksgiving!

Use the recipe for "White Spelt Cinnamon Raisin Bread," "Rice Cinnamon Raisin Bread," or "Whole Spelt Cinnamon Raisin Bread," pages 126 to 127, except substitute an equal amount of dried cranberries (craisins) for the raisins. For the cinnamon, substitute 1 tablespoon orange zest in the 1½ pound loaf or 2 teaspoons orange zest in the 1 pound loaf.

Blueberry Lemon Bread

**Gluten-Free IF
made with rice**

Use the recipe for "White Spelt Cinnamon Raisin Bread," "Rice Cinnamon Raisin Bread," or "Whole Spelt Cinnamon Raisin Bread," pages 126 to 127, except substitute an equal amount of dried blueberries for the raisins. For the cinnamon, substitute 1 tablespoon lemon zest in the 1½ pound loaf or 2 teaspoon lemon zest in the 1 pound loaf.

Sugarplum Bread

¾ cup water
¼ cup agave, Fruit Sweet™ or honey
2 tablespoons oil
½ teaspoon salt
½ teaspoon nutmeg
3 to 3½ cups white spelt flour
2¼ teaspoons active dry yeast
½ cup raisins
½ cup dried fruit (small pieces of cherries, pineapple, or papaya)

To make this bread by hand or with a mixer, make the dough according to the directions on pages 121 to 124. Add the dry fruit by hand at the end of the kneading time.

To use a bread machine, add the ingredients except for the raisins and dried fruit to the pan in the order listed. Use 3 cups of white spelt flour to start. (Add more as needed as the cycle progresses). Start the dough cycle. When the "beep" to add raisins sounds, or 5 to 8 minutes before the end of the last kneading time, add the raisins and dried fruit to the machine.

After the cycle ends or the dough has risen once, remove the dough and shape it into a ball. Place it on a well oiled baking sheet, or line the sheet with oiled parchment paper for easiest removal of the loaf. Allow it to rise in a warm place until double, about 50 to 70 minutes. Bake at 350°F for 35 to 50 minutes, covering it with foil if it browns too quickly. Allow the loaf to cool completely on a wire rack. Glaze with "Creamy Glaze," page 148, if desired.

Mexican Holiday Bread

¾ cup water
¼ cup agave, Fruit Sweet™ or honey
2 tablespoons oil
¾ teaspoon salt
1½ teaspoons orange zest
3 to 3½ cups white spelt flour
2¼ teaspoons active dry yeast
½ cup dried sweet (Bing) cherries, plus a few more for topping the loaf if
    desired

To make this bread by hand or with a mixer, make the dough according to the directions on pages 121 to 124. Add the dry fruit by hand at the end of the kneading time.

To use a bread machine, add the ingredients except for the raisins and dried fruit to the pan in the order listed. Use 3 cups of white spelt flour to start. (Add more as needed as the cycle progresses). Start the dough cycle. When the "beep" to add raisins sounds, or 5 to 8 minutes before the end of the last kneading time, add the dried cherries to the machine.

After the cycle ends or the dough has risen once, remove the dough and shape it into a ball. Place it on a well oiled baking sheet, or line the sheet with oiled parchment paper for easiest removal of the loaf. Allow it to rise in a warm place until double, about 50 to 70 minutes. Bake at 350°F for 35 to 50 minutes, covering it with foil if it browns too quickly. Allow the loaf to cool completely on a wire rack. Glaze with "Creamy Glaze," page 148, and top it with additional cherries if desired.

Pannetone

⅞ cup water

3 tablespoons agave, Fruit Sweet™ or honey

2 tablespoons oil

¾ teaspoon salt

1 teaspoon lemon zest

3⅜ to 4 cups white spelt flour

2¼ teaspoons active dry yeast

¼ cup golden raisins

¼ cup currants or dark raisins

3 tablespoons chopped citron (optional – or add additional raisins and
    currants instead)

To make this bread by hand or with a mixer, make the dough according to the directions on pages 121 to 124. Add the dry fruit by hand at the end of the kneading time.

To use a bread machine, add the ingredients except for the dried fruit to the pan in the order listed. Use 3⅜ cups of white spelt flour to start. (Add more as needed as the cycle progresses). Start the dough cycle. When the "beep" to add raisins sounds, or 5 to 8 minutes before the end of the last kneading time, add the dried fruit to the machine.

Oil a baking sheet, lining it with parchment paper if desired, or oil a 7 to 8-inch round casserole dish or pannetone pan and line it with parchment or wax paper After the cycle ends or the dough has risen once, remove the dough and shape it into a ball. Place it on the prepared baking sheet or in the prepared pan. Allow it to rise in a warm place until double, about 30 to 45 minutes. Bake at 375°F for 40 to 50 minutes, covering it with foil if it browns too quickly. Remove it from the baking sheet or casserole dish immediately. Allow the loaf to cool completely on a wire rack. Glaze with "Creamy Glaze," page 148, if desired.

Hawaiian Bread

½ cup coconut milk

¼ cup pineapple juice concentrate, thawed

½ cup pureed or thoroughly mashed banana (about 1 medium banana)

1 tablespoon oil

½ teaspoon salt

3 to 3½ cups white spelt flour

2 teaspoons active dry yeast

⅓ cup dry diced pineapple

¼ cup unsweetened coconut (optional)

To make this bread by hand or with a mixer, make the dough according to the directions on pages 121 to 124. Add the dried pineapple and coconut by hand at the end of the kneading time.

To use a bread machine, add the ingredients except for the dried pineapple and coconut to the pan in the order listed. Use 3 cups of white spelt flour to start. (Add more as needed as the cycle progresses). Start the dough cycle. When the "beep" to add raisins sounds, or 5 to 8 minutes before the end of the last kneading time, add the dried pineapple and coconut to the machine.

After the cycle ends or the dough has risen once, remove the dough and shape it into a ball. Place it in a well oiled pie dish, or line the dish with oiled parchment paper for easiest removal of the loaf. Allow it to rise in a warm place until double, about 40 to 60 minutes. Bake at 375°F for 30 to 40 minutes. Cover it with foil for the last 20 minutes of baking to prevent excessive browning. Remove it from the pie dish immediately. Allow the loaf to cool completely on a wire rack. Glaze with "Creamy Glaze," page 148, if desired.

SWEET DOUGH FOR COFFEE CAKES, BUNS, AND DOUGHNUTS

The next six recipes are for sweet dough made with various types of flour. These sweet doughs are used in the recipes for coffee cakes, buns, and doughnuts on pages 134 to 144.

White Spelt Sweet Roll Dough

1 cup water
⅓ cup agave, Fruit Sweet™ or honey
2 tablespoons oil
¾ teaspoon salt
4½ cups white spelt flour
1¾ teaspoons active dry yeast

To make this dough by hand and/or with a mixer, use the directions on pages 121 to 122. To make it with a bread machine, use the dough cycle. Watch the dough while it is kneading and if it begins to soften, add more spelt flour. Do not be surprised if you have to add up to ¾ cup of additional flour. Shape and bake the dough as directed in the coffee cake, bun, or doughnut recipe you are using.

Rice Sweet Roll Dough

Gluten-Free

½ cup water
¼ cup agave, Fruit Sweet™ or honey
2 tablespoons oil
3 extra large eggs or enough smaller eggs to make ¾ cup of slightly beaten egg
1 teaspoon salt
⅛ teaspoon unbuffered vitamin C crystals
4 teaspoons guar gum
2 cups brown rice flour
⅓ cup potato flour
⅓ cup tapioca flour
2¼ teaspoons active dry yeast

To make this dough with a mixer, follow the directions on page 123. After the first rise, beat the dough for three minutes. To make it with a bread machine, use the dough cycle. After the cycle finishes, start it again and let the dough knead for three minutes. Shape and bake the dough as directed in the coffee cake or bun recipe you are using.

Buckwheat Sweet Roll Dough

Gluten-Free

⅜ cup water
⅜ cup agave, Fruit Sweet™ or honey
About 4 large or 3 extra large eggs*, or enough to measure ¾ cup in volume,
    at room temperature
3 tablespoons oil
1¼ teaspoon salt
1 tablespoon guar or xanthum gum
2 cups buckwheat flour
1¼ cup tapioca starch
2¼ teaspoons active dry yeast

To make this dough with a mixer, follow the directions on page 123. After the first rise, beat the dough for three minutes. To make it with a bread machine, use the dough cycle. After the cycle finishes, start it again and let the dough knead for three minutes. Shape and bake the dough as directed in the coffee cake recipe you are using.

Whole Spelt Sweet Roll Dough

1 cup water
⅓ cup agave, Fruit Sweet™ or honey
2 tablespoons oil
¾ teaspoon salt
4¾ cups whole spelt flour
2¼ teaspoons active dry yeast

To make this dough by hand and/or with a mixer, use the directions on pages 121 to 122. To make it with a bread machine, use the dough cycle. Watch the dough while it is kneading and if it begins to soften, add more spelt flour. Do not be surprised if you have to add up to ¾ cup of additional flour. Shape and bake the dough as directed in the coffee cake, bun, or doughnut recipe you are using.

Kamut Sweet Roll Dough

1⅛ cups water
⅜ cup agave, Fruit Sweet™ or honey
2 tablespoons oil
¾ teaspoon salt
3¼ cups kamut flour

To make this dough by hand and/or with a mixer, use the directions on pages 121 to 122. To make it with a bread machine, use the dough cycle. Shape and bake the dough as directed in the coffee cake, bun, or doughnut recipe you are using.

Barley Sweet Roll Dough

2 cups water
2 tablespoons agave, Fruit Sweet™ or honey
2 tablespoons oil
1 teaspoon salt
1 tablespoon guar or xanthum gum
3⅓ cups barley flour
2¼ teaspoons active dry yeast

To make this dough with a mixer, use the directions on page 123. To make it with a bread machine, use the dough cycle. Shape and bake the dough as directed in the coffee cake recipe you are using.

COFFEE CAKES

Streusel Coffee Cake

Gluten-Free IF
made with a GF dough

1 batch of any sweet roll dough, pages 131 to 133

1 teaspoon lemon or orange zest (optional)

¼ cup flour, the same kind as used in the dough recipe

⅓ cup date sugar

1 teaspoon cinnamon

1 to 2 tablespoons oil (use larger amount with rice and other low-gluten or gluten-free flours)

2 tablespoons finely chopped walnuts or other nuts

Make the dough for this recipe by hand and/or with a mixer adding the lemon or orange zest to the ingredients in the dough recipe. Use the directions on pages 121 to 123. To make it with a bread machine, use the dough cycle, adding the zest to the machine with the liquids. When the dough cycle finishes, punch down the spelt or kamut dough. For rice, buckwheat, or barley dough, when the dough cycle finishes, re-start the machine and allow the dough to knead for 3 minutes. Then stop the machine. If you make the dough by hand and/or mixer, after it has risen punch down the spelt or kamut dough or beat the rice, barley, or buckwheat dough for three minutes.

Spread the dough in a lightly oiled 9-inch by 9-inch baking pan. In a bowl, stir together the flour, date sugar, and cinnamon. With a fork or pastry cutter, cut in the oil, adding the second tablespoon of oil if necessary to get the mixture to stick together and form crumbs. Stir in the nuts. Sprinkle the topping over the dough. Allow it to rise in a warm place until double, 25 to 35 minutes for gluten-free or low-gluten dough or 30 to 45 minutes for high-gluten dough such as spelt or kamut. Watch the rising carefully for gluten-free or low-gluten dough and bake the coffee cake when it is just under doubled in volume. If it over-rises, it will collapse in baking. Bake at 375°F for 25 to 40 minutes, or until the coffee cake is browned on the top and bottom. Check to see if the top is browning occasionally starting at about 20 minutes into the baking time. If the top it getting brown before the coffee cake is done through, cover it with foil. Makes about 8 to 10 servings of coffee cake.

Fruit Kuchen

**Ask your doctor about
eating oats on a gluten-free diet
and make this with a GF dough**

1 batch of any sweet roll dough, pages 131 to 133
4 to 5 cups fresh or frozen blueberries or peeled, sliced apples or peaches
½ cup flour, the same kind as used in the dough recipe
½ cup quick cooking oats, uncooked
½ cup date sugar
3 teaspoons cinnamon
2 tablespoons oil

Make the dough for this recipe by hand and/or with a mixer using the ingredients in the dough recipe and the directions on pages 121 to 123. To make it with a bread machine, use the dough cycle. When the dough cycle finishes, punch down the spelt or kamut dough. For rice, buckwheat, or barley dough, when the dough cycle finishes, re-start the machine and allow the dough to knead for 3 minutes. Then stop the machine. If you make the dough by hand and/or mixer, after it has risen punch down the spelt or kamut dough or beat the rice, barley, or buckwheat dough for three minutes.

Spread the dough in a lightly oiled 9-inch by 13-inch pan. Arrange the fruit evenly over the dough. In a bowl, stir together the flour, oats, date sugar, and cinnamon. Sprinkle the mixture with the oil and mix it in with your fingers. Sprinkle the oat topping over the fruit. Allow the kuchen to rise in a warm place until double, 30 to 60 minutes, depending on the kind of dough used. Bake at 350°F for 40 to 50 minutes, or until browned on the top and bottom.

Easy Lattice Coffee Cake

**Gluten-Free IF
made with a GF dough**

1 batch of any sweet roll dough, pages 131 to 133
Oil
1 cup of all-fruit jam or preserves
1 cup chopped nuts

Make the sweet roll dough for this recipe by hand and/or with a mixer using the ingredients in the dough recipe and the directions on pages 121 to 123. To make it with a bread machine, use the dough cycle. When the dough cycle finishes, punch down the spelt or kamut dough. For rice, buckwheat, or barley dough, when the dough cycle finishes, re-start the machine and allow the dough to knead for 3 minutes. Then stop the machine. If you make the dough by hand and/or mixer, after it has risen punch down the spelt or kamut dough or beat the rice, barley, or buckwheat dough for three minutes.

Oil an 8 or 9 inch square baking pan. Divide the dough and set aside about one-fourth of it. For spelt or kamut dough, roll out the larger piece to fit the bottom of the baking pan and lay it in the pan. For the other types of dough, put three-fourths of the dough in the pan and stretch it out with your oiled fingers to cover the bottom of the pan. Stir together the fruit jam or preserves and the nuts and spread them over the dough.

For spelt or kamut dough, roll the smaller piece of dough into a rectangle and cut it into 8 to 10 strips. Roll each strip into a round "snake" with your hands. Weave the strips of dough into a lattice on top of the preserve-nut mixture. If you are using any of the other types of dough, drop teaspoonfuls of the dough onto the fruit preserves. Let the coffee cake rise in a warm place until it just doubles in volume, about 30 to 60 minutes, depending on the type of dough used. Preheat your oven to 375° F. Bake the coffee cake for 30 to 45 minutes or until it is browned. Remove it from the pan immediately.

Monkey Bread

Gluten-Free IF made with rice dough

1 batch of any white spelt, whole spelt, rice, or kamut sweet roll dough,
    pages 131 to 133
Cooking oil
½ cup date sugar
2 teaspoons cinnamon

Make the dough for this recipe by hand and/or with a mixer using the ingredients in the dough recipe and the directions on pages 121 to 123. To make it with a bread machine, use the dough cycle. When the dough cycle finishes, re-start it and allow the dough to knead for 3 minutes. Then stop the machine. After the dough has risen if you make it by hand and/or mixer, knead the spelt or kamut dough briefly on a lightly floured board or beat the rice dough for 3 minutes.

Oil a 10-inch tube pan or a 2 to 3-quart round casserole dish. Stir together the date sugar and cinnamon. Divide the dough into 45 to 50 1-inch balls. Brush each ball lightly with cooking oil. Then roll the balls in the cinnamon mixture. Place the balls in the prepared pan. Sprinkle any remaining cinnamon mixture over the top of the balls.

Let the bread rise in a warm place until double, about 35 to 50 minutes. Bake at 375°F for 35 to 45 minutes, or until brown. Remove from the pan immediately.

Jam Crescents or Tea Ring

1 batch of white spelt, whole spelt, or kamut sweet roll dough, pages 131 or 133
⅓ to ½ cup all-fruit (sugar-free) jam
⅓ cup chopped walnuts or other nuts
2 teaspoons cinnamon

Make the dough for this recipe by hand and/or with a mixer using the ingredients in the dough recipe and the directions on pages 121 to 122. To make it with a bread machine, use the dough cycle. When the dough cycle finishes, re-start it and allow the dough to knead for 3 minutes. Then stop the machine. After the dough has risen if you make it by hand and/or mixer, knead the dough briefly on a lightly floured board. Oil a baking sheet. To make two crescents, divide the dough in half and roll each out to an 8 inch square. Spread the squares with the jam and sprinkle with the nuts and cinnamon, leaving about ¾-inch of dough plain around the edges. Roll up jelly-roll fashion, crimp the outer edge to the roll, and squeeze the ends together. Lay the rolls on the baking sheet with the seam down and curve them into crescent shapes. Using a sharp knife, make 7 cuts from the outer edge of the crescent to within about 1½-inch of the inner edge. Turn the slices on their sides, all facing the same direction.

To make a tea ring, roll the dough out to a 12 inch square. Spread all but a 1-inch margin on one edge of the square with jam, and sprinkle it with the nuts and cinnamon. Roll the square up jelly-roll fashion, beginning with the edge opposite the edge without jam. Lay the roll seam side down on the baking sheet. Using a sharp knife, make 11 cuts (at 1-inch intervals) through one side of the roll to within about 1½-inch of the other side of the roll. Form the roll into a circle with the cut edge on the outside. Turn the slices on their sides, all facing the same direction.

Allow the crescents or ring to rise in a warm place until double, about 40 to 50 minutes. Bake at 375°F until nicely browned, about 18 to 25 minutes for the crescents and 20 to 30 minutes for the ring. Remove from the baking sheet immediately and drizzle with "Creamy Glaze," page 148, if desired.

BUNS, ROLLS AND DOUGHNUTS

Sticky Buns

Gluten-Free IF
made with rice dough

1 batch of white spelt, whole spelt, rice,* or kamut sweet roll dough, pages 131
    to 133
1½ cups of sticky agave (on the next page) or honey
1 tablespoon maple flavoring or 1 teaspoon vanilla extract
1½ teaspoons cinnamon
1¼ cups whole pecans or 1 cup pecan pieces
½ cup raisins (optional)
Oil

Before you begin making the dough, make the sticky agave as directed on the next page. Make the dough for this recipe by hand and/or with a mixer using the ingredients in the dough recipe and the directions on pages 121 to 123. To make it with a bread machine, use the dough cycle. If you have made the sticky agave syrup far enough ahead of time that it is cool, when the dough is almost done rising, heat the syrup to barely warm by microwaving it on high power for ½ to 1 minute or warming it over low heat in a saucepan. If you are using the honey, while the dough is in the early stage of rising, bring the honey to a boil over high heat. When it comes to a full boil, turn it down to low heat and boil it for four minutes. Stir the flavoring into the honey or warmed sticky agave. Oil a 13 inch by 9 inch baking pan. Pour half of the agave syrup or honey into the pan and sprinkle with the pecans. Stir the cinnamon into the remaining agave syrup or honey and let it cool to near room temperature.

When the dough is finished rising, punch down the high-gluten doughs and knead or beat the rice dough for three minutes. Oil your work surface and a rolling pin. Roll the dough out into a 10 inch by 12 to 15 inch rectangle if you are using any type of dough except rice dough. (See the next patagraph for directions fo the rice dough). Spread the dough with the remaining agave syrup and sprinkle it with the raisins. Roll it up starting with the long side. Slice the roll into 12 to 15 1-inch segments. Lay each segment cut side down in the prepared pan. Let the buns rise in a warm place draft-free place until doubled in volume, about 30 to 40 minutes to an hour. Heat your oven to 375° F near the end of the rising time. Bake the buns for 25 to 35 minutes or until they are browned. Immediately after removing the buns from the oven, turn the pan over on to a large platter or a piece of aluminum foil.

To make sticky buns with gluten-free rice dough, make a 1 cup batch of sticky agave or use 1 cup of honey. Add 2 teaspoons maple flavoring or ¾ teaspoon vanilla. Oil an 8 or 9-inch square cake pan and put half of the sticky agave or honey in the pan and sprinkle it with ¾ cup of pecans. Mix 1 teaspoon of cinnamon into the remaining sweetener. After the dough has risen, pat it out into a 6-inch by 12-inch rectangle on a very well oiled board. Spread it with the remaining sticky agave or honey and ¼ cup raisins. Roll it up carefully starting at the long edge and cut it into 9 slices. Put them in the oiled baking pan and allow to rise until double, about 30 minutes. Bake as above. Makes 9 rice buns or 12 to 15 buns with any other dough.

*Note on rice dough: Use ⅔ of the amounts of all ingredients in this recipe because the rice dough makes a smaller batch of buns.

Sticky Agave

Gluten-Free

> 1⅝ cup agave to make one batch of sticky buns (or you may make a larger batch of sticky agave)

Attach a candy thermometer to a saucepan which is at least 2½ to 3 times the volume of the agave you are using. Put the agave in to the pan and bring it to a boil over high heat. Turn the heat down to medium and cook it until the candy thermometer reaches 245° to 250°F* if you live near sea level. See the note below if you live at high altitude. Remove the pan from the heat and cool the agave syrup. Allow enough time for it to cool to just warm before you roll it into the bun dough.

If you are a sticky bun fan and will be making these buns often, you can make a larger batch of syrup and store it at room temperature until you are ready to make buns. Use any amount of agave up to a little over one-third of the volume of the saucepan you are using.

*Note on candy thermometer use at high altitude: Since this is not a candy recipe, the final temperature or the agave syrup is not extremely critical, but a thermometer helps to quantitate how sticky the agave becomes. If it is too thin, it will soak into the buns rather than forming a glaze. If you live at high altitude, measure the boiling point of water with your candy thermometer. Subtract that number from 212 °F. For example, if your water boils at 207 °F, the difference is 5°. Subtract that difference from the final temperature of the agave. In the example given, subtract 5° from 245° to 250°F F. The result, 240° to 245°F, is the temperature to which you should cook the syrup for the desired results at your altitude.

Cinnamon Rolls

Gluten-Free IF
made with rice dough

1 batch of white spelt, whole spelt, rice, or kamut sweet roll dough, pages 131
   to 133
1 tablespoon oil (omit with sticky agave)
½ cup date sugar or sticky agave or ¼ cup maple sugar
2 teaspoons cinnamon
½ cup raisins

Make the dough for this recipe by hand and/or with a mixer using the ingredients in the dough recipe and the directions on pages 121 to 123. To make it with a bread machine, use the dough cycle. When the dough cycle finishes, re-start it and allow the dough to knead for 3 minutes. Then stop the machine. After the dough has risen if you make it by hand and/or mixer, punch down the spelt or kamut dough or beat the rice dough for 3 minutes. If you made rice dough in the bread machine, re-start the cycle and allow it to mix for 3 minutes. Lightly oil your work surface and rolling pin.

If you are using spelt or kamut dough, transfer the dough to the work surface and roll it out to a 12-inch by 15-inch rectangle. If you are using sticky agave, warm it slightly by microwaving it for ½ to 1 minute or warming it in a saucepan. Mix the cinnamon into it and spread it on the rectangle of dough. If you are using the date sugar or maple sugar, brush the rectangle of dough with oil and sprinkle it with the sweetener and cinnamon. Sprinkle it with the raisins if desired. Starting at the long side, roll the dough up jelly roll fashion. Cut the roll into 12 to 15 slices and put them cut side down in an oiled 13-inch by 9-inch pan. (Or for individual cinnamon rolls, cut the dough into 15 slices and put each slice cut side down into an oiled muffin cup). Allow them to rise in a warm place until double, about 35 to 50 minutes. Bake at 375°F for 20 to 30 minutes. Remove the buns from the pan and cool them on a wire rack. Drizzle them with "Creamy Glaze," page 148, if desired. Makes 12 to 15 rolls.

To make cinnamon rolls with gluten-free rice dough, when you remove the dough from the machine, pat it out into a 6-inch by 10-inch rectangle on a very well oiled board. Spray or brush it with oil. Sprinkle it with ¼ cup date sugar or ⅛ cup sugar, 1½ teaspoons cinnamon, and ¼ cup raisins. Roll it up carefully starting at the long edge and cut it into 9 slices. Put them in an oiled 8-inch or 9-inch square baking pan and allow to rise until double, about 30 minutes. Bake as above. Remove the buns from the pan and cool them on a wire rack. Drizzle them with "Creamy Glaze," page 148, if desired. Makes 9 rolls.

Low-Fat Danish

1 batch of white spelt, whole spelt, or kamut sweet roll dough, pages 131
    or 133
2 teaspoons oil
⅓ cup plus ¼ cup date sugar or maple sugar
2½ teaspoons cinnamon, divided
Cooking oil spray or cooking oil
½ cup chopped walnuts or other nuts
¼ cup all fruit (sugar-free) jam

Make the dough for this recipe by hand and/or with a mixer using the ingredients in the dough recipe and the directions on pages 121 to 122. To make it with a bread machine, use the dough cycle. When the dough cycle finishes or after the dough has risen once if you make it by hand and/or mixer, divide the dough in half. On an oiled board, use a lightly oiled rolling pin to roll each half out to a 12-inch square. Brush each half with 1 teaspoon oil. Sprinkle each half with about ⅙ cup sweetener and ¾ teaspoon cinnamon. Roll the dough up jelly roll fashion. Cut the roll into 12 slices and put them cut side down at least 3 inches apart on an oiled baking sheet. Oil your hand and flatten the slices with your fingers to make them about 3 inches in diameter. (They may spring back some after you remove your hand). Allow them to rise in a warm place until double, about 30 to 40 minutes. Brush or spray the tops of the rolls lightly with cooking oil. Then cover them with a piece of waxed or parchment paper. Use a rolling pin to flatten them to ¼-inch to ⅜-inch thickness. Remove the paper. Mix together the remaining ¼ cup sweetener, 1 teaspoon cinnamon, and nuts. Sprinkle the rolls with the mixture. Cover them with the waxed or parchment paper and flatten them to ¼-inch to ⅜-inch thickness again. Let them rise until double again, about 30 to 40 minutes. Make an indentation in the center of each roll with your fingertip and fill it with ½ teaspoon jam. Bake at 375°F for 8 to 12 minutes. Makes 24 small Danish.

Hot Cross Buns

**Gluten-Free IF
made with rice dough**

1 batch of white spelt, whole spelt, rice, or kamut sweet roll dough, pages 131
    to 133
½ cup currants or dried blueberries
1 slightly beaten egg white or "Bread or Bun Wash," below
"Creamy Glaze," page 148, optional

Make the dough for this recipe by hand and/or with a mixer using the ingredients in the dough recipe and the directions on page 121 to 123. To make it with a bread machine, use the dough cycle. Add the currants or raisins to the machine at the "beep" for adding raisins or 5 to 10 minutes before the end of the last kneading time. At the end of the cycle, remove the spelt or kamut dough from the machine and knead it a few times on a lightly oiled board. For the rice dough, restart the cycle and allow the dough to knead for three minutes. Then stop the machine. If you made the dough by hand and/or mixer, at the end of the rising time, punch down the spelt or kamut dough and beat the rice dough for 3 minutes.

Transfer the dough to a lightly oiled work surface. Pat or roll it to ½-inch thickness with a lightly oiled rolling pin. Cut rounds of dough with a 2½-inch biscuit cutter or glass. Place them on a baking sheet that has been lightly oiled and allow them to rise in a warm place until double, about 40 minutes. For the spelt or kamut dough, snip a shallow cross in the top of each bun with a very sharp scissors, knife, or lamé. Brush the tops of the rolls with the egg white or wash. Bake at 375°F for 15 minutes, or until lightly browned. If desired, use sweet roll glaze to pipe a cross into the cross cut on the top of each roll. Makes about 12 buns.

Bread or bun wash: Combine ¼ cup water with 1 teaspoon arrowroot or tapioca starch in a small saucepan, bring them to a boil, reduce the heat, and simmer until the mixture is clear and the consistency of egg white. Or, combine the water and starch in a glass container and microwave them for 45 seconds to 1 minute, stirring every 15 seconds. Allow the wash to cool to lukewarm. Brush it on bread or buns after shaping them. Allow them to rise and bake as directed in the bread or bun recipe.

Cinnamon Crisps

1 batch of white spelt, whole spelt, or kamut sweet roll dough, pages 131
    or 133
2 teaspoons oil
⅓ cup plus ¼ cup date sugar or maple sugar
2½ teaspoons cinnamon, divided
Cooking oil spray or cooking oil
½ cup chopped walnuts or other nuts

Make the dough for this recipe by hand and/or with a mixer using the ingredients in the dough recipe and the directions on page 121 to 122. To make it with a bread machine, use the dough cycle. When the dough cycle finishes or after the dough has risen once if you make it by hand and/or mixer, divide the dough in half. On an oiled board, use a lightly oiled rolling pin to roll each half out to a 12-inch square. Brush each half with 1 teaspoon oil. Sprinkle each half with about ⅙ cup sweetener and ¾ teaspoon cinnamon. Roll the dough up jelly roll fashion. Cut the roll into 12 slices and put them cut side down at least 3 inches apart on an oiled baking sheet. Oil your hand and flatten the slices with your fingers to make them about 3-inch in diameter. (They may spring back some after you remove your hand). Allow them to rise in a warm place until double, about 30 minutes. Brush or spray the tops of the rolls lightly with cooking oil. Then cover them with a piece of waxed or parchment paper. Use a rolling pin to flatten them to ⅛-inch to ¼-inch thickness. Remove the paper. Mix together the remaining ¼ cup sweetener, 1 teaspoon cinnamon, and nuts. Sprinkle the cinnamon crisps with the mixture. Cover them with the waxed or parchment paper and flatten them to ⅛-inch to ¼-inch thickness again. Immediately bake them at 400°F for 10 to 12 minutes. Makes 24 pastries.

Orange Rolls

Gluten-Free IF
made with rice dough

1 batch of white spelt, whole spelt, rice, or kamut sweet roll dough, pages 131
     133
4 teaspoons orange zest
3 teaspoons oil
½ cup date sugar or ⅓ cup maple sugar
"Creamy Glaze," page 148 (optional)

Make the dough for this recipe by hand and/or with a mixer adding 2 teaspoons of the orange zest to the ingredients in the dough recipe and using the directions on pages 121 to 122. To make it with a bread machine, use the dough cycle adding 2 teaspoons of the orange zest to the liquid ingredients. When the dough cycle finishes, for the rice dough, re-start it and allow the dough to knead for 3 minutes. Then stop the machine. After the dough has risen if you make it by hand and/or mixer, beat the rice dough for three minutes. Punch down the spelt or kamut dough. Divide the dough in half. On a lightly oiled board roll or pat each half out to a 12 by 7 inch rectangle for the spelt or kamut dough or a 9 by 7 inch rectangle for the rice dough. Brush each half with 1½ teaspoons oil. Sprinkle each half with ¼ cup date sugar and 1 teaspoon grated orange zest. Roll each half jelly roll fashion starting with the long side. Cut each roll into 1-inch slices and place them cut side down on an oiled or nonstick baking sheet. Let rise until double, about 30 to 35 minutes. Bake at 375°F for 12 to 18 minutes. Cool and drizzle with orange-flavored "Creamy Glaze," page 148, if desired. Makes 18 rice rolls or 24 spelt or kamut rolls.

Lemon Rolls

Gluten-Free IF
made with rice dough

Make the same as "Orange Rolls" on the previous page except substitute lemon zest for the orange zest and drizzle with lemon-flavored "Creamy Glaze," page 148, if desired.

No-Fry Raised Doughnuts

Gluten-Free IF
made with a GF dough

One batch of sweet roll dough from this list:

1 batch of white spelt, whole spelt, rice (GF), or kamut sweet roll dough, pages 131 to 133
Additional oil
Doughnut coating, topping or glaze, pages 148 to 149 (optional)

Quinoa cinnamon doughnut dough (GF):

½ cup apple juice concentrate, thawed
½ cup water
2¼ teaspoons active dry yeast
2½ cups quinoa flour
1¾ teaspoons guar gum
1 teaspoon cinnamon
⅛ teaspoon salt (optional)
3 tablespoons oil
Additional oil
Optional coating: ¼ cup maple sugar plus 1 teaspoon cinnamon

Rye maple doughnut dough:

1 cup water
⅓ cup maple syrup or agave
2¼ teaspoons active dry yeast
3¼ to 3¾ cups rye flour
¼ tsp salt (optional)
3 tablespoons oil

Additional oil

Optional coating: ¼ cup maple sugar or 1 batch of any doughnut topping
   or glaze, pages 148 to 149

Carob doughnut dough:

⅔ cups apple juice concentrate, thawed

⅔ cup water

2¼ teaspoons active dry yeast

3 cups rye flour

⅓ cup carob powder

¼ teaspoon salt (optional)

3 tablespoons oil

Additional oil

Optional coating: ½ cup carob powder, ¼ cup maple sugar, or "Creamy
   Glaze," page 148

Choose one set of ingredients above. Make the dough by hand or mixer as described on pages 121 to 123 or use the dough cycle on a bread machine, omitting the last two ingredients (additional oil and coating or topping) from the dough itself. When the cycle is finished or the dough has raised once if made by hand or mixer, punch down the high-gluten doughs or beat the quinoa or rice dough for three minutes. Roll the dough out to about ½-inch thickness on a lightly oiled board with an oiled rolling pin. Cut into doughnuts with a floured doughnut cutter. Lightly oil a baking sheet. Transfer the doughnuts to the sheet with a spatula and spray them lightly with a cooking oil sprayer or brush them with oil. Let them rise in a warm place until double, about 30 to 40 minutes. Bake at 375°F for 10 to 15 minutes or until the doughnuts are just beginning to brown. Spray or brush both the top and bottom of each doughnut with oil and immediately shake each doughnut in one of the coatings listed here or the toppings on page 149. Or if you wish to frost the doughnuts, oil them while warm and then allow them to cool before frosting them with "Creamy Glaze," page 148. Makes about 10 to 15 doughnuts.

Rice Cake Doughnuts

Gluten-Free

To make these doughnuts and the following three recipes for cake doughnuts, you will need a special doughnut pan. See "Sources," page 231, for information on ordering the pan from The King Arthur Flour Baker's Catalogue.

> 1 cup brown rice flour
> ¼ cup tapioca starch
> ⅛ teaspoon salt
> ¾ teaspoon baking soda
> ⅛ teaspoon unbuffered vitamin C powder
> 1 teaspoon cinnamon (optional)
> 2 large eggs
> 3 tablespoons oil
> ⅜ cup agave

Preheat your oven to 375°F. Grease a 6-doughnut pan with a solid fat such as butter, coconut oil, or Spectrum Naturals™ non-hydrogenated shortening. In a large bowl, stir together the flour, starch, salt, baking soda, vitamin C and cinnamon. Beat the eggs thoroughly with a fork until the white and yolk are well blended and combine them with the oil and agave. Stir the liquid ingredients into the dry ingredients until just mixed. Fill the wells of the doughnut pan about three-fourths full with the batter. Bake for 10 to 12 minutes. Remove the doughnuts from the pan after taking them from the oven and allow them to cool completely on a wire rack. Frost them with "Creamy Glaze," page 148, if desired. Makes 6 doughnuts.

Barley Cake Doughnuts

My husband says these barley doughnuts are so tender and light that they almost fly off the plate.

> 1⅛ cups barley flour
> ⅛ teaspoon salt
> ¾ teaspoon baking soda
> ⅛ teaspoon unbuffered vitamin C powder
> 1 teaspoon cinnamon (optional)
> 2 large eggs
> 3 tablespoons oil
> ⅜ cup agave

Preheat your oven to 375°F. Grease a 6-doughnut pan with a solid fat such as butter, coconut oil, or Spectrum Naturals™ non-hydrogenated shortening. In a large bowl, stir together the flour, salt, baking soda, vitamin C and cinnamon. Beat the eggs thoroughly with a fork until the white and yolk are well blended and combine them with the oil and agave. Stir the liquid ingredients into the dry ingredients until just mixed. Fill the wells of the doughnut pan about three-fourths full with the batter. Bake for 10 to 12 minutes. Remove the doughnuts from the pan after taking them from the oven and allow them to cool completely on a wire rack. Frost them with "Creamy Glaze," page 148, if desired. Makes 6 doughnuts.

Chocolate Rice Cake Doughnuts

Gluten-Free

⅞ cup brown rice flour
¼ cup tapioca starch
¼ cup cocoa
⅛ teaspoon salt
¾ teaspoon baking soda
⅛ teaspoon unbuffered vitamin C powder
1 large egg
1 egg white from a large egg
3 tablespoons oil
⅜ cup plus 1 tablespoon agave

Preheat your oven to 375°F. Grease a 6-doughnut pan with a solid fat such as butter, coconut oil, or Spectrum Naturals™ non-hydrogenated shortening. In a large bowl, stir together the flour, starch, cocoa salt, baking soda, vitamin C and cinnamon. Beat the egg and egg white thoroughly with a fork until the white and yolk are well blended and combine them with the oil and agave. Stir the liquid ingredients into the dry ingredients until just mixed. Fill the wells of the doughnut pan about three-fourths full with the batter. Bake for 10 to 12 minutes. Remove the doughnuts from the pan after taking them from the oven and allow them to cool completely on a wire rack. Frost them with "Creamy Glaze," page 148, if desired. Makes 6 doughnuts.

Chocolate Barley Cake Doughnuts

1⅛ cups barley flour
¼ cup cocoa
⅛ teaspoon salt
¾ teaspoon baking soda
⅛ teaspoon unbuffered vitamin C powder
1 large egg
1 egg white from a large egg
3 tablespoons oil
⅜ cup plus 1 tablespoon agave

Preheat your oven to 375°F. Grease a 6-doughnut pan with a solid fat such as butter, coconut oil, or Spectrum Naturals™ non-hydrogenated shortening. In a large bowl, stir together the flour, cocoa, salt, baking soda, vitamin C and cinnamon. Beat the egg and egg white thoroughly with a fork until the white and yolk are well blended and combine them with the oil and agave. Stir the liquid ingredients into the dry ingredients until just mixed. Fill the wells of the doughnut pan about three-fourths full with the batter. Bake for 10 to 12 minutes. Remove the doughnuts from the pan after taking them from the oven and allow them to cool completely on a wire rack. Frost them with "Creamy Glaze," page 148, if desired. Makes 6 doughnuts.

Creamy Glaze for Doughnuts and Sweet Rolls

Gluten-Free

3 ounces of cream cheese
¼ cup (½ stick) butter
¼ cup agave or honey
½ teaspoon vanilla extract, orange zest, or lemon zest (optional)

Allow the cream cheese and butter to come to room temperature. The butter will soften more quickly if you cut it into 4 or 5 slices. Combine all of the ingredients with a hand blender, mixer, blender or food processor. Makes a scant cup of glaze. Refrigerate rolls or doughnuts that have been frosted, or refrigerate the glaze and frost the rolls or doughnuts right before serving.

Cinnamon "Sugar" Doughnut Topping

Gluten-Free

¼ cup date sugar or maple sugar
1 tsp cinnamon

Mix the sweetener and cinnamon in a plastic bag. Immediately after baking the doughnuts, spray or brush each doughnut with oil and shake the doughnuts one at a time in the bag with the cinnamon mixture while they are still warm.

Powdered "Sugar" Doughnut Topping

Gluten-Free

¼ cup banana powder* OR, if you must, powdered sugar

Put the banana powder or powdered sugar in a plastic bag. Immediately after baking the doughnuts, spray or brush each doughnut with oil and shake the doughnuts one at a time in the bag with the powder while they are still warm.

*__Note:__ Banana powder, which is dehydrated ground bananas, can be purchased from The King Arthur Flour Baker's Catalogue. (See "Sources," page 231).

NON-YEAST SWEET BREADS

Banana Bread

This sweet and moist bread can be made in either grain or non-grain versions. The millet and amaranth breads are gluten-free.

Barley

2½ cups barley flour
½ teaspoon salt
2 teaspoons baking soda
½ teaspoon unbuffered vitamin C powder
1 teaspoon cinnamon or ½ teaspoon ground cloves
½ cup chopped nuts (optional)
1¾ cups mashed ripe bananas (about 3½ bananas)
¼ cup oil

Spelt

3 cups whole spelt flour
½ teaspoon salt
2 teaspoons baking soda
½ teaspoon unbuffered vitamin C powder
1 teaspoon cinnamon or ½ teaspoon ground cloves
½ cup chopped nuts (optional)
1¾ cups mashed ripe bananas (about 3½ bananas)
¼ cup oil

Amaranth (GF)

2 cups amaranth flour
½ cup arrowroot
2 teaspoons baking soda
½ teaspoon unbuffered vitamin C powder
1 teaspoon cinnamon or ½ teaspoon ground cloves
½ cup chopped nuts (optional)
1¾ cups mashed ripe bananas (about 3½ bananas)
¼ cup oil

Millet (GF)

> 1½ cups millet flour
> 1 cup tapioca starch
> ½ teaspoon salt
> 2 teaspoons baking soda
> ½ teaspoon unbuffered vitamin C powder
> 1 teaspoon cinnamon or ½ teaspoon ground cloves
> ½ cup chopped nuts (optional)
> 1¾ cups mashed ripe bananas (about 3½ bananas)
> ¼ cup oil

Choose one set of ingredients above. Preheat your oven to 350°F. Oil and flour a loaf pan. Stir together the flour(s), salt (if called for), baking soda, vitamin C powder, spice, and nuts in a large bowl. Combine the mashed bananas and oil and stir them into the dry ingredients until they are completely mixed in, but be careful not to over-mix. (The batter will be stiff). Put the batter into the prepared pan and bake for 55 to 60 minutes, or until the bread is lightly browned and a toothpick inserted in the center comes out dry. Remove it from the oven and allow it to cool in the pan for 10 minutes. Remove it from the pan to cool completely. Makes one loaf of bread.

Spelt Date-Nut Bread

> 5 cups white spelt flour
> 1¼ cups date sugar
> ¼ teaspoon salt
> 2½ teaspoons baking soda
> ½ teaspoon unbuffered vitamin C powder
> 1½ cups chopped dates
> 1½ cup chopped nuts
> 1⅔ cup apple juice concentrate, thawed
> ½ cup oil

Preheat your oven to 375°F. Oil and flour an 8 or 9 inch square cake pan or two loaf pans. Stir together the flour, date sugar, salt, baking soda, vitamin C powder, chopped dates, and nuts in a large bowl. Combine the juice and oil and stir them into the dry ingredients until they are completely mixed in, but be careful not to over-mix. Put the batter into the prepared pan(s) and bake for 30 to 40 minutes, or until the bread is lightly browned and a toothpick inserted in the center comes out dry. Remove it from the oven and allow it to cool in the pans for 10 minutes. Remove it from the pans to cool completely. Makes two loaves or one round or square pan of bread.

Barley Date-Nut Bread

4 cups barley flour
1 cup date sugar
¼ teaspoon salt
2 teaspoons baking soda
½ teaspoon unbuffered vitamin C powder
1½ cups chopped dates
½ cup chopped nuts
2 cups apple juice concentrate, thawed
¾ cup oil

Preheat your oven to 375°F. Oil and flour two loaf pans. Stir together the flour, date sugar, salt, baking soda, vitamin C powder, chopped dates, and nuts in a large bowl. Combine the juice and oil and stir them into the dry ingredients until they are completely mixed in, but be careful not to over-mix. Put the batter into the prepared pans and bake for 30 to 40 minutes, or until the bread is lightly browned and a toothpick inserted in the center comes out dry. Remove it from the oven and allow it to cool in the pans for 10 minutes. Remove it from the pans to cool completely. Makes two loaves of bread.

Cookies

Who can resist cookies? For most of us, our first experiences with dessert are of eating cookies. They are sweet, easy to hold, and the most delightful thing a child has ever eaten. I have some great pictures of each of my sons with his first fruit-sweetened homemade cookie at about one year of age.

Nutritious fruit-sweetened or agave-sweetened cookies can be a mother's best friend. They round out a child's brown bag lunch or are a good between-meal snack that will not ruin you child's appetite for the next meal. Best of all, your child will enjoy them. Don't tell your kids that the cookies you make are actually nutritious and just maybe you can use them to motivate good behavior! Cookies are easy to make, easy to store, and come in serving-size portions. They can make a restricted diet seem livable. Nutritious cookies are truly a treat for kids of all ages.

Chocolate chip cookies are the most common favorite cookie. They can be made with a variety of different kinds of chips. If can't have chocolate, use carob chips. This book contains a recipe for homemade carob or chocolate chips if you cannot find commercially made chips that will work on your diet. (See page 201 for this recipe). If you want some variety from chips, substitute raisins, currants, other small or chopped dry fruit, nuts, or you can even make them without any additions for a basic vanilla drop cookie.

The recipes in this chapter use the healthiest sweeteners to make these cookies something you can eat often without guilt. Apple juice concentrate is used in many of the recipes, as is agave. Agave has a score of 11 on the glycemic index so it will not provoke large swings in blood sugar and may be acceptable for weight watchers and diabetics if your doctor allows. When baking cookies with agave, line your baking sheets with parchment paper to save time and breakage when you remove the cookies from the baking sheets.

A few cookie recipes are sweetened with whole fruit which includes all of its health promoting fiber. See "Sorghum Banana Cookies," page 158, and "Fiber-Full Oatmeal Cookies," page 160.

For those with severe candidiasis or diabetes, this chapter contains stevia-sweetened versions of the recipes for "Quinoa Chocolate or Carob Chip Cookies," page 156, "Carrot Cookies," page 166, "Carob Wafers," page 181, and "Amaranth Carob Brownies," page 171.

It is my hope that all readers will find a cookie recipe or two here that fits their diet and that will add enjoyment to their lives.

DROP COOKIES

White Spelt Chocolate or Carob Chip Cookies

These cookies are near normal yet healthy and are great for children's lunches and every-day use. For a recipe for butter and egg-containing white spelt chocolate or carob chip cookies to use for guests, see page 218.

    3½ cups white spelt flour
    1 teaspoon baking soda
    ¼ teaspoon vitamin C powder
    ½ teaspoon baking soda
    ¼ teaspoon salt
    1 cup agave, Fruit Sweet™, or honey
    1 cup oil
    2 teaspoons vanilla extract (optional)
    1 cup chocolate or carob chips (optional)

Preheat your oven to 375°F. If you are using the agave, line your baking sheets with parchment paper for easy cookie removal or oil the baking sheets. If you are using the other sweeteners, lining or oiling the sheets is optional.

In a large bowl, stir together the flour, baking soda, vitamin C, and salt. In a separate bowl thoroughly combine the sweetener, oil, and vanilla extract. Stir the liquid ingredients into the dry ingredients until they are just mixed. Fold in the chocolate or carob chips. Drop the batter by heaping teaspoonfuls 2 to 3 inches apart on the prepared baking sheets. Bake the cookies for 9 to 13 minutes or until they are golden brown. Slide the parchment paper and cookies off onto a cooling rack or remove the cookies from the baking sheets with a spatula and put them on paper towels to cool. Makes 3 to 4 dozen cookies.

Rice Chocolate or Carob Chip Cookies

Gluten-Free

    1½ cups brown or white rice flour
    1¼ cups arrowroot or tapioca starch
    1½ teaspoons baking soda
    ⅜ teaspoon unbuffered vitamin C powder
    ½ teaspoon salt
    ¾ cup agave or Fruit Sweet™

3 tablespoons water
⅜ cup oil
1 teaspoon vanilla extract (optional)
¾ cup chocolate or carob chips (optional)

Preheat your oven to 375°F. Lightly oil your baking sheets or, if you are using the agave, line your baking sheets with parchment paper for easiest cookie removal.

In a large bowl, stir together the flour, starch, baking soda, vitamin C, and salt. In a separate bowl thoroughly combine the sweetener, oil, and vanilla extract. Stir the liquid ingredients into the dry ingredients until they are just mixed. Fold in the chocolate or carob chips. Drop the batter by heaping teaspoonfuls 2 to 3 inches apart on the prepared baking sheets. Bake the cookies for 7 to 11 minutes or until they are golden brown. Slide the parchment paper and cookies off onto a cooling rack or remove the cookies from the baking sheets with a spatula and put them on paper towels to cool. Makes 3 to 4 dozen cookies.

Amaranth Chocolate or Carob Chip Cookies

Gluten-Free

2¼ cups amaranth flour
¾ cup arrowroot
1 teaspoon baking soda
¼ teaspoon unbuffered vitamin C powder
¼ teaspoon salt
¾ cup agave or Fruit Sweet™
½ cup water
¼ cup oil
2 teaspoons vanilla extract (optional)
¾ cup chocolate or carob chips (optional)

Preheat your oven to 375°F. If you are using the agave, line your baking sheets with parchment paper for easiest cookie removal or lightly oil the baking sheets.

In a large bowl, stir together the flour, arrowroot, baking soda, vitamin C, and salt. In a separate bowl thoroughly combine the sweetener, water, oil, and vanilla extract. Stir the liquid ingredients into the dry ingredients until they are just mixed. Fold in the chocolate or carob chips. Drop the batter by heaping teaspoonfuls 2 to 3 inches apart on the baking sheets. Bake the cookies for 10 to 13 minutes or until they are golden brown. Remove them from the baking sheets and put them on paper towels to cool. Makes 3 to 4 dozen cookies.

Quinoa Chocolate or Carob Chip Cookies

Gluten-Free

The high protein content of quinoa flour makes these cookies very satisfying. If made with unsweetened carob chips and stevia rather than apple juice, they may be acceptable as a reduced-carb snack.

    3 cups quinoa flour
    1 cup tapioca starch
    1½ teaspoons baking soda
    ⅜ teaspoon unbuffered vitamin C powder
    2 cups apple juice concentrate
    ½ cup oil
    1¼ cups chocolate or carob chips (optional)

Boil the apple juice down to 1⅜ cups in volume and allow it to cool to room temperature or cooler. If you are in a hurry, put it in the refrigerator to cool.

Preheat your oven to 350°F. In a large bowl, combine the quinoa flour, tapioca starch, baking soda, and vitamin C. In a separate bowl or cup, stir together the juice and oil. Immediately stir them into the dry ingredients until they are just mixed in. Fold in the chocolate or carob chips. Drop the dough by tablespoonfuls onto an ungreased baking sheet and flatten them to about ¼ inch thickness with your fingers held together. Bake for 10 to 15 minutes, or until the cookies are lightly browned. Makes about 5 dozen cookies.

Stevia-sweetened quinoa chocolate or carob chip cookies: Instead of the apple juice, use 1⅜ cups water plus ¾ to 1 teaspoon pure stevia powder and increase the amount of vitamin C to ½ teaspoon. When you are mixing the cookies, thoroughly stir the stevia into the dry ingredients. These cookies will not brown much when they are baked but will feel dry to the touch when they are done.

Barley Chocolate or Carob Chip Cookies

    3½ cups barley flour
    1 teaspoon baking soda
    ¼ teaspoon unbuffered vitamin C powder
    ½ teaspoon salt
    1 cup oil

1 cup agave or Fruit Sweet™
2 teaspoons vanilla extract (optional)
1 cup chocolate or carob chips (optional)

Preheat your oven to 375°F. If you are using the agave, line your baking sheets with parchment paper for easiest cookie removal or lightly oil the baking sheets.

In a large bowl, stir together the flour, baking soda, vitamin C, and salt. In a separate bowl thoroughly combine the sweetener, oil, and vanilla extract. Stir the liquid ingredients into the dry ingredients until they are just mixed. Fold in the chocolate or carob chips. Drop the batter by heaping teaspoonfuls 2 to 3 inches apart on the baking sheets. Bake the cookies for 8 to 10 minutes or until they are golden brown. Remove them from the baking sheets and put them on paper towels to cool. Makes 3 to 4 dozen cookies.

Whole Spelt Chocolate or Carob Chip Cookies

These nutritious cookies provide fiber and extra vitamins because they are whole grain. You can vary the sweetness to suit your taste.

2⅓ cups whole spelt flour
½ teaspoon baking soda
¾ cup agave, Fruit Sweet™, or apple juice concentrate, thawed, OR
    1¼ cups apple juice concentrate (Use the larger amount of apple juice
    for sweeter juice-sweetened cookies).
½ cup oil
2 teaspoons vanilla extract (optional)
¾ cup chocolate or carob chips (optional)

If you want to use apple juice for the sweetener and like your cookies fairly sweet, boil 1¼ cup apple juice concentrate down to ¾ cup in volume and allow it to cool to room temperature or cooler. (If you are in a hurry, put it in the refrigerator to cool). For minimally sweetened cookies, use ¾ cup apple juice concentrate.

Preheat your oven to 350°F. Lightly oil the baking sheets or, if you are using the agave, line your baking sheets with parchment paper for easiest cookie removal.

Stir together the spelt flour and baking soda in a large bowl. Mix the oil, sweetener, and vanilla and stir them into the flour mixture until they are just mixed in. Fold in the chocolate or carob chips. Drop the dough by heaping teaspoonfuls onto the prepared baking sheets and bake them for 10 to 14 minutes, or until they begin to brown. Slide the parchment paper and cookies off onto a cooling rack or remove the cookies from the baking sheets with a spatula and put them on paper towels to cool. Makes 3 dozen cookies.

Kamut Chocolate or Carob Chip Cookies

These are a golden take-off on your favorite cookie.

> 3¼ cups kamut flour
> 1 teaspoon baking soda
> ¼ teaspoon unbuffered vitamin C powder
> ¾ cup honey, agave, or Fruit Sweet™
> ¾ cup water
> ¼ cup oil
> 2 teaspoons vanilla extract (optional)
> 1 cup chocolate or carob chips (optional)

Preheat your oven to 350°F. Lightly oil the baking sheets or, if you are using the agave, line your baking sheets with parchment paper for easiest cookie removal.

Stir together the flour, baking soda, and vitamin C powder in a large bowl. Mix together the sweetener, water, oil, and vanilla and stir them into the flour mixture until they are just mixed in. Fold in the chocolate or carob chips. Drop heaping teaspoonfuls of the dough onto the prepared baking sheets. If you prefer flat rather than domed cookies, flatten them with your an oiled glass bottom or your oiled fingers held together. Bake for 15 to 20 minutes, or until they begin to brown. Slide the parchment paper and cookies off onto a cooling rack or remove the cookies from the baking sheets with a spatula and put them on paper towels to cool. Makes about 5 dozen cookies.

Vanilla Cookies

**Gluten-Free IF
made with a GF grain**

Make any of the chocolate or carob chip cookie recipes on pages 154 to 158 except omit the chocolate or carob chips, nuts, and other additions. Bake as directed. The number of cookies the recipes yields may be slightly fewer.

Sorghum Banana Cookies

Gluten-Free

> 3 cups sorghum (milo) flour
> 1 teaspoon baking soda
> ¼ teaspoon unbuffered vitamin C powder
> ¼ teaspoon salt
> 1 teaspoon cinnamon (optional)

⅛ teaspoon ginger (optional)
1½ cups thoroughly mashed or pureed bananas (about 3 large bananas)
½ cup oil
2 teaspoons vanilla extract (optional)

Preheat your oven to 350°F. Mash or use a hand blender to puree the bananas and measure out 1½ cups of puree. Lightly oil your baking sheets or line them with parchment paper.

Stir together the flour, baking soda, vitamin C, salt, and spices in a large bowl. Mix together the banana puree, oil, and vanilla and stir them into the flour mixture until they are just mixed in. Drop heaping teaspoonfuls of the dough onto the prepared baking sheets. Bake the cookies for 12 to 17 minutes, or until they begin to brown. Makes about 3 to 4 dozen cookies.

Chocolate or carob chip cookie variation: Omit the cinnamon and ginger and fold 1 cup of carob chips or chocolate chips into the cookie dough.

White Spelt Banana Cookies

This cookies are a moist and flavorful change from "plain" chocolate chip cookies.

3¼ cups white spelt flour
1 teaspoon baking soda
¼ teaspoon salt
1 cup agave or Fruit Sweet™
½ cup oil
¾ cup pureed or thoroughly mashed ripe banana (about 1½ large bananas)
1½ teaspoons banana or vanilla extract* (optional)
½ to 1 cup chopped walnuts (optional - use the smaller amount if you're also using the chocolate or carob chips)
¾ to 1¼ cups chocolate or carob chips (optional - use the smaller amount if you are also using nuts)

Preheat the oven to 350°F. Lightly oil your baking sheets or, if you are using the agave, line your baking sheets with parchment paper for easiest cookie removal. Mash the bananas or puree them using a hand blended and measure out ¾ cup of puree.

In a large bowl, stir together the flour, baking soda, and salt. In a smaller bowl stir together the sweetener, oil, banana puree, and banana or vanilla extract. Stir the liquid ingredients into the dry ingredients until they are just mixed. Quickly fold in the chocolate or carob chips and/or nuts if you are using them. Drop the cookie dough onto the prepared baking sheets by heaping teaspoonfuls. Bake for 12 to 15 minutes, or until they are golden brown. Slide the parchment paper and cookies off onto a cooling rack or remove the cookies from the baking sheets with a spatula and put them on paper towels to cool. Makes 4 to 5 dozen cookies.

*Note: If you want banana-nut cookies or banana cookies with no added chocolate or carob chips, the banana extract makes the banana flavor more pronounced. This recipe also makes great chocolate or carob chip cookies if you use the vanilla extract.

Fiber-Full Oatmeal Raisin Cookies

Ask your doctor about eating oats on a gluten-free diet

These cookies are fragile but delicious and are an excellent source of fiber. Since the only grain they contain is oats, celiacs whose doctors allow oats on a gluten-free diet may be able to eat them.

> 2 cups white raisins
> 2 cups white grape juice*
> ½ cup oil
> 2 cups oat flour
> 2 cups oatmeal
> 1 teaspoon baking soda
> 1½ teaspoons cinnamon
> 1 cup brown raisins
> ½ cup chopped nuts (optional)

Soak the white raisins in the grape juice overnight. In the morning, puree them using a hand blender, blender or food processor. Add the oil and blend again briefly. Preheat your oven to 375°F. Lightly oil your baking sheets or line them with parchment paper.

Combine the oat flour, oatmeal, baking soda, cinnamon, brown raisins, and nuts in a mixing bowl. Add the white raisin mixture and stir until it is just mixed into the flour mixture. Drop the batter by heaping teaspoonfuls onto an ungreased baking sheet and bake for 15 to 18 minutes, or until the cookies are lightly browned. Remove the cookies from the baking sheets with a spatula and put them on paper towels to cool. Makes about 6 dozen cookies.

*Whole fruit variation: To sweeten this recipe with whole fruit only, substitute water for the grape juice and add ¼ teaspoon unbuffered vitamin C powder to the dry ingredients. The cookies will be less sweet but still are delicious.

Oatmeal Treasures

2½ cups white spelt flour
2 cups oatmeal, regular or quick-cooking (not instant)
1 teaspoon baking soda
½ teaspoon salt
1 teaspoon cinnamon
1¼ cups agave or Fruit Sweet™ or 1 cup honey plus ¼ cup water
½ cup oil
2 teaspoons lemon juice
1 teaspoon vanilla extract (optional)
1 cup raisins or ½ cup raisins plus ½ cup chocolate or carob chips

Preheat your oven to 375°F. Lightly oil your baking sheets or, if you are using the agave, line your baking sheets with parchment paper for easiest cookie removal.

In a large bowl stir together the flour, oatmeal, baking soda, cinnamon, and salt. In a separate bowl thoroughly combine the agave, Fruit Sweet™, or honey plus water, oil, lemon juice, and vanilla extract. Stir the liquid ingredients into the dry ingredients until they are just mixed. Quickly fold in the raisins and chocolate or carob chips. Drop the batter by heaping teaspoonfuls 2 to 3 inches apart on the prepared baking sheets. Bake the cookies for 8 to 13 minutes or until they are golden brown. Let them cool on the baking sheets for about five minutes after you take them out of the oven. Remove them from the baking sheets and put them on paper towels to cool. Makes 3½ to 4 dozen cookies.

Peanut Butter Oatmeal Cookies

1½ cups white spelt flour
1 cup oatmeal, regular or quick-cooking (not instant)
1 teaspoon baking soda
½ cup natural peanut butter
¼ cup oil
1 cup agave or Fruit Sweet™ or ¾ cup honey plus ¼ cup water
1 teaspoon vanilla (optional)

Preheat your oven to 375°F. If you are using the agave, line your baking sheets with parchment paper for easiest cookie removal or lightly oil the baking sheets.

In a large bowl, combine the flour, oatmeal, and baking soda. Thoroughly stir the oil which is at the top of the peanut butter jar into the peanut butter before measuring the peanut butter. In another bowl or cup, thoroughly combine the peanut butter; oil; agave, Fruit Sweet™, or honey plus water; and vanilla. (If you have a hand blender, use it to mix the liquid ingredients). Stir them into the dry ingredients until they are just mixed. Drop the dough by heaping teaspoonfuls 2 to 3 inches apart on an ungreased baking sheet. Bake for 7 to 11 minutes. Cool the cookies for about five minutes on the baking sheet. Slide the parchment paper and cookies off onto a cooling rack or use a spatula to transfer the cookies to paper towels to cool. Makes about 3½ dozen cookies.

Cashew Butter Cookies

This delicious alternative to peanut butter cookies is gluten-free when made with the amaranth flour. My husband, a wheat-eater who doesn't like peanut butter cookies, comes back for second and third servings of these cookies made with amaranth flour.

Gluten-Free IF
made with amaranth

2 cups rye flour OR 1½ cups amaranth flour plus ½ cup arrowroot or tapioca
   starch
½ teaspoon baking soda
⅛ teaspoon unbuffered vitamin C powder
⅔ cup cashew butter
¼ cup oil
¾ cup agave or maple syrup
1 teaspoon vanilla (optional)

Preheat your oven to 400°F. If you are using the agave, line your baking sheets with parchment paper for easiest cookie removal or lightly oil the baking sheets.

Combine the flour(s), baking soda, and vitamin C powder in a large bowl. In a small bowl, thoroughly mix together the cashew butter, oil, agave or maple syrup, and vanilla. (A hand blender is helpful for thorough mixing especially if the cashew butter is fairly solid from having been refrigerated). Stir and mash the cashew butter mixture into the dry ingredients. Drop the dough by heaping teaspoonfuls onto an ungreased baking sheet. Use an oiled fork to flatten the balls of dough, making an "X" on the top of them with the fork tines. Bake the cookies for 8 to 10 minutes, or until they are golden brown. Makes about 3 dozen cookies.

Quinoa Almond Cookies

Gluten-Free

This cookie has several different "personalities" depending on which sweetener and how much liquid you use. Try all the varieties – they're delicious in different ways.

1½ cups quinoa flour
½ cup almond meal/flour
¾ teaspoon baking soda
¼ teaspoon unbuffered vitamin C powder
¼ cup sliced almonds (optional)
½ cup oil
½ teaspoon almond flavoring (optional)
½ cup agave or honey (for crisp cookies, with honey being more crisp)
    OR ½ cup agave or honey plus ½ cup water (for soft cookies)
    OR 1 cup apple juice concentrate, thawed (for fruit-sweetened soft cookies)

Preheat your oven to 375°. Oil your baking sheets or, if you are using the agave, line your baking sheets with parchment paper for easiest cookie removal. Combine the flour, almond meal, baking soda, vitamin C, and almonds in a large bowl. Thoroughly mix the oil and almond flavoring with the agave, honey, agave or honey plus water, or juice in a measuring cup or small bowl. Immediately pour the liquid ingredients into the dry ingredients and stir the dough until it is just mixed. Drop it by teaspoonfuls onto the prepared baking sheets. For the crisp cookies, flatten the cookies with an oiled glass bottom or your fingers held together. Bake the cookies at for 7 to 10 minutes or until golden brown. Makes about 1½ to 2 dozen crisp or 2 to 3 dozen soft cookies.

Very crisp cookie variation: Make the "crisp cookie" variation of this recipe using ½ cup agave or honey for the sweetener and no water, but also decrease the flour to 1 cup. If you are using the agave, be sure to line your baking sheets with parchment paper to avoid struggling to remove the cookies. There is no need to flatten the cookies with your fingers or a glass because the batter will be much thinner and will spread readily. Place the cookies at least 3 to 4 inches apart on the baking sheet. Bake at 375°F for 6 to 9 minutes. Slide the parchment paper and cookies off onto a cooling rack or let the cookies cool on the cookie sheet for about 2 minutes before removing them with a spatula to paper towels to cool. Makes about 1½ dozen cookies.

Tropical Delights

2⅛ cups white spelt flour or 2 cups kamut or rye flour
½ teaspoon baking soda
¼ teaspoon salt
1 cup unsweetened coconut
1 cup pineapple canned in its own juice with the juice (crushed, chunks, or
       tidbits work well)
¾ cup pineapple juice concentrate, thawed
½ cup oil

Preheat your oven to 375°F. Lightly oil your baking sheets. Put the pineapple in the narrow cup of your hand blender and puree it, or puree it with a food processor or standard blender. Add the pineapple juice concentrate to the puree and blend briefly.

In a large bowl, stir together the flour, baking soda, salt, and coconut. Stir the liquid ingredients into the dry ingredients until they are just mixed. Drop the batter by heaping teaspoonfuls 2 to 3 inches apart on the prepared baking sheets. Bake the cookies for 15 to 19 minutes or until they are golden brown on the bottom and just beginning to brown on the top. Remove them from the baking sheets with a spatula and put them on paper towels to cool. Makes 2½ to 3 dozen cookies.

Gluten-Free Applesauce Cookies

Gluten-Free

These fruit-sweetened cookies are fragile but delicious especially when made with the chocolate or carob chips.

2 cups millet or teff flour
½ teaspoon baking soda
½ cup unsweetened applesauce
¾ cup apple juice concentrate, thawed
½ cup oil
¾ cup chopped nuts or chocolate or carob chips (optional)

Preheat your oven to 350°F. You may want to line your baking sheets with parchment paper for easiest removal of these fragile cookies.

Combine the flour and baking soda in a large bowl. Mix together the applesauce, juice, and oil in a small bowl, and then stir them into the flour until they are just mixed in. Quickly fold in the nuts or chocolate or carob chips. Drop the batter by heaping teaspoonfuls onto an ungreased or parchment-lined baking sheet. Bake for 15 to 20 minutes, or until the cookies begin to brown. Slide the parchment paper and cookies off onto a cooling rack or remove the cookies from the baking sheets with a spatula and put them on paper towels to cool. Makes about 3½ dozen 1½ inch cookies.

Gluten-Free Banana Chocolate Cookies

Gluten-Free

2 1-ounce squares of unsweetened baking chocolate
3 cups sorghum (milo) flour
1 teaspoon baking soda
¼ teaspoon vitamin C powder
Dash of salt
¾ cups mashed banana (about 1½ large bananas)
¾ cup agave
¼ cup oil
1 cup chocolate chips (optional)

Preheat your oven to 350°F. Melt the chocolate in a double boiler over boiling water or carefully microwave it in a glass bowl, stirring often, until it is just melted. Let it cool while preparing the other liquid ingredients. Oil the baking sheets or line them with parchment paper for easiest removal of the cookies.

Thoroughly mash the banana or puree it with a hand blender. Combine the banana, agave, oil, and melted chocolate. In a separate bowl, stir together the flour, baking soda, vitamin C, salt, and optional chocolate chips if you are using them. Stir the liquid ingredients into the dry ingredients until just mixed. The dough will be stiff. Drop the dough by heaping teaspoonfuls onto the prepared baking sheet. If you like your cookies flat rather than like balls, oil your fingers of the bottom of a glass and flatten the cookies. Bake for 10 to 12 minutes or until the cookies are set to the touch and a toothpick inserted into the center of one of the larger cookie comes out dry. Slide the parchment paper and cookies off onto a cooling rack or remove the cookies from the baking sheets with a spatula and put them on paper towels to cool. Makes about 3½ dozen cookies.

Carrot Cookies

These cookies are as nutritious as they are delicious! The carrots make them a good source of vitamin A, and if they are made with quinoa flour these cookies are also high in protein and calcium. Diabetics and weight watchers may be able to enjoy these treats by using stevia for the sweetener.

    2 cups quinoa or spelt flour
    ⅔ cup tapioca starch or arrowroot
    1 teaspoon baking soda
    ¼ teaspoon vitamin C powder
    1 teaspoon cinnamon
    ½ cup raisins (optional)
    ⅞ cups apple juice concentrate, thawed
    ⅓ cup oil
    1½ cups grated carrots

Preheat your oven to 350°F. Mix together the flour, starch, baking soda, vitamin C, cinnamon and raisins in a large bowl. Combine the juice, oil, and carrots and stir them into the flour mixture until they are just mixed in. Drop the batter by heaping teaspoonfuls onto an ungreased baking sheet. If you like flat rather than round cookies, flatten the balls of dough with an oiled glass bottom or your fingers held together. Bake for 12 to 15 minutes or until the cookies begin to brown on the bottom. Remove the cookies from the baking sheets with a spatula and put them on paper towels to cool. Makes 2 to 3 dozen cookies.

Stevia-sweetened carrot cookies variation: Instead of the apple juice, use ⅞ cups water plus ½ to ¾ teaspoon pure stevia powder and increase the amount of vitamin C to ⅜ teaspoon. When you are mixing the cookies, thoroughly stir the stevia into the dry ingredients. These cookies will not brown much when they are baked but will feel dry to the touch when they are done.

Barley Lemon Cookies

    3½ cups barley flour
    1 teaspoon baking soda
    ½ teaspoon salt
    1⅛ cups agave
    ¾ cup oil

2 tablespoons lemon juice

½ teaspoon lemon oil (See "Sources," page 229) or the zest from two medium-sized lemons (about ¾ to 1 tablespoon of zest, pressed into the spoon)

Preheat your oven to 350°F. Lightly oil your baking sheets or line them with parchment paper for easiest cookie removal.

In a large bowl stir together the flour, baking soda, and salt. In a separate bowl or cup, combine the agave, oil, lemon juice, and lemon oil or lemon zest. Add the liquid ingredients to the dry ingredients and stir until they are just mixed in. Drop the dough by teaspoonfuls onto baking sheets, allowing room for the dough to spread out as the cookies bake. Bake for 10 to 13 minutes or until they are just beginning to brown. Cool the cookies on the baking sheets for a few minutes and then remove them with a spatula to paper towels or, if you used parchment paper, slide the parchment paper and cookies off onto a cooling rack. Allow them to cool completely. Makes about 4 dozen 2 to 3 inch cookies.

Oat Lemon Cookies

Ask your doctor about eating oats on a gluten-free diet

3 cups oat flour

1 cup tapioca starch

1 teaspoon baking soda

½ teaspoon salt

1 cup agave

½ cup oil

2 tablespoons lemon juice

¼ teaspoon lemon oil (See "Sources," page 229) or the zest from one medium-sized lemon (about 1 to 1½ teaspoons of zest, pressed into the spoon)

Preheat your oven to 350°F. Lightly oil your baking sheets or line them with with parchment paper for easiest cookie removal.

In a large bowl stir together the flours, baking soda, and salt. In a separate bowl or cup, combine the agave, oil, lemon juice, and lemon oil or lemon zest. Add the liquid ingredients to the dry ingredients and stir until they are just mixed in. Drop the dough by teaspoonfuls onto baking sheets, allowing room for the dough to spread out as the cookies bake. Bake for 8 to 12 minutes or until they are just beginning to brown. Cool the cookies on the baking sheets for a few minutes and then remove them with a spatula to paper towels or, if you used parchment paper, slide the parchment paper and cookies off onto a cooling rack. Allow them to cool completely. Makes about 3 dozen 3 inch cookies.

Gluten-Free Lemon Cookies

3 cups sorghum (milo) flour

1 teaspoon baking soda

½ teaspoon salt

1 cup agave

½ cup oil

2 tablespoons lemon juice

2 extra large eggs or three large eggs (to yield ½ cup of slightly beaten egg)

¼ teaspoon lemon oil (See "Sources," page 229) or the zest from one medium-sized lemon (about 1 to 1½ teaspoons of zest, pressed into the spoon)

Preheat your oven to 350°F. Lightly oil your baking sheets or line them with parchment paper for easiest cookie removal. Beat the eggs slightly with a fork and measure out ½ cup of beaten egg.

In a large bowl stir together the flour, baking soda, and salt. In a separate bowl or cup, combine the agave, oil, lemon juice, eggs, and lemon oil or lemon zest. Add the liquid ingredients to the dry ingredients and stir until they are just mixed in. Drop the dough by heaping teaspoonfuls onto baking sheets. Bake for 14 to16 minutes or until they are just beginning to brown. Cool the cookies on the baking sheets for a few minutes and then remove them with a spatula to paper towels or, if you used parchment paper, slide the parchment paper and cookies off onto a cooling rack. Allow them to cool completely. Makes about 3 dozen 2 inch cookies.

Gingersnaps

These spicy cookies are delicious and easy to make gluten-free.

2 cups barley flour OR 2½ cups amaranth flour plus ½ cup arrowroot or tapioca starch

1 teaspoon baking soda

¼ teaspoon unbuffered vitamin C powder

½ teaspoon ginger

1 cup light molasses OR ¾ cup agave or Fruit Sweet™ plus ¼ cup blackstrap molasses

½ cup oil

Preheat your oven to 350°F. Lightly oil your baking sheets or, especially if you are using the agave, line them with parchment paper. Combine the flour(s), baking soda, vitamin C powder, and ginger in a large bowl. Mix together the sweetener(s) and oil and stir them into the dry ingredients until they are just blended in. Drop the dough by heaping teaspoons onto the prepared baking sheets, being sure to place the amaranth cookies at least 3 inches apart. Flatten the barley cookies to about ¼ inch thickness with your fingers held together; the amaranth cookies will spread readily. Bake the barley cookies for 10 to 15 minutes or the amaranth cookies for 9 to 11 minutes or until they begin to brown. Slide the parchment paper and cookies off onto a cooling rack or remove the cookies from the baking sheets with a spatula and put them on paper towels to cool. Makes 3 to 4 dozen cookies.

BAR COOKIES

Bar cookies are quick and easy to make. There's no dropping of the dough by teaspoonfuls, rolling, or shaping. Just spread the dough in a pan and bake. You will find recipes for ever-popular brownies made with a wide range of grains, grain alternatives and sweeteners below. For brownies that cannot be distinguished from those made by a bakery, see the recipe on page 217 of the "Especially for Guests" chapter.

Buckwheat Chocolate Brownies

Gluten-Free

I have a gluten-intolerant friend who is quite discriminating about how things taste who loves these brownies. If you're not sure about buckwheat, you might want to try it for the first time in this recipe.

> 2 1-ounce squares unsweetened chocolate
> ⅜ cup oil
> 1 cup fine maple sugar
> 2 large eggs
> ½ teaspoon salt
> ¾ cup buckwheat flour
> ½ teaspoon baking powder*

Preheat your oven to 350°F. Oil an 8-inch square metal baking pan. Line the bottom and two opposite sides of the pan with an 8-inch wide strip of parchment or waxed paper. Also oil the paper. Melt the chocolate in a double boiler over boiling water or carefully microwave it in a glass bowl, stirring often, until it is just melted. Stir the oil into the melted chocolate thoroughly. Add the maple sugar, eggs, and salt and stir thoroughly. In a separate bowl, stir together the flour and baking powder. Add the dry ingredients to the chocolate mixture and stir until just mixed. Spread the batter in the prepared pan. Bake for 30 minutes or until the top has a dull crust and a toothpick inserted into the brownies comes out with just a few moist crumbs on it. Cool completely in the pan, then cut into squares. Makes 16 brownies.

* Note on baking powder: Use Featherweight™ brand baking powder if you are allergic to corn. It contains potato starch instead of cornstarch.

Amaranth Chocolate Brownies

Gluten-Free

Amaranth brownies rise and then fall in baking which makes it possible to produce delicious brownies with a chewy (rather than cake-like) texture without using eggs or a dry granulated sweetener.

> 1 cup amaranth flour
> ¼ cup arrowroot
> ¼ cup cocoa
> ½ teaspoon baking soda
> ¾ cup agave
> ¼ cup oil

Preheat your oven to 350°F. Oil and flour a 9 inch by 5 inch metal loaf pan. Combine the amaranth flour, arrowroot, cocoa, and baking soda in a bowl. In another bowl or measuring cup, thoroughly mix the agave and oil. Before the liquid ingredients can separate, stir them into the dry ingredients until just mixed. Immediately put the batter into the prepared pan and pop it into the oven. Bake for 22 to 28 minutes. When they are close to done, insert a toothpick into the center of the pan. It should come out with a few moist crumbs on it. Do not over bake. The batter will puff up during baking and then collapse after you remove the brownies from the oven which gives them a moist, chewy texture. Makes 8 to 10 brownies.

Barley Chocolate Brownies

     2 1-ounce squares unsweetened chocolate
     ⅓ cup oil
     2 eggs
     1 cup fine maple sugar
     ¾ barley flour
     ½ teaspoon salt
     ½ teaspoon baking powder*

Preheat your oven to 350°F. Oil the bottom only of an 8 inch square cake pan. Melt the chocolate in a double boiler over boiling water or carefully microwave it in a glass bowl, stirring often, until it is just melted. Stir the oil into the melted chocolate thoroughly. Add the maple sugar, eggs, and salt and stir thoroughly. In a separate bowl, stir together the flour and baking powder. Add the dry ingredients to the chocolate mixture and stir until just mixed. Spread the batter in the prepared pan. Bake for 22 to 25 minutes or until the top has a dull crust and a toothpick inserted into the brownies comes out with a few moist crumbs on it. Do not over bake. Cool completely in the pan, then cut into squares. Makes 16 brownies.

* **Note on baking powder:** Use Featherweight™ brand baking powder if you are allergic to corn. It contains potato starch instead of cornstarch.

Amaranth Carob Brownies

Gluten-Free

When made with stevia, these brownies can be a nutritious treat for diabetics and weight watchers.

     1 cup amaranth flour
     ¼ cup arrowroot
     ⅓ cup carob powder
     ½ teaspoon baking soda
     ¾ cup apple juice concentrate, thawed
     ¼ cup oil

Preheat your oven to 350°F. Oil and flour a 9 inch by 5 inch metal loaf pan. If your carob powder contains lumps, press it through a strainer with the back of a spoon to remove the lumps before measuring it. Combine the amaranth flour, arrowroot, carob powder, and baking soda in a bowl. In another bowl or measuring cup, stir together the apple juice concentrate and oil. Stir the liquid ingredients into the dry ingredients until just mixed and immediately put the batter into the prepared pan. Bake for 20 minutes. The batter will puff up during baking and then collapse either near the end of the baking time or after you remove the brownies from the oven which gives them a moist, chewy texture. Do not over bake. The "toothpick test" does not apply to these brownies; if you test them with a toothpick, the toothpick will come out with wet dough on it. Makes 8 to 10 brownies.

Stevia-sweetened amaranth brownies variation: Instead of the apple juice, use ¾ cup water. Increase the baking powder to 1 teaspoon and also add ⅛ teaspoon pure stevia powder and ¼ teaspoon unbuffered vitamin C powder to the dry ingredients. When you are mixing the cookies, thoroughly stir the stevia into the dry ingredients.

Oatmeal Bars

**Ask your doctor about
eating oats on a gluten-free diet**

2¾ cups white spelt flour
1 cup oatmeal, regular or quick-cooking
1 teaspoon baking soda
¼ teaspoon salt
1¼ cups agave or Fruit Sweet™ or 1 cup honey plus ¼ cup water
½ cup oil
1 cup raisins, chopped nuts, carob chips, or chocolate chips, or any
    combination of these ingredients (optional)

Preheat your oven to 350°F. Oil and flour a 13-inch by 9-inch baking pan. In a large bowl, combine the flour, oatmeal, baking soda, and salt. In a separate bowl or cup, stir together the oil with the agave, Fruit Sweet™, or honey plus water until thoroughly combined. (The mixture will look granular). Stir the liquid ingredients into the dry ingredients until just mixed. Quickly fold in the raisins, nuts, or chips, if you are using them. Spread the batter in the prepared pan. Bake for 20 to 28 minutes, or until the cookies are golden brown. Do not over bake or they will be dry. Cool the cookies for 15 minutes in the pan; then cut them into 1½ to 2-inch squares. If your cake pan has a lid, you can store the cookies in the pan, or remove them from the pan at this point if desired. Makes 2 to 3 dozen cookies. For fewer cookies, halve this recipe and bake it in an 8 inch square cake pan.

Date Squares

These cookies require minimal clean-up – no mixing bowl is required! If you make them with apple butter, you do not need to wash a saucepan either.

Filling ingredients:

> 2 cups pitted natural (unsweetened) dates
> ½ cup water
> 2 tablespoons lemon juice

Crust ingredients:

> 1¼ cups white spelt flour
> 1½ cups oatmeal, old fashioned (thick rolled), regular or quick-cooking
>   (not instant)
> ½ teaspoon baking soda
> Dash of salt
> ¼ cup agave, Fruit Sweet™, or slightly warmed honey
> ⅜ cup oil
> 2 teaspoons vanilla extract

To make the filling, cut the dates into halves or quarters. Combine the dates, water, and lemon juice in a small saucepan. Cook them over medium heat, stirring often, until the dates form a smooth, very thick paste. If they dry out, add more water as necessary while they are cooking.

Preheat your oven to 350°F. In an 8 inch square cake pan, stir together the flour, oatmeal, baking soda, and salt. Mix together the oil, sweetener, and vanilla in a cup or bowl. Stir the liquids into the flour mixture in the pan. Remove about one third of the crumbs from the pan. Press the remaining crumbs into a thin layer of dough which covers the whole bottom of the pan. Bake for five minutes or until set. Let the pan cool on a wire rack until the crust is lukewarm; being cooler is all right also. Spread the date mixture on top of the crust in the pan. Crumble the remaining dough over the date mixture. Bake for 20 to 25 minutes or until lightly browned. Put the pan on a wire rack to cool. Cut the cookies in the pan into 16 squares. Makes 16 cookies.

Apple butter squares variation: Substitute 1 cup of thick apple butter plus ½ teaspooon cinnamon for the cooked dates. Thoroughly stir the cinnamon into the apple butter before spreading it on the crust.

ROLLED COOKIES

Shortbread

These cookies are easy to make in several different varieties to fit any day of an allergy rotation diet. For "good enough for guests" white spelt shortbread, see page 218.

Amaranth (GF):

1¼ cups amaranth flour
1 cup arrowroot
½ teaspoon baking soda
⅜ cup oil
½ cup pineapple juice concentrate, thawed

Date-Oat:

2¼ cups oat flour
½ cup date sugar, pressed through a strainer to remove any lumps
½ teaspoon baking soda
⅛ teaspoon unbuffered vitamin C powder
⅜ cup oil
½ cup water

Whole Spelt:

1½ cups whole spelt flour
1 cup arrowroot or tapioca starch
½ teaspoon baking soda
⅜ cup oil
½ cup apple juice concentrate, thawed

Pineapple-Oat:

2½ cups oat flour
½ teaspoon baking soda
⅜ cup oil
½ cup pineapple juice concentrate, thawed

Barley:

> 2 cups barley flour
> ½ teaspoon baking soda
> ⅜ cup oil
> ½ cup apple juice concentrate, thawed

Teff (GF):

> 2 cups teff flour
> ½ teaspoon baking soda
> ⅛ teaspoon unbuffered vitamin C powder
> ½ cup oil
> ¼ cup agave or Fruit Sweet™
> 1 extra-large egg or 1 large egg plus enough water to bring its volume up
>   to ¼ cup

Rice-Date (GF):

> 2¼ cups rice flour
> ½ cup date sugar
> ½ teaspoon baking soda
> ⅛ teaspoon unbuffered vitamin C powder
> ½ cup oil
> ½ cup water

Quinoa (GF):

> 1¼ cups quinoa flour
> 1 cup tapioca starch
> ½ teaspoon baking soda
> ⅜ cup oil
> ½ cup apple juice concentrate, thawed

Choose one set of ingredients above. Preheat your oven to 350°F. If you are using the agave, line the baking sheets with parchment paper for easiest cookie removal or lightly oil the baking sheets. (Lining the baking sheets is less important with this recipe than most because it is generous in oil). If you are making the teff shortbread, break the egg into a measuring cup and beat it slightly with a fork. If needed, add water to the cup to bring the volume up to ¼ cup.

Combine the flour(s), baking soda, vitamin C powder (if the recipe calls for it), and date sugar (if called for) in a large bowl. Stir together the oil, sweetener or water, and egg (if called for) and add them to the dry ingredients, mixing with a spoon and your hands until the dough sticks together. If necessary, add 1 to 2 tablespoons of water to help it stick together. Roll the dough out to ¼ inch thickness on a baking sheet and cut it into 1 by 3-inch rectangular bars with a sharp knife. Bake at 350°F until the cookies are set and beginning to brown. This will take about 15 to 20 minutes for the amaranth, oat, teff, quinoa, and spelt varieties and 20 to 25 minutes for the barley and rice cookies. Cut the cookies again on the same lines after you remove them from the oven. Remove the cookies from the baking sheet with a spatula. Put them on paper towels to cool completely. Makes 2½ to 3 dozen bars.

Gluten-Free Gingerbread Diamonds

Gluten-Free

2½ cups amaranth flour
½ cup arrowroot
¾ teaspoon baking soda
¼ teaspoon unbuffered vitamin C powder
½ teaspoon ginger
¼ teaspoon nutmeg
¾ cup light molasses OR ¼ cup blackstrap molasses plus ½ cup agave or
      Fruit Sweet™
½ cup oil

Preheat your oven to 350°F. Lightly oil your baking sheets or, if you are using the agave, line your baking sheets with parchment paper for easiest cookie removal.

In a large bowl stir together the flours, baking soda, vitamin C powder, and spices. In a separate bowl or cup, stir together the sweetener(s) and oil. Immediately add the liquid ingredients to the dry ingredients and mix them in using a spoon and then your hands to make a stiff dough. You may add a teaspoon or two of water if necessary to get the dough to stick together. Divide the dough between two baking sheets. Sprinkle your rolling pin and the top of the dough with a little amaranth flour and roll the dough to between ⅛ and ¼ inch thickness. Cut it into dough into diamonds with a knife. Bake the cookies for 12 to 16 minutes or until they begin to brown. Remove them from the oven. Slide the parchment paper off onto a cooling rack or use a spatula to transfer the cookies to paper towels to cool. Makes 2 to 3 dozen cookies

Gingerbread Men

Whole spelt:

3 cups spelt flour

¾ teaspoon baking soda

¼ teaspoon unbuffered vitamin C powder

½ teaspoon ginger

¼ teaspoon nutmeg

¾ cup light molasses OR ¼ cup blackstrap molasses plus ½ cup agave or
    Fruit Sweet™

½ cup oil

Raisins or dried fruit (optional)

Kamut:

3 cups kamut flour

1 teaspoon baking soda

¼ teaspoon unbuffered vitamin C powder

¾ teaspoon ginger

½ teaspoon nutmeg

1 cup light molasses OR ¼ cup blackstrap molasses plus ¾ cup agave or
    Fruit Sweet™

⅜ cup oil

Raisins or dried fruit (optional)

Choose one set of ingredients above. Preheat your oven to 350°F. If you are using the agave, line the baking sheets with parchment paper for easiest cookie removal or lightly oil the baking sheets.

Combine the flour, baking soda, vitamin C powder, and spices in a large bowl. Stir together the sweetener(s) and oil and mix them into the dry ingredients using a spoon and then your hands to make a stiff dough. Roll the dough out to between ⅛ and ¼ inch thickness on a floured board. Cut it into gingerbread men or other cookie cutter shapes and transfer them to a baking sheet with a spatula. Decorate them with raisins or small pieces of dried fruit if desired. Bake for 11 to 15 minutes or until they are beginning to brown. Remove them from the oven and slide the parchment paper off onto a cooling rack or use a spatula to transfer the cookies to paper towels to cool. Makes about 14 to 18 6-inch tall gingerbread men.

Cut-Out "Sugar" Cookies

Yes, you can make "sugar" cookies in special shapes without using sugar or shortening! The white spelt version of this recipe is so close to "normal" that no one will know that the cookies are sugar and wheat-free.

3⅞ to 4 cups barley flour OR 4 to 4⅛ cups white spelt flour
¼ teaspoon salt
½ teaspoon baking soda
⅛ teaspoon unbuffered vitamin C powder
⅜ cup agave
½ cup oil
1 teaspon vanilla extract

Preheat your oven to 375°F. Line two to three baking sheets with parchment paper. Measure the flour and reserve about ⅛ cup of it in the measuring cup. (The "trick" with this recipe is to get the dough firm enough to handle but not so firm that the cookies are hard). Put the rest of the flour in a large bowl with the salt, baking soda and vitamin C powder and stir them together. Stir together the agave, oil and vanilla thoroughly and add them to the flour mixture quickly before they have a chance to separate. Mix the dough together with a spoon and, if necessary, also use your hands until the flour is worked in. If the dough is very stiff, add a tablespoon or two of water. If it is too soft to handle, add the reserved flour. If it is still quite soft, add an additional tablespoon or two of flour. Divide the dough in half and sprinkle the top of the dough with flour. Roll each half of the dough out on a well floured pastry cloth to just under ¼ inch thickness. Cut it into shapes with cookie cutters and transfer them to the baking sheets with a spatula. Bake the cookies at for 8 to 11 minutes or until they are just beginning to brown. Watch them closely as the baking time nears completion so they do not become overly browned. Makes 3 to 4 dozen 3-inch cookies.

Drop "Sugar" Cookies

Gluten-Free

These cookies give those on gluten-free diets an alternative to the cookies above. They do not contain sugar, but you would never know it because of the "pure sweet" flavor of agave, and they are crisp like rolled sugar cookies.

2½ cups amaranth flour
½ cup arrowroot or tapioca starch
1 teaspoon baking soda

¼ teaspoon unbuffered vitamin C powder
1 cup agave
½ cup oil
½ teaspoon vanilla extract

Preheat your oven to 350ºF. Line your baking sheets with parchment paper. Combine the flours, baking soda, and vitamin C powder in a large bowl. Thoroughly mix together the agave, oil, and vanilla. Immediately stir them into the dry ingredients until they are just blended in. Drop the dough by heaping teaspoons onto the prepared baking sheets, being sure to place the cookies at least 3 inches apart. Bake for 9 to 11 minutes or until they begin to brown. Remove them from the oven. Slide the parchment paper off onto a cooling rack or use a spatula to transfer the cookies to paper towels to cool. Makes 3 to 4 dozen cookies.

SHAPED COOKIES

No Grain Coconut Cookies

Gluten-Free

2 cups finely grated unsweetened coconut (see "Sources, page 233)
¼ cup tapioca starch or arrowroot
¼ teaspoon vanilla extract (optional)
½ cup agave or Fruit Sweet™ (or more depending on the fineness of the coconut)

Preheat your oven to 325°F. Line your baking sheet with parchment paper for easiest cookie removal or oil the baking sheet with a teaspoon or two of melted coconut oil. If necessary, you can substitute another kind of oil. However, these cookies are very fragile. They are most easily removed from the baking sheet if parchment paper is used, and the second best option is greasing the baking sheet with coconut oil.

In a bowl, stir together the coconut and starch. In a separate bowl or cup, combine the agave or Fruit Sweet™ with the vanilla. Stir the liquid ingredients into the coconut mixture. Press the mixture into walnut-sized balls with your hands. If the mixture does not stick together, add more sweetener, up to about 2 tablespoons, until it sticks together. Put the balls on the prepared baking sheet and flatten them to about ½ inch thickness with your fingers held together. Bake the cookies for 12 to 15 minutes or until they are golden on the top. (The bottoms of the cookies will brown first; do not remove them when the bottom only is brown). Allow them to cool on the baking sheet for a few minutes. Slide the parchment paper and cookies onto a cooling rack or carefully remove the cookies from the baking sheet with a metal spatula. Put them on a wire cooling rack to cool; they will stick to paper towels. Makes about 1½ dozen cookies

Cookie Press Cookies

No one will feel deprived at Christmas time if you have some of these cookies made in the shape of Christmas trees on hand. For spritz cookies made with white spelt flour that are "near normal" to serve to guests, see page 222.

Oat:

    2 cups oat flour
    1 cup date sugar
    1 teaspoon baking soda
    ¼ teaspoon unbuffered vitamin C powder
    ½ cup coconut oil
    ⅝ cup water
    1 teaspoon vanilla extract or other flavoring (optional)

Whole Spelt:

    2½ cups spelt flour
    1 cup date sugar
    1 teaspoon baking soda
    ¼ teaspoon unbuffered vitamin C powder
    ½ cup coconut oil
    ¾ cup water
    1 teaspoon vanilla extract or other flavoring (optional)

Amaranth (GF):

    2 cups amaranth flour
    ½ cup arrowroot
    ½ cup Fruit Sweet™
    1 teaspoon baking soda
    ¼ teaspoon unbuffered vitamin C powder
    ½ cup coconut oil
    ¼ cup water
    1 teaspoon vanilla extract or other flavoring (optional)

Quinoa (GF):

> 2 cups quinoa flour
> ½ cup Fruit Sweet™
> 1 teaspoon baking soda
> ¼ teaspoon unbuffered vitamin C powder
> ½ cup coconut oil
> ¼ cup water
> 1 teaspoon vanilla extract or other flavoring (optional)

Choose one set of ingredients above. Preheat your oven to 375°F. Melt the coconut oil and allow it to cool until it is just very slightly warm. If you are using date sugar, press it through a wire mesh strainer with the back of a spoon to remove any small lumps or they will clog the cookie press.

Combine the flour(s), date sugar (if called for), baking soda, and vitamin C powder in a large bowl. Mix together the oil, Fruit Sweet™ (if called for), water, and flavoring and stir them into the dry ingredients. Put the dough into a cookie press and press out the cookies onto an ungreased baking sheet. Bake until the bottoms of the cookies begin to brown. If you make them as trees, hearts, etc. this takes about 10 to 12 minutes for the oat and amaranth cookies and about 11 to 15 minutes for the spelt and quinoa cookies. If you make them as spritz strips, which are thinner, reduce the baking time by 2 to 4 minutes for each type of cookie. When the cookies begin to brown, remove them from the oven. Immediately use a spatula to transfer the cookies to paper towels to cool. Makes 4 to 5 dozen cookies.

Carob Wafers or Sandwich Cookies

Gluten-Free

You can put these sandwich cookies together with sugar-free jam or carob chips or eat them plain. For a special event, if you can tolerate a little sugar occasionally, fill the sandwiches with white fondant and they will remind you of Oreos™. For people at the opposite end of the sugar tolerance spectrum, make these cookies with stevia.

> 1½ cups carob powder
> 1½ cups tapioca starch or arrowroot
> 3 teaspoons baking powder
> 1 cup apple juice concentrate
> ½ cup oil
> About ⅔ cup all-fruit (sugarless) jam or jelly OR 1 cup carob chips (optional)

Preheat your oven to 350ºF. Combine the carob powder, tapioca starch, and baking powder in a large bowl. Mix together the juice and oil and stir them into the dry ingredients until they are thoroughly mixed in. Roll the dough into 1 inch balls and place them on an ungreased baking sheet. Flatten each ball to ⅛ to ¼ inch thickness with an oiled glass bottom or your fingers held together. Bake the cookies for 10 to 12 minutes or until they feel set when you touch them. Remove them from the baking sheet with a spatula and cool them completely. If you are using the carob chips, melt them in the top of a double boiler over water that is just below the boiling point, stirring them frequently. As soon as they are melted, remove the top of the double boiler from the pan. Another option is to microwave the carob chips, stirring often, until melted. Put the cookies together in pairs with their bottoms together using the melted carob chips, jelly or jam. Makes about 2 dozen sandwich cookies or 4 dozen carob wafers.

"Oreos™" variation: See page 148 of *Allergy Cooking with Ease* (described on the last pages of this book), a general purpose cookbook such as *Joy of Cooking,* or a candy cookbook for a white fondant recipe. Make fondant and use it to put these cookies together in pairs to make sandwich cookies that will remind you of Oreos™.

Stevia-sweetened carob wafers variation: Instead of the apple juice, use 1 cup water plus ¾ teaspoon pure stevia powder. When you are mixing the cookies, thoroughly stir the stevia into the dry ingredients.

Fig Bars

**Gluten-Free IF
made with amaranth**

These cookies will remind you of Fig Newtons™.

Filling:

8 ounces dried figs
1 cup water
2 teaspoons vanilla extract (optional)

Dough:

Amaranth:

3 cups amaranth flour
1 cup arrowroot
¾ cup oil
⅜ cup to ½ cup cold water

White Spelt:

> 3 cups white spelt flour
> 1 cup Spectrum Naturals™ non-hydrogenated shortening or butter (2 sticks)
> 2 tablespoons agave or Fruit Sweet™
> ¼ to ⅜ cup cold water

To make the filling, remove the stems from the figs. Combine the figs and water in a saucepan, bring them to a boil, reduce the heat, and simmer them on low heat for 30 minutes. Cool the figs, stir in the optional vanilla, and puree them with a hand blender or in a blender or food processor until they are smooth. While the filling is cooking, make the dough.

For the amaranth dough, mix together the amaranth flour and arrowroot in a large bowl. Add the oil and cut it in with a pastry cutter until the mixture is crumbly. Gradually add enough of the water to make a soft pie crust-like dough. Divide the dough in half and flatten each half unto a small square.

For the spelt dough, measure the flour into a large bowl. Add the shortening or butter and cut it in with a pastry cutter until the mixture is crumbly. Stir together ¼ cup of the water and the sweetener. Gradually add this mixture to the crumbs. Then, if the dough is not coming together, adding enough of the remaining water to the crumbs to make a soft pie crust-like dough. Divide the dough in half and flatten each half unto a small square. Place one square for the top layer of dough in the freezer to chill briefly while you are preparing the bottom layer and spreading it with the filling.

For either type of dough, preheat your oven to 400°F. Roll out one half of the dough into an 8 by 12 inch rectangle on an ungreased cookie sheet and spread it with the filling. Remove the other half of the spelt dough from the freezer. Roll the second half of the dough out into an 8 by 12 inch rectangle on a well-floured pastry cloth or roll it out between two pieces of waxed or parchment paper and peel off the top piece. Invert the pastry cloth or waxed or parchment paper with the dough on it onto the top of the fig filling. Peel off the pasty cloth or paper from the dough. Bake the amaranth cookies for 25 to 30 minutes or the spelt cookies for 20 to 25 minutes or until they begin to brown. Cool for 10 minutes, then carefully cut it into 1½ inch squares with a sharp knife. Remove the cookies from the baking sheets with a spatula and put them on paper towels to cool. Makes about 3 dozen cookies.

COOKIES FOR HOLIDAYS AND SPECIAL OCCASIONS

Pfeffernusse

Gluten-Free IF made with amaranth

White spelt:

1¾ cups white spelt flour

¼ cup almond meal/flour

½ teaspoon baking soda

¼ teaspoon salt

1 teaspoon cinnamon

½ teaspoon each freshly ground black pepper, cloves, nutmeg, and allspice

½ cup agave

¼ cup oil

½ teaspoon anise flavoring

1½ tablespoons lemon zest or ¼ teaspoon lemon oil

Rye:

1½ cups rye flour

¼ cup pecan or almond meal/flour

½ teaspoon baking soda

¼ teaspoon salt

1 teaspoon cinnamon

½ teaspoon each freshly ground black pepper, cloves, nutmeg, and allspice

½ cup agave

¼ cup oil

½ teaspoon anise flavoring

1½ tablespoons lemon zest or ¼ teaspoon lemon oil

Amaranth (GF):

1¼ cups amaranth flour

⅓ cup arrowroot

¼ cup pecan or almond meal/flour

½ teaspoon baking soda

¼ teaspoon salt

1 teaspoon cinnamon

½ teaspoon each freshly ground black pepper, cloves, nutmeg, and allspice
½ cup agave
¼ cup oil
½ teaspoon anise flavoring
1½ tablespoons lemon zest or ¼ teaspoon lemon oil

Preheat your oven to 350°F. Oil your baking sheets or, for easiest removal of the cookies, line them with parchment paper. Combine the flour(s), nut meal, baking soda, salt, and spices in a large bowl. Mix together the agave, oil, anise flavoring, and lemon oil or zest and stir them into the dry ingredients until they are just blended in. Drop the dough by heaping teaspoons onto the prepared baking sheets. If you prefer flat rather than rounded cookies, flatten the rye or spelt cookies with an oiled glass bottom or your fingers held together. The amaranth cookies will spread readily. Bake until the cookies are lightly browned, or for 10-12 min for amaranth and rye cookies or 13 to 15 minutes for white spelt cookies. Slide the parchment paper and cookies off onto a cooling rack or remove the cookies from the baking sheets with a spatula and put them on paper towels to cool. Makes 1½ to 2 dozen 1½ to 2 inch cookies.

Amaranth Biscotti

Gluten-Free

These cookies are a gluten-free variation of my favorite cookies that my aunt made for Christmas every year. For a white spelt version of these cookies, see page 221.

2 cups amaranth flour
1 cup arrowroot
½ teaspoon baking soda
¼ teaspoon unbuffered vitamin C powder
¼ teaspoon salt (optional)
½ cup sliced almonds
¾ cup agave or Fruit Sweet™
⅓ cup oil
1 teaspoon almond extract
1 teaspoon vanilla extract

Preheat your oven to 350°F. If you are using the agave, line your baking sheet with parchment paper for easiest removal of the cookies. Stir together the flours, salt, baking soda, vitamin C, and almonds in a large bowl. In a small bowl, mix the sweetener, oil, and flavorings; then stir them into the dry ingredients. Put the dough on a lightly oiled baking sheet, and use your hands to form it into a flat-topped loaf about 14 inches long, 3 inches wide, and 1 inch tall. Bake it at 350°F for 25 to 30 minutes, or until it is set and is barely beginning to brown. Remove it from the oven. Using a serrated knife, cut the loaf down the middle lengthwise and slice it crosswise into ¾ to 1 inch slices. Lay the slices down on their cut sides on the cookie sheet. Bake the slices and additional 15 to 20 minutes, or until they are hard and lightly browned. Slide the parchment paper and cookies off onto a cooling rack or remove the cookies from the baking sheets with a spatula and put them on paper towels to cool. Makes 2½ dozen cookies.

**Gluten-Free IF
made with amaranth or quinoa**

Yes, you can have these traditional Italian cookies on your special diet! Since they are cooked in an iron, they are a bit of work, but if you've made them before, you'll find making them wheat- and sugar-free is a lot like making "normal" pizzelles. This is one of the rare recipes in which what kind of oil you use makes a difference. They are less likely to stick to the iron if you use coconut oil, although you can use other kinds of oil if necessary. If you can tolerate butter or goat butter occasionally, substitute melted butter for the oil and they will be easy to remove from the iron. For a "just like Grandma's" white spelt version of this recipe, see page 223.

Amaranth (GF):

> 1 cup amaranth flour
> 1 cup arrowroot
> 1 teaspoon baking soda
> ⅛ teaspoon unbuffered vitamin C powder
> ¼ cup melted coconut oil or other oil
> ¼ cup honey or Fruit Sweet™
> ⅝ cup water
> 2 teaspoons anise extract

Quinoa (GF):

> 1½ cups quinoa flour
> ½ cup tapioca flour
> ½ teaspoon baking soda
> ½ cup melted coconut oil or other oil
> ½ cup apple juice concentrate, thawed
> 2 teaspoons anise extract

Rye:

2 cups rye flour
½ cup melted coconut oil or other oil
1¼ cups apple juice concentrate, thawed OR ½ cup water plus ¾ cup apple
    juice concentrate, thawed, depending on the amount of sweetness desired
2 teaspoons anise extract

Spelt:

3 cups whole spelt flour
½ cup melted coconut oil or other oil
1¼ cups apple juice concentrate, thawed OR ½ cup water plus ¾ cup apple
    juice concentrate, thawed, depending on the amount of sweetness desired
2 teaspoons anise extract

Choose one set of ingredients, above. Begin heating the pizzelle iron. Combine the flour(s), baking soda (if used), and vitamin C powder (if used) in a large electric mixer bowl. In a small bowl, stir together the oil, juice or sweetener, water (if used), and anise flavoring and pour them into the dry ingredients. Beat the dough on low speed until the flour is all moistened, then beat it on medium speed for one minute. Brush the top and bottom grids of the iron with oil. When the iron's light goes off, indicating that it is sufficiently heated, put one heaping tablespoon of dough in the iron. (You may need more – this is a starting point as you determine how much dough you should put in to fill the iron when you close it). Cook each pizzelle for 20 to 30 seconds, or until it is golden brown, remove it from the iron using two forks, and lay it on a paper towel to cool. If you are using a type of oil other than coconut oil or butter or if the cookies stick at all, brush both the top and the bottom plates of the iron with oil before cooking each cookie or set of cookies.

You may have to experiment to determine what cooking time makes the cookies easiest to remove. Sometimes the pizzelles stick even if you used coconut oil in the batter, and will need to brush the iron with melted coconut oil before cooking each set of cookies. Makes about 2 to 3 dozen 6-inch pizzelles or about 15 pizzelles which are 8-inch circles that break apart into quarter-circles.

Carob Pizzelles

Gluten-Free

We always had anise-flavored pizzelles when I was a young child, but in my teens, chocolate pizzelles became popular, so we had both for Christmas. This recipe is a take-off on chocolate pizzelles.

 1 cup quinoa flour
 ½ cup carob powder
 ½ cup tapioca starch
 ½ teaspoon baking soda
 ½ cup melted butter or coconut oil or other oil
 1 cup apple juice concentrate, thawed

Begin heating the iron. Brush the plates with melted butter or coconut oil or the oil you are using to make your pizzelles. Combine the flour, starch, carob powder, and baking soda in a large electric mixer bowl. In a small bowl, stir together the oil and juice, and pour them into the dry ingredients. Beat the dough on low speed until the flour is all moistened, then beat it on medium speed for one minute. If you are using a type of oil other than coconut oil or butter, brush both the top and the bottom of the iron with oil before cooking each cookie. Put one heaping tablespoon of dough in the iron. (You may need more – this is a starting point as you determine how much dough you should put in to fill the iron when you close it). Cook each cookie for 20 to 30 seconds, or until it is beginning to brown, and remove it from the iron using two forks. (You may have to experiment to determine what cooking time makes the cookies easiest to remove). Lay them flat on paper towels to cool. Makes about 3 dozen 6-inch pizzelles or about 18 pizzelles which are 8-inch circles that break apart into quarter-circles.

Sauces and Toppings

There are desserts, and then there are fancy, dressed-up, very special occasion desserts. The difference is in the toppings, sauces, and other dessert accompaniments that are added to an ordinary dessert. This chapter embodies the differences between chocolate ice cream and a hot fudge sundae with whipped cream and a coconut-and-nut topping, or a sweet dessert waffle and the same waffle topped with warm pineapple sauce and piña colada ice cream. Use the recipes here to make your desserts extra special!

Fudge Sauce

Gluten-Free

2 ounces (2 1-ounce squares) of unsweetened baking chocolate
½ cup agave

Melt the chocolate in a double boiler over simmering water or in your microwave oven. To melt chocolate in the microwave, place it in a glass bowl and microwave it, checking it at 30-second intervals, until it is mostly melted with just a few solid parts remaining. Remove it from the microwave and stir it to melt the remaining solid chocolate

Add the melted chocolate to the agave and blend it with a hand blender or blender. Serve immediately or refrigerate. This sauce will become quite thick when refrigerated, so microwave it for a few seconds and stir it to liquefy it for serving. Makes about ⅔ cup of sauce.

Chocolate Syrup

Gluten-Free

Although not a thin syrup, this is less thick and intensely flavored than the sauce above. My family enjoys this on vanilla ice cream with sliced bananas.

2 ounces (2 1-ounce squares) of unsweetened baking chocolate
1 tablespoon tapioca starch
¾ cup agave
½ cup water
1 teaspoon vanilla (optional)

Finely chop the chocolate. Stir it together with the tapioca starch in a saucepan. Add the agave and water and whisk the ingredients together until well combined. Cook the syrup over medium-high heat, whisking continually, until it comes to a full boil which is not dissipated by the whisking. Reduce the heat slightly and whisk continually while allowing the sauce to boil for one minute. Remove the pan from the heat and whisk it occasionally for about 20 minutes while it cools. Whisk in the vanilla after it has cooled. Serve at room temperature or slightly above if you are going to be using it soon. If not, refrigerate the syrup and microwave it for a few seconds to return it to a thinner, syrup-like consistency if desired. Makes about 1⅓ cups of syrup.

Carob Syrup

Gluten-Free

Try this on vanilla, strawberry or carob ice cream or as a topping for cake or waffles.

½ cup agave or honey
¼ cup carob powder

Press the carob powder through a wire mesh strainer with the back of a spoon to remove any lumps. Mix the sweetener and carob powder together thoroughly and serve the sauce. Refrigerate any leftovers. Makes about ⅔ cup of syrup.

Butterscotch Sauce

Gluten-Free

I have debated – with myself and others – about whether this recipe should be in this book. It is not the usual golden color of butterscotch topping and the some of the butter may separate out into tiny pieces after refrigeration. Despite these problems, my butterscotch-fan husband says, "It's great made with Fruit Sweet™." Other devotees of butterscotch have voted with him rather than with me, so here it is for those of you whose favorite sundae has always been butterscotch.

¼ cup water
3 to 4 tablespoons arrowroot* with Fruit Sweet™ or 4 to 5 tablespoons with
    honey
¾ cup Fruit Sweet™ or honey
4 teaspoons vanilla extract
2 to 4 tablespoons butter, goat butter or ghee, to taste

Stir together the water and arrowroot in a saucepan. (Use the larger amount of arrowroot for thicker sauce). When they are completely mixed, stir in the Fruit Sweet™ or honey. Cook the sauce over medium heat, stirring often. As the sauce begins to steam and nears boiling, stir it continuously. When the sauce comes to a full rolling boil, cook it for one more minute, stirring continuously. It will thicken during this time. Cool the sauce to near room temperature. Using a hand blender or electric mixer, beat in the vanilla and butter or ghee. The sauce will lighten in color and texture during beating. Serve immediately. Refrigerate and stir or re-beat (to redistribute the butter) before serving. Makes about 1 cup of sauce of a light beige color unless you use dark-colored (but be sure it is mild tasting) honey.

Note on substitutions: This is one of the rare recipes in which arrowroot and tapioca starch are not interchangeable. If you use tapioca, the sauce will be quite ropy. Also, do not substitute agave for the other sweeteners or it will be extremely sticky. Even if it turns out at its best, it will not be like butterscotch topping from Dairy Queen™ but it is sugar-free, gluten-free, and delicious.

Strawberry Sauce

Gluten-Free

This easy sauce is delicious served on lemon cake, pancakes, waffles and many kinds of ice cream and sorbet. If you keep a bag of strawberries in your freezer, you can make it at any time.

> 1 pound fresh strawberries or unsweetened frozen strawberries, thawed
>   (about 3½ cups)
> ½ cup apple juice concentrate, thawed, or ¼ cup agave, Fruit Sweet™ or honey
>   plus ¼ cup water
> 2 teaspoons arrowroot or tapioca starch

If you are using fresh strawberries, wash and stem them. Cut them in half if they are large. Stir the arrowroot or tapioca starch into the juice or sweetener plus water in a saucepan. Add the strawberries and cook the mixture over medium heat, stirring the sauce often. If the frozen strawberries are large, break up the strawberries with the spoon a little as you stir. When the sauce thickens and boils, remove it from the heat. Serve it warm or cold. Refrigerate leftover sauce. Makes about 2½ cups of sauce.

Fresh Peach Sauce

Gluten-Free

This is delicious made with freshly picked in-season peaches.

> 4 to 6 peaches, or about 3 cups chopped peaches
> ¾ teaspoon cinnamon (optional)
> ⅞ cup thawed apple juice concentrate, divided
> 2 teaspoons arrowroot or tapioca starch

Peel the peaches and make a cut around the "equator" of each peach cutting all the way down to the pit. Slice the peaches. (Each slice will be cut into two pieces). Combine them with ¾ cup of the apple juice and the cinnamon in a saucepan and bring them to a boil. Reduce the heat and simmer for about 10 to 15 minutes or until the peaches are tender. Combine the remaining 2 tablespoons apple juice with the starch and stir it into the pan. Cook the mixture over medium heat, stirring the sauce often. When the sauce thickens and boils, remove it from the heat. Serve it warm or cold. Refrigerate leftover sauce. Makes about 2½ cups of sauce.

Pineapple Sauce

Gluten-Free

This all-fruit sauce is excellent on "Piña Colada Ice Cream," page 104, cake, pancakes, or waffles.

> 1 8-ounce can crushed pineapple packed in its own juice OR ¾ cup finely
>   chopped fresh pineapple
> ⅓ to ½ cup pineapple juice concentrate plus water to make 1 cup OR 1 cup
>   pineapple juice
> 2 teaspoons arrowroot or tapioca starch

If you are using canned pineapple, drain the juice to use as part of the 1 cup pineapple juice called for in the ingredient list or to save for another use. Measure the pineapple juice into a saucepan or if you are using the pineapple juice concentrate and water, combine them in a saucepan. Stir the arrowroot or tapioca flour into the juice. Cook the mixture over medium heat, stirring it often, until it thickens and boils. Remove it from the heat and stir in the drained pineapple. Serve the sauce warm or cold. Refrigerate leftover sauce. Makes about 1¾ cup of sauce.

Cherry Sauce

Gluten-Free

This is delicious on chocolate or carob cake or dessert pancakes or waffles. For a special treat, also top the cake, pancakes, or waffles with vanilla, chocolate, or carob ice cream.

1 15-ounce can tart pie cherries, packed in water
1 cup apple juice concentrate OR ½ cup agave, Fruit Sweet™ or honey plus
½ cup juice reserved from the cherries
3 teaspoons arrowroot or tapioca starch

Begin preparing this sauce at least ½ hour before you want to serve it or, for best flavor, a day ahead. Drain the cherries, reserving the liquid if you are using agave, Fruit Sweet™ or honey. Combine ½ cup of the cherry liquid with agave, Fruit Sweet™ or honey if you are using them. In a saucepan, stir together the cherry juice mixture or apple juice concentrate with the arrowroot or tapioca starch. Stir in the drained cherries. Cook this mixture over medium heat until it thickens and begins to boil. Refrigerate the sauce. Cherry sauce is best made a day before you plan to serve it so the sweetener or apple juice can permeate the cherries. You can reheat it right before serving time if you wish to serve it warm. Refrigerate leftover sauce. Makes about 2½ cups of sauce.

Blueberry or Raspberry Sauce

Gluten-Free

1 pound fresh blueberries or raspberries or 1 pound unsweetened frozen
blueberries or raspberries
½ cup apple juice concentrate, thawed, or ¼ cup agave, Fruit Sweet™ or honey
plus ¼ cup water
2 teaspoons arrowroot or tapioca starch

If you are using fresh berries, wash them and remove and discard any stems or bad berries. Stir the arrowroot or tapioca starch into the juice or sweetener plus water in a saucepan. Add berries and cook the mixture over medium heat, stirring the sauce often. When the sauce thickens and boils, remove it from the heat. Serve it warm or cold. Refrigerate leftover sauce. Makes about 2½ cups of sauce.

Apple Topping

This is delicious served on gingerbread or spice cake, pages 80 to 83.

2 large apples, or about 3 cups chopped apples
¾ teaspoon cinnamon
⅞ cup thawed apple juice concentrate, divided
2 teaspoons arrowroot or tapioca starch

Peel, core, and slice the apples. Cut each slice into two or three pieces. Combine them with ¾ cup of the apple juice and the cinnamon in a saucepan and bring them to a boil. Reduce the heat and simmer for 15 to 20 minutes or until the apples are tender. Combine the remaining 2 tablespoons apple juice with the starch and stir it into the pan. Cook the mixture over medium heat, stirring the sauce often. When the sauce thickens and boils, remove it from the heat. Serve it warm or cold. Refrigerate leftover sauce. Makes about 2½ cups of sauce.

Easy Coconut Topping

There is almost no clean up when you make this recipe because it can be mixed in the measuring cup.

½ cup agave
1 tablespoon coconut oil
About 1½ to 1¾ cups finely shredded unsweetened coconut (See "Sources,"
    page 233).

Measure the agave in a 2 cup glass measuring cup. Add the coconut oil. Microwave the mixture on high power until it just begins to boil. While it is coming to a boil, preheat your oven to 400°F and line a baking sheet which has an edge with parchment paper. (If the paper comes up the edge enough, the baking sheet clean up will be minimal). Add 1 cup of the coconut to the agave mixture and stir. Continue adding more coconut, stirring after each addition, until the liquid is completely absorbed by the coconut. (How much you will need to add depends on how finely shredded the coconut is). Spread the coconut mixture on the prepared baking sheet and bake it for 6 to 10 minutes or until it is medium brown in the middle. The coconut at the edges of the pan will be darker. Allow it to cool completely. Break it up into small pieces and sprinkle it on ice cream, sorbet, fresh berries, or other desserts. Makes about 1¾ cups of topping.

Nutty Topping

Gluten-Free

This is delightful on top of ice cream, or if you keep a jar of this topping on hand, you will be able whip up a cobbler very quickly. Just cook the any cobbler filling in a saucepan until thickened and sprinkle it with this topping for an "instant" cobbler, page 55.

⅔ cup unsweetened coconut (shredded to a medium coarseness)
⅓ cup chopped almonds or pecans or ½ cup sliced almonds
¼ cup almond or pecan meal/flour (See "Sources," page 232 or 233)
¼ teaspoon cinnamon (optional)
2 tablespoons oil
2 tablespoons agave, Fruit Sweet™ or apple juice concentrate, thawed

Preheat your oven to 400°F. Stir together the coconut, nuts, nut meal, and optional cinnamon in a bowl. Add the oil and sweetener and stir until the nut mixture is well moistened throughout. If there are still dry particles after thorough mixing, the coconut used may have been more finely shredded than what was used to develop this recipe. Add a little more oil until all the particles are moistened. If the mixture is quite wet, the coconut may have been coarsely shredded. Add more coconut until the topping is no longer excessively wet.

Oil an 8 or 9 inch square metal cake pan. Spread the nut mixture evenly in the pan. Bake it for 5 to 10 minutes, or until the coconut is just beginning to brown. Remove the pan from the oven and stir the nut mixture. Bake an additional 2 to 10 minutes, watching it carefully, until it is all lightly browned. Stir the mixture again when you remove it from the oven. Cool it completely in the pan. Store it in a jar with an air-tight lid at room temperature or in the freezer. Serve it on a batch of warm or cooled cobbler filling (pages 47 or 51 to 54) for an "instant" cobbler. (This makes dessert quickly because there is no baking of the fruit and topping together required). Makes enough topping for one batch of any fruit cobbler filling on pages 51 to 54 or double cherry or berry filling on page 47. It is also delicious served on ice cream or sorbet (pages 100 to 113 or store-bought), pudding or tapioca (pages 39 to 42 and 44), or fruit sauce and/or ice cream-topped dessert pancakes or waffles (pages 114 to 117),

Sugar-Free Whipped Cream

Gluten-Free

This is delicious on all kinds of desserts – pumpkin pie, ice cream sundaes, cake, ginger-bread or almost any dessert you might like to dress up.

    1 cup heavy or whipping cream
    2 to 4 teaspoons of Fruit Sweet™, agave, or honey, to taste.

Pour the whipping cream into the narrow bowl of your electric mixer and beat it at the whipped cream setting. Whip it until soft peaks form. Add sweetener to taste and continue to whip it until the peaks become firm. Serve immediately. Makes 8 to 12 servings.

Nutty "Whipped Cream"

Gluten-Free

This topping is great for those who cannot have dairy products or soy-based cream substitutes but want something like whipped cream on gingerbread or pumpkin pie.

    ¼ cup water
    ¼ cup cashew, macadamia, or other mild-tasting nut butter*
    ⅛ cup (2 tablespoons) agave
    ½ cup oil
    1 teaspoon vanilla

Put the water in a 2-cup measuring cup for liquids. Add the nut butter up to the ½ cup line. Add the agave. Combine them in the measuring cup using a hand blender. (If you do not have a hand blender, use a regular blender, or food processor). Slowly add the oil while processing until the topping becomes thicker and creamy. Briefly blend in the vanilla. Refrigerate any leftover topping; it will become thicker as it chills. Makes about 1¼ cups of topping.

*Note on the nut butter: If you make this topping with light colored macadamia nut butter it will be light colored. It is more brown made with cashew butter but has great flavor.

Peanut butter topping variation: When made with peanut butter (natural peanut butter containing only peanuts and salt – no hydrogenated fat, please!) this topping tastes like peanuts rather than being a general dessert topping. However, paired with a carob or chocolate sauce, it is delicious on many desserts (ice cream, waffles, chocolate, carob or vanilla cake, etc.)

Confections, Snacks and Miscellaneous Recipes

Desserts, cookies, sweet snacks – Is there a line between these categories of treats? Although not strictly desserts, I think you will enjoy these recipes for sweet snacks, confections, and "graham" crackers. Most of the recipes can stand alone as snacks. Some, such as the chocolate or carob chips and crackers, can be used in other recipes. This chapter gives you recipes for fun foods that can add to your enjoyment of life's "smaller" yet memorable special occasions.

Spicy Glazed Nuts

Gluten-Free

These nuts are great to take on a hike. The protein in the nuts plus low-glycemic index carbohydrate in the agave will keep you going to your destination and back.

½ cup agave or honey
1 tablespoon butter or oil
⅛ teaspoon salt
1 teaspoon cinnamon
2 to 3 cups of pecan halves, almonds, or other nuts of your choice

Preheat your oven to 350°F. Line a baking sheet with parchment paper. Combine the agave or honey, oil or butter and salt in a saucepan and bring it to a boil over medium heat. Boil it until the color begins to darken, about 4 to 5 minutes for the honey or 6 to 10 minutes for the agave. Remove it from the heat, quickly stir in the cinnamon, and quickly add 2 cups of the nuts and stir. If the nuts do not "absorb" most of the liquid, stir in another ½ to 1 cup of the nuts. (How many nuts you use depends on the size and shape of the pieces; pecans absorb more of the syrup than smooth nuts like almonds and smaller nuts absorb more of the syrup than larger nuts).

Immediately spread the nuts on the prepared baking sheet and bake them for 10 minutes, stirring after 5 minutes. If the nuts are not in a single layer when you stir them, spread them out more. Remove the baking sheet from the oven and put in on a cooling rack. When the nuts are completely cool, break them into pieces and store them in an air-tight tin. Makes about 3 to 4 cups.

Caramel Corn

Gluten-Free

This recipe will remind you of Cracker Jack™ but is made with healthy sweeteners.

2 to 2½ quarts air-popped popcorn or one batch of "Good and Healthy
    Popcorn," page 199
1 cup slivered almonds or chopped nuts of any kind (optional)
¼ cup (½ stick) of butter, goat butter, ghee, or Earth Balance™ margarine
½ cup agave, honey or Fruit Sweet™
½ teaspoon salt (optional – decrease or omit if you use salted butter or
    margarine)
1 teaspoon vanilla extract, almond flavoring, butter flavoring, or flavoring of
    your choice (optional)
¼ teaspoon baking soda

Make the popcorn as directed in "Good and Healthy Popcorn" on the next page or
as directed in the instructions for your popcorn popper. Stir together the popcorn and
nuts in a large bowl. Oil a 13 by 9 inch cake pan, a jelly roll pan, or two square or round
cake pans. Preheat your oven to 250°F.

In a saucepan, combine the butter or margarine, sweetener, and salt. (You may omit
the salt if you use salted butter or margarine). Heat the mixture over medium heat until
it begins to bubble. Reduce the heat to low and let it simmer for 5 minutes if you are
using honey or Fruit Sweet™ or 4 minutes if you are using agave. (If you are using agave,
watch it closely and remove it from the heat when it becomes darker, being careful not
to let it get so dark that it is slightly burnt. If it is in danger of burning, skip adding the
flavoring and add the baking soda quickly to stop the further darkening).

Remove the pan from the stove when the simmering time is completed. Immediately
stir in the flavoring. Then quickly stir in the baking soda. The liquid will become a very
fine foam. Immediately pour the liquid over the popcorn and nuts and stir thoroughly
to coat the popcorn and nuts uniformly. Put the popcorn mixture in the prepared pan(s)
and bake the popcorn for 30 minutes, stirring it every 10 minutes. Remove it from the
oven and allow it to cool. Stir it a couple of times while it is cooling to break it up. When
it is completely cooled, store it in a tin or other tightly covered container or plastic bag.
Makes about 2 quarts of caramel corn.

Nutty Caramel Corn

Gluten-Free

The nut butter in this recipe makes this caramel corn especially flavorful and adds some extra protein as well.

    6 to 7 cups unsalted popped corn (about ¼ cup unpopped corn) or about
        ¾ batch of "Good and Healthy Popcorn," below
    ¾ cup sliced almonds, chopped peanuts, or other nuts
    ¾ cup agave or honey
    ¼ cup natural almond butter, peanut butter, or other nut butter
    ¼ to ½ teaspoon salt (optional or to taste depending on the nut butter)

Make the popcorn as directed in the "Good and Healthy Popcorn" recipe below or as directed in the instructions for your popcorn popper. Preheat your oven to 250°F. Stir together the popcorn and nuts in a large bowl. Oil a 13 by 9 inch cake pan, a jelly roll pan, or two square or round cake pans.

Combine the sweetener, nut butter and salt in a saucepan. Bring it to a boil over medium heat. When it becomes frothy throughout, begin timing it, and boil it, stirring constantly, for 1 minute for the honey or 2 minutes for the agave. Immediately pour it over the popcorn mixture and stir it to coat the popcorn. Pour the popcorn in the prepared pans and put it in the oven. Remove it in 8 minutes and stir it to more evenly coat the popcorn. Bake it for another 8 minutes and stir it again. Remove it from the oven and allow it to cool completely in the pans. Break up any chunks of caramel corn and store it in a tin or plastic bag. Makes about 1½ quarts of caramel corn.

Good and Healthy Popcorn

Gluten-Free

This and the previous two recipes are great to serve for a movie night at home.

    2 tablespoons olive oil
    ⅓ cup unpopped popcorn
    ⅛ teaspoon salt, or to taste

Put the oil in a 3 quart or slightly larger saucepan. Add three kernels of popcorn to the pan and heat it over medium heat. When you hear the three kernels of popcorn pop, add the rest of the popcorn to the pan. Shake the pan back and forth on the burner while it is heating until the popping slows down and nearly stops. Pour the popcorn into a bowl. Sprinkle it with the salt. Makes 2 to 2½ quarts of popcorn.

Nut Balls

¾ cup agave or honey
¼ cup natural almond butter, peanut butter, or other nut butter
Dash of salt (optional – use only with unsalted nut butter)
½ cup chopped almonds, peanuts, or other nuts

Combine the sweetener, nut butter and salt in a saucepan. Bring it to a boil over medium heat. When it becomes frothy throughout, begin timing and boil, stirring constantly, for 3 to 4 minutes or until it thickens a little begins to darken slightly. Immediately pour it into a bowl to remove it from the heat of the pan. Allow the mixture to cool to warm. Then drop teaspoons of the mixture into a bowl containing the chopped nuts and roll the balls in the nuts. Put them on an oiled baking sheet and allow them to harden. If they are too soft, store them in the refrigerator and cook them a little longer the next time you make them. Makes about 1½ dozen balls.

Fudgey Nut Balls

2 squares (2 ounces) unsweetened baking chocolate
¾ cup agave or honey
¼ cup natural almond butter, peanut butter, or other nut butter
Dash of salt (optional – use only with unsalted nut butter)
½ cup chopped almonds, peanuts, or other nuts

Melt the chocolate in a double boiler over boiling water or carefully microwave it in a glass bowl, stirring often, until it is just melted. When it is melted, set it aside to cool.

Combine the sweetener, nut butter and salt in a saucepan. Bring it to a boil over medium heat. When it becomes frothy throughout, begin timing and boil, stirring constantly, for 3 to 4 minutes or until it thickens a little begins to darken slightly. Immediately pour it into the chocolate and stir. Allow the mixture to cool to warm. Then drop teaspoons of the mixture into a bowl containing the chopped nuts and roll the balls in the nuts. Put them on an oiled baking sheet and allow them to harden. If they are too soft, store them in the refrigerator and cook them a little longer the next time you make them. Makes about 1½ to 2 dozen balls.

Milk-free Chocolate or Carob Chips

Gluten-Free

Milk-free chocolate and carob chips are getting harder to find in health food stores and often contain grain sweeteners or other sweeteners. If you can't find any you can tolerate, here is a recipe for homemade carob or chocolate chunks to use in cookies, ice cream, and other desserts.

Unsweetened carob chips:

> 1 cup carob powder, sieved
> ⅝ cup melted coconut oil

Sweetened carob chips:

> ¾ cup carob powder, sieved
> ⅜ cup sorbitol, xylitol, or erythritol* or fine maple sugar**
> ½ cup plus 1 tablespoon melted coconut oil

Sweetened chocolate chips:

> 8 ounces unsweetened baking chocolate
> 1½ cups sorbitol, xylitol, or erythritol* or fine maple sugar** or date sugar***
> 3 tablespoons oil

Chose one set of ingredients, above. If you are using maple sugar or date sugar and it is not finely ground, process it in a blender or food processor until it is a fine powder.

If you are making carob chips, press the carob powder through a wire mesh strainer with the back of a spoon to break up all lumps. Then measure the sieved powder. Melt the coconut oil in your microwave oven or over low heat a saucepan and measure out the required amount. Stir together the carob powder, coconut oil, and sweetener if you are using it. The mixture should be a very thick paste. Because of the variations in carob powder, the amount needed may vary and you may need to add a little more melted coconut oil or carob powder to achieve the desired consistency.

To make the chocolate chips, melt the chocolate over boiling water in the top of a double boiler. Add half of the sugar alcohol, maple sugar** or date sugar and stir it in thoroughly. Add the oil and stir. Then thoroughly stir in the rest of the sweetener.

Generously grease a baking sheet with butter or melted coconut oil. Spread the carob or chocolate mixture on the sheet to a thickness of between ⅛ and ¼ inch. Chill it in the refrigerator for at least 30 minutes or until it is hard. Remove the baking sheet from the refrigerator and let it sit at room temperature for a few minutes. Use a long knife, such as a butcher or chef's knife, to cut the carob or chocolate into strips about ¼ inch wide. Then cut the carob or chocolate strips in a direction perpendicular to the first cut to form ¼ inch squares. Remove the squares from the baking sheet with a spatula and store them in a glass jar or plastic bag in the refrigerator.

Makes about 2 cups unsweetened carob chips, 1⅔ cups sweetened carob chips, or 3½ cups chocolate chips.

*Note on sugar alcohols: Most sugar alcohols such as sorbitol, mannitol, xylitol, erythritol, etc. are made from corn. However, The Ultimate Life™ xylitol is derived from birch trees. See "Sources," page 234 for purchasing information.

**Maple sugar sweetened chocolate or carob chips variation: Although maple sugar contains sucrose like white table sugar, it has not had nutrients removed. If desired, you may use finely ground maple sugar, such as India Tree™ brand, in this recipe in the same quantity as the other sweeteners. See "Sources," page 234 for purchasing information.

***Date sugar sweetened chocolate chips variation: These chips are not especially sweet. They are similar to bittersweet chocolate and are good in cookies and ice cream but may not be sweet enough for some to enjoy alone.

Chocolate Chips for Ice Cream

Gluten-Free IF made with GF chips

These chips are better than regular chocolate chips in ice cream because they don't freeze to rock-like hardness. They're creamy and melt in your mouth in the ice cream.

> 2 ounces chocolate chips (preferrably sugar-free*), semi-sweet* chocolate chips, or semi-sweet* baking chocolate
> 1 tablespoon oil
> 1 teaspoon liquid lecithin or additional oil
> Butter or coconut oil

Thoroughly butter a small metal tray such as a toaster-oven baking pan. Melt the chocolate in a double boiler or microwave. If you are microwaving the chocolate, use medium power and stir it every 30 seconds; it will take about 1½ minutes to melt. Stir the oil and lecithin into the melted chocolate until well combined. Pour the chocolate mixture onto the tray. Put it in the freezer for a few hours or overnight. Remove it from the freezer and quickly cut the chocolate into ¼-inch or smaller squares. Return the tray to the freezer and process your ice cream. When the ice cream is frozen, remove the chocolate chips from the tray with a spatula and immediately stir them into the ice cream. These chips are not rock-hard in frozen ice cream so are good to use when you will be keeping leftover ice cream in the freezer for a few days.

*Note: Semi-sweet baking chocolate and chips contain sugar. Grain-sweetened chocolate chips are usually not gluten-free. See page 228 to order maltitol-sweetened chocolate chips.

Spelt "Graham" Crackers

These are great for snacks as well as for making graham cracker pie crusts. The recipe gives several options for the sweetener and fat so you can choose between an easy-to-make healthy graham cracker or a "for guests" type of cracker.

Honey or agave sweetened:

2½ cups whole spelt flour plus additional flour for the baking sheet and rolling
½ teaspoon salt
¾ teaspoon baking soda
¼ teaspoon unbuffered vitamin C powder
½ cup oil* OR ½ cup solid fat* at room temperature – choose from butter, goat butter, Earth Balance™ trans fat-free and milk-free margarine, or Spectrum Naturals™ trans-fat free shortening
⅜ cup agave or honey
⅛ cup water

Apple juice sweetened:

¾ cup apple juice concentrate, thawed
2½ cups whole spelt flour plus additional flour for the baking sheet and rolling
½ teaspoon salt
¾ teaspoon baking soda
⅛ teaspoon unbuffered vitamin C powder
½ cup oil* OR ½ cup solid fat* at room temperature – choose from butter, goat butter, Earth Balance™ trans fat-free and milk-free margarine, or Spectrum Naturals™ trans-fat free shortening

If you are using butter or margarine, remove it from the refrigerator and allow it to come to room temperature. It will warm up more quickly if it is cut into small pieces. If you are making these crackers with apple juice, put the juice in a saucepan and bring it to a boil. Measure the volume of the juice every few minutes while it is boiling. When the volume reaches ½ cup, set it aside in the measuring cup and let it cool to room temperature. Rub two baking sheets with oil, butter, margarine or shortening (whatever fat you are using in the crackers) and sprinkle them with spelt flour; shake off the excess flour.

Combine the 2½ cups spelt flour, salt, baking soda, and vitamin C powder in a bowl. If you are using the agave or honey, mix it thoroughly with the water in a small bowl or cup.

If you are using the solid fat, cut the butter, margarine or shortening into the flour mixture with a pastry cutter until well blended. Stir the cooled apple juice or water plus agave or honey into the flour-fat mixture, using the spoon and your hands to mix until it forms a soft dough.

If you are using the oil, stir it into the cooled apple juice concentrate or the water plus sweetener mixture thoroughly. Pour the combined liquids into the flour mixture and stir. Use your hands if needed to form a soft dough.

Divide the dough in half and place each half on a prepared baking sheet. Flour the top of the dough and a rolling pin and roll the dough to about ⅛ inch thickness. Cut it into 1½ inch by 3 inch rectangles and prick them with a fork. Bake at 350°F for 8 to 11 minutes, or until they begin to brown. Remove them from the oven and re-cut them on the original cut lines if necessary. Cool on paper towels. Makes 3 to 4 dozen crackers.

Note on the fat: Although the crackers have a more flaky traditional graham cracker texture when made with solid fat, it is healthier and less work to use the oil in this recipe.

Especially For Guests

If you have been on a special diet for more than a few weeks, you have probably developed an appreciation for many new grains and other foods. You have discovered they are delicious and sustaining. Now you enjoy foods that may look different and taste different from the standard fare you used to eat.

But what happens when you have guests? You hope they will enjoy what you serve. Therefore you may be searching for dessert recipes that look and taste as much like bakery fare as possible. This chapter gives you "normal" looking and tasting impressive desserts to serve guests – flaky-crusted pies, melt-in-the-mouth lemon cake with creamy frosting, rich cookies, lemon meringue pie, strawberry shortcake, chocolate layer cake, custard-based rich ice cream, cheesecake, pecan pie for Thanksgiving, traditional Christmas cookies, and a host of other favorite desserts.

Many of these recipes are made with white spelt flour because desserts baked with white spelt have a texture and appearance that is very close to those made with wheat. Some of them contain eggs, butter, and other more-allergenic ingredients to produce a taste and texture that your guests will find familiar. However, none of the recipes are made with the sugar, high fructose corn syrup, wheat, or "ugly" (hydrogenated) fat that you will find in almost every dessert that you can buy.

At the beginning of each category of desserts in this chapter you will find a list of less-allergenic recipes for that dessert category in other parts of this book that also make impressive desserts to serve to guests. Whether you use the recipes here or those from other chapters, have a wonderful time enjoying good food and building pleasant memories and lasting relationships with your guests.

Wickedly Rich Cheesecake

Gluten-Free IF
crust is made with GF crackers

2 8-ounce packages cream cheese or low-fat (Neufchatel) cream cheese
⅔ cup agave, Fruit Sweet™ or honey
4 eggs
2 tablespoons lemon juice
¼ teaspoon salt
1 teaspoon vanilla extract
One baked "graham" cracker crust, page 68
2 cups fresh blueberries, raspberries, or sliced strawberries

Remove the cream cheese from the refrigerator an hour or two before you want to make this cheesecake and let it come to room temperature. Prepare the crust and let it cool completely.

Preheat your oven to 450°F. In a bowl, combine the cream cheese, sweetener, eggs, lemon juice, salt, and vanilla. Blend them with a hand blender or electric mixer until they are thoroughly mixed. Pour the filling into the crust. Bake the cheesecake for 10 minutes. Then turn the oven temperature down to 300°F. Bake the cheesecake for another 40 to 50 minutes or until it is set in the center. Allow the cheesecake to cool on a cooling rack for about a half hour and then refrigerate it. At serving time, top it with the fresh fruit. Makes 8 to 10 servings.

Sumptuous Shortcake

Ask your doctor about eating oats on a gluten-free diet

This dessert is as impressive-looking as it is delicious. It made the cover of this book!

Shortcake

2⅜ white spelt flour OR 2 cups barley flour OR 2 cups oat flour (If you are using light coconut milk, add an additional 1 tablespoon of flour).

½ cup finely shredded unsweetened coconut

2½ teaspoons baking powder* with spelt OR 2 teaspoons baking powder* with oat or barley flour

½ teaspoon baking soda

⅛ teaspoon salt

1 stick (4 ounces) cold unsalted butter or ½ cup non-hydrogenated Spectrum Naturals™ shortening

½ cup regular or light* coconut milk

¼ cup agave or Fruit Sweet™

Baked coconut topping (optional)

1 egg (optional - may be omitted)

1 tablespoon coconut milk

Additional coconut, about 1 tablespoon

Fruit topping and/or filling

> 4 cups of sliced strawberries, sliced peaches or other fruit of your choice
> 2 tablespoons agave or Fruit Sweet™, to taste (optional - use if the fruit is not
>   very sweet)
> "Sugar-free Whipped Cream," page 196 (optional)

Preheat your oven to 375°F. Lightly rub a baking sheet with butter or shortening or line it with parchment paper. Stir or blend the coconut milk until it is thoroughly mixed. Taste the strawberries or peaches. If they are not as sweet as you like them, mix them with the sweetener.

In a large bowl, stir together the flour, coconut, baking powder, baking soda and salt. (If you are using light coconut milk add an additional tablespoon of flour to the bowl). Cut the butter into small pieces and add it or the shortening to the flour mixture. Cut the fat into the flour mixture with a pastry cutter until it resembles coarse meal. It is all right if a few larger pieces of fat remain which are about the size of a small pea. In a separate bowl or cup, stir together the coconut milk and sweetener. Add them to the flour mixture and stir until just mixed. You will have a soft dough. Transfer the dough to a generously floured surface and knead it a few times. Pat the dough to ½ to ¾ inch thickness. Cut it into rounds with a 3-inch biscuit or cookie cutter or a floured glass. Transfer the shortcakes to the prepared baking sheet with a spatula.

If you wish to have a classy-looking topping on your shortcakes, beat the egg and coconut milk and brush it on the top of the shortcakes. (If you can't have eggs, just brush the shortcakes with plain coconut milk). Sprinkle the tops of the shortcakes with coconut.

Bake the shortcakes for 17 to 20 minutes or until they are brown and set to the touch. Cool them on the baking sheet for a few minutes and then transfer them to a cooling rack with a spatula. When they are completely cool, use a serrated knife to slice the spelt or barley shortcakes into two layers if desired. (The oat shortcakes do not slice well). Fill and/or top them with fruit and whipped cream. Makes 6 to 8 3-inch shortcakes.

*Notes on baking powder and coconut milk: Most baking powder contains corn and some contain aluminum. Featherweight™ baking powder is corn- and gluten-free as well as being free of aluminum and sodium. It is available at most health food stores, but if you need to order it, see "Sources," page 232.

If you use **light coconut milk** in this recipe, add an additional 1 tablespoon of flour.

PIES

Below are some of the most impressive pie recipes you could ever want. See pages 63 to 73 for other favorite pie recipes that are equally delicious but take less time and effort to make than, for example, the lemon meringue pie recipe on page 210.

Extra Flaky Pie Crust

This pie crust is the flakiest I have ever made and is easier to handle than crust made with butter. For pie crusts made with oil or for gluten-free pie crusts, see pages 63 to 68.

> 2¼ cups white spelt flour
> ½ teaspoon salt
> 1 cup Spectrum Naturals™ non-hydrogenated shortening ("Sources," page 232)
> ¼ to ⅜ cup cold water

In a large mixing bowl, stir together the flour and salt. Blend the shortening into the flour using a pastry cutter until the mixture resembles coarse meal. (It is all right if there are still a few pieces of shortening the size of small peas left). Slowly add about 3 tablespoons of the water, stirring with a large fork or spoon while you add it, and if necessary adding more water until the dough begins to hold together. Press the dough together. Divide it in half. Press each half into a 5-inch disc.

To make two one-crust pie shells, preheat the oven to 400°F. Using one half of the dough at a time, place each piece of dough on a well-floured pastry cloth. Cover your rolling pin with the "sock" that comes with a pastry cloth and flour it. Sprinkle flour on the top of the dough and roll it out into about an 11 to 12-inch round. Because Spectrum Naturals™ shortening is a little stiffer than hydrogenated shortening, transferring the dough to the pie plate can be interesting. The easiest method to try is to fold the pastry cloth, with the dough on it, in half. (If the dough cracks when folded, ignore the "cosmetics" – it will be delicious. Just press it together when you get it in the pie plate and try adding a little more water the next time). Then peel back the top of the pastry cloth, leaving the dough folded in half. Lift the folded dough into a 9-inch glass pie plate and unfold it. A second method is to flip the pastry into the dish as described on page 62. The ideal method (and a good investment if you wish to make this impressive pie crust often for guests) is to lift the rolled pastry with an 8-inch pie crust spatula.*

After you have moved the pie crust, fit each half of the pastry into a pie plate, prick all over with a fork, fold the edge under, and crimp or flute the edge. If you have pie weights, add them to the crusts to help them retain their shape as they bake. Bake the crusts for 15 to 20 minutes or until they are lightly browned on the bottom. Cool the crusts completely before filling them.

For a two-crust pie, prepare your pie filling according to the recipes on pages 68 to 73. Preheat your oven to the temperature directed in the filling recipe. Roll one piece of the dough out into an 11 to 12-inch round on a floured pastry cloth as directed above. Fit it into a 9-inch glass pie plate and trim the edge even with the plate. Fill the crust with the filling. Roll out the other piece of dough into an 11 to 12-inch round and place it on the top of the pie. Turn the edge of the top crust under the edge of the bottom crust and crimp it or press it together with the tines of a fork. Prick the top crust with a fork or knife to allow steam to escape from the pie as it bakes. Bake as directed in the filling recipe. Makes enough crust for one two crust pie or two single pie crusts.

*Note on transferring the crust to the pie dish. The best way to get this pie crust from the pastry cloth to the pie dish without breaking it is to use an 8-inch spatula which can be purchased from the King Arthur Flour Baker's Catalogue. See "Sources," page 231.

Pecan Pie

Gluten-Free IF made with a GF crust

1 unbaked pie shell, 9 inches or larger, made using the recipe above or a crust
    recipe from pages 63 to 67
3 eggs
¾ cup agave or Fruit Sweet™ OR ⅝ cup honey plus 2 tablespoons water
⅓ cup unsweetened applesauce
1 teaspoon vanilla
⅛ teaspoon salt
¼ cup tapioca starch
3 tablespoons water
2 cups pecan halves

Prepare the pie crust as directed in the recipe above or in the recipes on pages 63 to 67. Preheat your oven to 375°F. Beat the eggs with a fork or eggbeater until the white and yolk are thoroughly mixed. Add the agave, Fruit Sweet™ or honey plus 2 tablespoons of water, applesauce, vanilla, and salt to the eggs and mix them together. Stir the starch into the 3 tablespoons of water. Stir the starch mixture into the egg mixture thoroughly. Stir in the pecans and pour the filling into the pie shell. Put the pie in the oven and bake it for 45 to 55 minutes or until the crust is nicely browned and the filling is set in the middle of the pie. Makes 8 servings.

Lemon Meringue Pie

Filling

⅓ cup tapioca starch

⅛ teaspoon salt

1 cup agave, Fruit Sweet™ or honey

½ cup water

⅜ cup lemon juice

2 teaspoons to 1 tablespoon lemon zest, to taste (from 1½ to 3 lemons
    depending on their size)

5 egg yolks at room temperature

Meringue

⅓ cup agave, Fruit Sweet or honey

5 egg whites at room temperature

¼ teaspoon cream of tartar

1 baked pie crust, pages 63 to 68 and 208

Remove 5 eggs from the refrigerator an hour or two before you plan to make this pie, or put them in a bowl of warm water for a few minutes and allow them to come to room temperature. Make the crust and let it cool. Remove the zest from the lemons, being careful to only take the outer yellow portion of the peel. Juice the lemons. Separate the egg yolks from the egg whites, being careful not to break the yolks.

For the meringue, combine the ⅓ cup sweetener and 1 tablespoon tapioca starch in a small saucepan. Bring them to a boil over medium heat. Boil the agave mixture for about 15 seconds and the honey or Fruit Sweet™ mixture for 1 to 2 minutes. Set the sweetener mixture aside to cool while you are making the filling.

For the filling, in the top of a double boiler stir together the ⅓ cup tapioca starch and ⅛ teaspoon salt. Stir in the 1 cup of sweetener, water, lemon juice, and lemon zest. Cook over simmering water, stirring often, until the mixture steams and begins to thicken. Add about one tablespoon of the lemon mixture to the egg yolks and stir. Continue adding the lemon mixture to the egg yolks a tablespoon at a time until you have added about ½ cup. Then stir the egg yolk mixture into the remaining lemon mixture in the top of the double boiler. Cook and stir continuously for about four or five minutes or until the mixture steams and becomes quite thick. Remove the top of the double boiler from the pan and allow it to cool a little while you are making the meringue.

Preheat your oven to 350°F. In a large mixer bowl, beat the egg whites on high speed until they are frothy. Add the cream of tartar. Beat until you begin to see lines where the mixer is going through the egg whites and soft peaks have formed. Add the sweetener a tablespoon at a time, beating after each addition, until it has all been added. Continue beating until the meringue holds stiff peaks. Put the filling in the baked pie crust. Top it with the meringue. Bake the pie for 12 to 15 minutes, or until the meringue is golden brown. If your oven does not heat perfectly evenly, turn the pie front-to-back halfway through the baking time. Makes one pie, about 6 servings.

Lemon Chiffon Pie

**Gluten-Free IF
made with a GF crust**

¼ cup cold water
1 envelope unflavored gelatin
4 eggs, near room temperature
¾ cup agave, Fruit Sweet™ or honey
¼ cup lemon juice, freshly squeezed if possible*
1 teaspoon grated lemon zest*
¼ teaspoon salt
½ teaspoon cream of tartar
1 baked pie crust, pages 63 to 68 or 208, 9 inches in diameter or larger

Remove 4 eggs from the refrigerator an hour or two before you plan to make this pie, or put them in a bowl of warm water for a few minutes and allow them to come to room temperature. Sprinkle the gelatin over the cold water and allow it to dissolve. Separate the eggs. In the top of a double boiler, beat the egg yolks slightly. Stir in the gelatin mixture, sweetener, lemon juice, lemon zest, and salt. Heat over simmering water, stirring constantly, until the mixture thickens enough to coat a spoon. (Since this custard is made without milk, it's a little harder to tell when it coats a spoon. When it has been steaming for a few minutes and is beginning to thicken, lift your stirring spoon from the pan. Run your finger along the back of the spoon. If a dry swath remains, the custard has been cooked long enough. If the liquid flows back in from where you ran your finger, keep cooking it). Cool the custard in the refrigerator until it reaches lukewarm which will take about 15 to 25 minutes. When it is cool, beat the egg whites at high speed until foamy. Add the cream of tartar and continue beating them until they are stiff. Fold in the lemon custard carefully. Put the filling into the pie shell and refrigerate it until it is cold and set. Makes one pie, about 6 servings.

Notes on the lemon juice and zest: Although I sometimes use bottled lemon juice and lemon oil instead of fresh juice and lemon zest in other recipes, this recipe and the preceeding lemon meringue pie recipe are not quick to make anyway, so I like to use freshly squeezed lemon juice and zest to add some interesting texture to the pie.

CAKES

These cakes below are fit for royalty! For more cakes that your guest will enjoy just as much, try a flavorful carrot cake, a gluten-free chocolate cake, or other types of cakes and frostings which you will find on pages 75 to 96.

White Spelt Pineapple Upside-Down Cake

The delicious fruit topping eliminates the need for frosting on this cake.

> 6 slices of fresh pineapple or pineapple canned in its own juice, drained
>   (about ⅔ of a 20-ounce can)
> A few seedless red grapes or cherries (optional)
> 3⅔ cups white spelt flour
> 1½ teaspoons baking soda
> ¼ teaspoon unbuffered vitamin C powder
> 1¼ cups pineapple juice concentrate, thawed
> ½ cup oil

Preheat your oven to 375°F. Oil a 9 inch square cake pan. Arrange the pineapple slices in the pan, cutting to fit as needed, and place a grape or pitted cherry in the center of each slice. Combine the flour, baking soda, and vitamin C powder in a large bowl. Stir together the pineapple juice concentrate and oil, add them to the flour mixture, and stir just until the liquid ingredients are mixed into the dry ingredients. Pour the batter into the prepared pan and bake the cake for 30 to 40 minutes or until it is golden brown. Cool the cake in the pan for 10 minutes; then run a knife around the edges of the pan and invert it onto a serving dish. Makes one 9 inch square cake, about 9 servings.

Luscious Lemon Layer Cake

6 cups white spelt flour

2¼ teaspoons baking soda

½ teaspoon unbuffered vitamin C powder

¼ teaspoon salt

2¼ cups apple juice concentrate, thawed, OR 1½ cups agave plus ¾ cup
water

¾ cup oil

2 teaspoons lemon zest (about the amount yielded by one large lemon) or
¼ teaspoon lemon oil (See "Sources," page 229)

Preheat your oven to 350°F. Cut parchment paper – or waxed paper if that is all you have on hand – to fit the bottom of two 9 inch (preferably) or 8 inch round cake pans. Oil the pans, put the parchment paper into the pans, and oil the paper. Then shake white spelt flour around the bottom and sides of the pans. If you are using lemon zest, remove it from a lemon being careful to take only the yellow outer layer. (The white layer is bitter). In a large bowl, stir together the flour, baking soda, vitamin C powder, and salt. In a small bowl or measuring cup combine the apple juice concentrate or agave plus water, oil and lemon zest or oil. Stir the liquid mixture into the flour mixture until they are just combined. Pour the batter into the prepared pans and bake the cake for 30 to 35 minutes or until a toothpick inserted into the center of the pan comes out dry. Remove the pans from the oven and allow them to cool on a cooling rack for 10 minutes. Then run a knife around the edges of the pans, put a rack over the top of each pan, and invert the pan, shaking a little to remove the cake from the pan. Allow the cake layers to cool completely and frost them with lemon cream cheese frosting, page 93. If you cannot have dairy products, use coconut frosting, page 90. Makes about 12 servings.

*Note on the color of this cake: When agave is baked with light-colored flour for a long time, the cake darkens in color especially near the sides and bottom where it is touching the pan. If you use agave, this cake will appear golden-brown on the inside, not yellow like you might expect from a lemon cake. However, the flavor is delicious. If the color is important to you, use the apple juice concentrate for sweetening.

Orange cake variation: Substitute 1½ tablespoons orange zest or ½ teaspoon orange oil for the lemon zest or oil in this cake, and frost it with orange flavored cream cheese frosting, page 93.

Devils Tower Fudge Cake

Science fiction movie fans will remember Devils Tower, a rock formation in Wyoming, where a close encounter occurred with aliens. This cake is "out of this world" as well. When it is made with three layers it is a dark chocolate delight worthy of the most special celebrations!

Ingredients for a three-layer cake

7⅜ cup white spelt flour
1 cup cocoa, preferably King Arthur's™ double Dutch dark cocoa* or Bensdorp
    Dutch-process cocoa*
3½ teaspoons baking soda
1⅛ teaspoons unbuffered vitamin C powder
¼ teaspoon salt
2¼ cups agave
1⅞ cups sugar-free applesauce (unsweetened or apple-juice sweetened)
½ cup plus 1 tablespoon oil
1½ teaspoons vanilla (optional)

Ingredients for a two-layer cake

5 cups minus 1 tablespoon white spelt flour
⅔ cup cocoa such as King Arthur's™ double Dutch dark cocoa* or Bensdorp
    Dutch-process cocoa*
2⅜ teaspoons baking soda
¾ teaspoon unbuffered vitamin C powder
Scant ¼ teaspoon salt
1½ cups agave
1¼ cups sugar-free applesauce (unsweetened or apple-juice sweetened)
⅜ cup oil
1 teaspoon vanilla (optional)

Preheat your oven to 350°F. Cut parchment paper – or waxed paper if that is all you have on hand – to fit the bottoms of two or three round cake pans. Oil the pans, put the parchment paper into the pans, and oil the paper. Then shake white spelt flour around the bottom and sides of the pans.

In a large bowl, stir together the flour, cocoa, baking soda, vitamin C powder, and salt. In a small bowl or measuring cup combine the agave, water, and oil. Stir the liquid mixture into the flour mixture until they are just combined. Scrape the batter, which will be thick, into the prepared pans and level it out with a spatula or back of the spoon you mixed with. Bake the cake for 23 to 30 minutes or until a toothpick inserted into the center of the pan comes out dry. Do not over bake this cake or it may become dry. Check the cake every two minutes with a toothpick to determine when it is done. If your oven bakes "hot" begin checking it before 23 minutes. When the cake is done, remove the pans from the oven and allow them to cool on a cooling rack for 10 minutes. Then run a knife around the edges of the pans, put a rack over the top of each pan, and invert the pan, shaking a little to remove the cake from the pan. Allow the cake layers to cool completely. The tops of the cake layers will be rough, so arrange the layers and level with a knife if needed to produce a stable 3-layer cake. The cream cheese frosting usually used for this cake is not stiff, so if the layers are not level, they may slide apart from each other. Frost the cake with chocolate cream cheese frosting, page 94, or dairy-free chocolate frosting, page 94. Use one batch of frosting for a 2-layer cake and 1½ batches of frosting for a 3-layer cake. Makes about 12 servings.

*Note on cocoa: This cake is very dark and flavorful made with double Dutch dark cocoa from the King Arthur Flour Baker's Catalogue. (See "Sources," page 228). Although not quite as dark, it is equally delicious made with Dutch cocoa such as Bensdorp Dutch process cocoa, which is also available from King Arthur Flour. It's great made with ordinary cocoa from the grocery store as well.

Traditional German Chocolate Cake

Gluten-Free IF
made with a GF cake

Frosting for German chocolate cake is usually made with egg yolks, milk, and butter as is this recipe. For similar frostings for German chocolate cake made without these allergenic ingredients, see pages 92 and 95.

Frosting

⅝ cup agave or Fruit Sweet™
2 egg yolks
3 tablespoons of butter cut into pieces
⅝ cup milk (cow's milk or alternative milk)
3 tablespoons tapioca starch
1 teaspoon vanilla (optional)
¾ cup chopped nuts such as pecans or almonds
¾ to 1 cup unsweetened coconut

Cake

2 layers of any chocolate or carob cake on pages 85 to 88 or 214

Bake the cake and allow the layers to cool completely. If you make the Devils Tower cake (an excellent choice if you tolerate spelt) you may wish to use ordinary cocoa to give the cake a lighter color which is more traditional for German chocolate cakes.

Stir together the agave or Fruit Sweet™, egg yolks and butter in a saucepan. Cook them over medium heat, stirring often, to bring them to a simmer. Turn the heat down and simmer, stirring often, for five minutes or until the mixture has thickened slightly.

In a separate bowl or cup, thoroughly mix together the milk and tapioca starch. Stir them into the egg mixture in the saucepan and cook until the mixture is very thick and the starch has become clear. Remove the pan from the heat and stir in the vanilla, nuts, and ¾ cup coconut. Depending on how coarsely or finely grated the coconut is, the frosting may not be thick enough. If so, stir in the remaining ¼ cup of coconut. Immediately, before the frosting cools, frost the top of the bottom cake layer. Add the top layer and frost the top of the cake.

This makes enough frosting to frost the tops of two or three round layers of a German chocolate layer cake. Use more frosting between the layers and on top if you are only making a two layer cake. Makes one cake or about 12 servings.

COOKIES

If you have eaten any of the cookies in the cookie chapter of this book you know that "delicious" does not have to mean sugar, eggs, butter, and light-colored flour. However, to please guests who have only eaten bakery cookies, the recipes in this section are made with white spelt flour, butter and eggs. If you are allergic to dairy products and eggs, do not despair. Just see the cookie recipes on pages 154 to 180 for many gluten-free and allergen-free cookies that are equally guest-worthy. Some favorite recipes in the cookie chapter include "Quinoa Almond Cookies," page 163, lemon cookies (barley, oat, or rice), pages 166 to 168, chocolate or carob brownies, pages 169 to 171, "Date Squares," page 173, "Fig Bars," page 182, and "Amaranth Biscotti," page 185.

Almond Cookies

½ cup (1 stick) butter at room temperature or ½ cup Spectrum Naturals™
    non-hydrogenated shortening (See "Sources," page 232)
¾ cup agave or Fruit Sweet™
1 egg
1 teaspoon almond extract
2¼ cups white spelt flour
¾ teaspoon baking soda
½ cup sliced almonds

Preheat your oven to 350°F. If you are using the agave, line your baking sheets with parchment paper for easiest cookie removal.

With an electric mixer, cream the butter or shortening. Add the sweetener and beat until it is thoroughly mixed into the butter or shortening. (For more about creaming butter with liquid sweeteners see page 15). Add the egg and almond extract and beat to mix them in. Stir the baking soda into the flour. Add the flour mixture to the bowl a little at a time and beat until it is thoroughly combined. Stir in the sliced almonds. Drop the dough by heaping teaspoons onto an ungreased or parchment lined baking sheet leaving at least 2 inches between the cookies for the batter to spread. If desired, sprinkle more sliced almonds on top of the cookies. Bake for 12 to 16 minutes or until the cookies are golden brown. Slide the parchment paper and cookies off onto a cooling rack or remove the cookies from the baking sheets with a spatula and put them on paper towels to cool. Makes about 2½ dozen cookies.

Rich Chocolate Brownies

For a decadent dessert, serve these with vanilla ice cream, page 100 or 224, and fudge sauce, page 189.

> 2 1-ounce squares unsweetened chocolate
> ⅓ cup oil
> 2 eggs
> 1 cup fine maple sugar such as India Tree™ brand
> ¾ cup white spelt flour
> ½ teaspoon baking powder*
> ½ teaspoon salt

Preheat your oven to 350°F. Oil the bottom only of an 8 inch square cake pan. Melt the chocolate in a double boiler over boiling water or carefully microwave it in a glass bowl, stirring often, until it is just melted. Stir the oil into the melted chocolate thoroughly. Add the maple sugar, eggs, and salt and stir thoroughly. In a separate bowl, stir together the flour and baking powder. Add the dry ingredients to the chocolate mixture and stir until just mixed. Spread the batter in the prepared pan. Bake for 21 to 25 minutes or until the top has a dull crust and a toothpick inserted into the brownies comes out with a few moist crumbs on it. Do not over-bake. Cool completely in the pan, then cut into squares. Makes 16 brownies.

* Note on baking powder: Use Featherweight™ brand baking powder if you are allergic to corn. It contains potato starch instead of cornstarch.

Favorite Chocolate Chip Cookies

Don't despair if you can't have spelt, butter, or eggs. There is a wide variety of scrumptious carob and chocolate chip cookie recipes on pages 154 to 158.

    1 cup (2 sticks) unsalted butter at room temperature
    1 cup agave
    2 large eggs
    1 teaspoon vanilla extract
    2¾ cups white spelt flour
    1 teaspoon baking soda
    ½ teaspoon salt
    1¼ cups chocolate or carob chips

Preheat your oven to 325°F. Line your baking sheets with parchment paper for easiest cookie removal or rub the baking sheets with butter.

Cream the butter with an electric mixer. Add the agave and continue creaming at high speed, stopping to scrape the bowl every minute or so, until it is thoroughly mixed in. (For more about creaming butter with liquid sweeteners see page 15). Add the egg and vanilla and beat again briefly. Stir together the flour, baking soda, and salt. Add them to the butter mixture about ½ cup at a time while beating. Briefly mix in the chocolate or carob chips. Drop the cookie dough onto the baking sheets by heaping teaspoonfuls leaving about three inches between cookies. Bake for 10 to 12 minutes or until they just begin to brown. Remove with a spatula and cool on paper towel. Makes about 4 to 5 dozen 2½ inch cookies.

Easy Shortbread

This shortbread has a delicate light texture and is very easy to make. Serve it with ice cream, sherbet, sorbet, or pudding for a simple but elegant dessert.

    1½ cups white spelt flour
    1 cup tapioca starch or arrowroot
    ½ teaspoon baking soda
    ¼ teaspoon salt
    ½ cup oil
    ⅜ cup agave, Fruit Sweet™ or slightly warmed honey

Preheat your oven to 350°F. Lightly oil a baking sheet or if you are using the agave, preferably line your baking sheet with parchment paper. In a large bowl, stir together the flour, starch, salt, and baking soda. In a measuring cup or small bowl, thoroughly stir together the oil and sweetener. (The mixture of the liquids should look granular). Immediately stir them into the dry ingredients. Put the dough on the prepared baking sheet and roll it out to ¼ inch thickness. Cut it into rectangles which are about 1 inch wide and 2 inches long. Bake for 12 to 18 minutes, or until the shortbread is golden brown. Remove the baking sheet from the oven and re-cut the shortbread on the lines where it was previously cut. Slide the parchment paper and cookies off onto a cooling rack or remove the cookies from the baking sheets with a spatula and put them on paper towels to cool. Makes about 3 dozen pieces of shortbread.

Lively Lemon Drops

For other delicious lemon cookie recipes, including egg-free and gluten-free recipes, see pages 166 to 168.

> 2 sticks (8 ounces) of butter at room temperature or 1 cup Spectrum™ Naturals non-hydrogenated shortening (See "Sources," page 232)
> 1 cup agave or Fruit Sweet™
> 1 egg
> 1 teaspoon vanilla extract
> ½ teaspoon pure lemon oil (See "Sources," page 229) or the zest from two medium-sized lemons (about ¾ to 1 tablespoon of zest)
> 2 tablespoons lemon juice
> 3¼ cups white spelt flour
> 1 teaspoon baking soda
> ¼ teaspoon salt

Preheat your oven to 350°F. Line your baking sheets with parchment paper for easiest cookie removal if you are using the agave.

Cream the butter or shortening with an electric mixer. Add the agave or Fruit Sweet™ and cream until it is thoroughly mixed in. (For more about creaming butter with liquid sweeteners see page 15). Add the egg, vanilla, lemon oil or zest, and lemon juice and beat again briefly. Stir together the flour, baking soda, and salt. Add them to the creamed mixture about ½ cup at a time while beating. Drop the cookie dough onto the baking sheets by heaping teaspoonfuls leaving a few inches between cookies because they will spread. Bake for 10 to 12 minutes or until they just begin to brown. Slide the parchment paper and cookies off onto a cooling rack or remove the cookies from the baking sheets with a spatula and put them on paper towels to cool. Makes about 4 to 5 dozen 2½ inch cookies.

Double Chocolate Cookies

If you can't have spelt, you may still be able to have cookies like these. For a gluten-free version of this recipe made with sorghum flour, see page 165.

> 1 ounce unsweetened baking chocolate
> ⅓ cup Spectrum Naturals™ non-hydrogenated shortening, and possibly
>   additional shortening for greasing the baking sheets ("Sources," page 232)
> ⅔ cup agave or Fruit Sweet™
> 1 teaspoon vanilla
> 1¾ cup white spelt flour
> 1½ teaspoons baking powder
> ¼ teaspoon salt
> ½ cup chocolate chips, nuts, or raisins, or a combination of these

Preheat your oven to 400°F. Rub your baking sheets with shortening or, if you are using the agave, line your baking sheets with parchment paper for easiest cookie removal.

Melt the chocolate carefully in a microwave oven, stirring often, or in a double boiler over simmering water. Allow it to cool while proceeding with the recipe. Cream the shortening with an electric mixer. Add the sweetener and cream thoroughly. (For more about creaming butter with liquid sweeteners see page 15). Mix in the vanilla and chocolate. Stir together the flour, baking powder and salt and add them to the mixer bowl gradually while mixing on medium speed. Mix in the chocolate chips, nuts, or raisins on low speed.

Drop the dough by heaping teaspoons on the baking sheets leaving at least 2 inches between the cookies for the batter to spread. Bake for 8 to 11 minutes or until the cookies are puffed up and dry looking but not browned. (The goal is to not have them brown much on the bottom). Remove them from the oven and cool them on the baking sheet for a few minutes. Then slide the parchment paper and cookies off onto a cooling rack or remove the cookies from the baking sheets with a spatula and put them on paper towels to finish cooling. Makes about 2½ dozen cookies.

HOLIDAY COOKIES

Here are some traditional holiday cookies made with spelt, butter, and other ingredients that some people with allergies might not be able to have. But take heart – there are many other holiday cookie recipes free of these ingredients in the cookie chapter of this book. See the recipes for "Pfeffernuse," page 184, "Pizzelles" made with a variety of grains including gluten-free alternatives, pages 186 to 188, "Gingerbread Men," page 177, and "Cookie Press Cookies" including gluten-free varieties, page 180.

White Spelt Biscotti

This recipe is based on my favorite of all the cookies which my aunt used to make at Christmas time when I was a child. For a gluten-free version, see page 185.

    3 cups white spelt flour
    ¼ teaspoon salt
    ¾ teaspoon baking soda
    ¼ teaspoon unbuffered vitamin C powder
    ½ cup sliced almonds
    ¾ cup agave or Fruit Sweet™
    ⅓ cup oil
    1 teaspoon almond extract
    1 teaspoon vanilla extract

Preheat your oven to 350°F. Lightly rub a baking sheet with oil, or if you are using the agave, preferably line your baking sheets with parchment paper. In a large bowl, stir together the flour, salt, baking soda, vitamin C, and almonds. In a separate bowl or cup, stir together the sweetener, oil, and flavorings. Add the liquids to the dry ingredients and stir until they are just mixed. Transfer the dough to a floured board and knead it about 20 times. Form the dough into a loaf about 12 inches long, 3½ inches wide, and 1 inch high on the prepared baking sheet. Bake the loaf for 20 to 25 minutes, or until it just barely starts to brown. Remove the baking sheet from the oven. Using a serrated knife, slice the loaf down the middle and then into about 1 inch slices crosswise. Lay the slices on their sides on the baking sheet. Return the sheet to the oven. Bake the cookies for 5 to 10 minutes. When they begin to brown, turn them over so the other side of each slice is down. Bake them for another 5 to 10 minutes. Slide the parchment paper and cookies off onto a cooling rack or remove the cookies from the baking sheets with a spatula and put them on paper towels to cool. Makes about 2 dozen cookies

Spritz

Made with Fruit Sweet™ and butter, this recipe is "near normal" and great for guests. For cookie press cookies made with oil and other types of flour and sweeteners, see page 180.

> 1 cup butter, goat butter, ghee or Spectrum Naturals™ non-hydrogenated shortening
> ⅔ cup Fruit Sweet™ (or agave* if you cannot get Fruit Sweet™)
> 1 teaspoon vanilla extract or almond flavoring
> 3⅔ to 4 cups white spelt flour
> ¼ teaspoon salt
> ⅜ teaspoon baking soda
> ⅛ teaspoon unbuffered vitamin C powder

An hour or so before you plan to make these cookies, take the butter or ghee out of the refrigerator to soften.

Preheat your oven to 375°F. Cream the butter, ghee, or shortening on medium speed with an electric mixer. Add the Fruit Sweet™ or agave* and flavoring and beat thoroughly. Stir together 3⅔ cups of the flour, baking soda, vitamin C and salt in another bowl. Add the flour mixture to the mixer bowl about ½ cup at a time, beating after each addition until all of the mixture been added. If the dough is soft, add the final ⅓ cup of flour, or enough to make the dough stiff. Put the dough into a cookie press following the directions that came with the press. Press out cookies or long spritz strips or other shapes onto an ungreased baking sheet. Bake the cookies for 6 to 11 minutes, depending on the size and thickness of the cookies, or until they are beginning to brown. If you make spritz strips, cut them into 2 to 3 inch segments while they are still warm. Remove them from the baking sheet and allow them to cool on paper towels. Makes about 4 dozen small cookies

*Note on agave: Agave is more sticky than Fruit Sweet™ which can cause problems with these cookies. For most agave-sweetened cookies, I line the baking sheet with parchment paper, but if you do that with cookie press cookies and are making trees, stars, or other shapes, the dough sticks to the cookie press rather than to the parchment paper on the baking sheet. To get them to stick to the baking sheet, it must be unlined and ungreased. However, you may have trouble removing agave-containing cookies after they are baked. If you wish to use parchment paper, make the cookies as spritz only. The agave-sweetened cookies are also more crunchy than delicate in texture. I prefer to use Fruit Sweet™ in these cookies, but since it is not as readily available, agave is included as an optional sweetener in this recipe.

Pizzelles Like Grandma's

When I was diagnosed with multiple food allergies and my husband heard the list of foods I could no longer eat, he said, "You've lost your Italian license." Although he was primarily thinking of pasta dishes, pizzelles also would have been hard to do without and have been ground for the loss of my license. However, there are several varieties, including gluten-free pizzelles, on pages 186 to 188. If you make this version with white spelt flour, your guests will find them "just like Grandma's." To get these pizzelles out of the iron easily, make them with butter.

3 cups white spelt or whole spelt flour

¾ cup butter or goat butter, melted, or if you must, substitute melted coconut oil*

⅝ cup Fruit Sweet™ or agave

⅜ cup water

1 tablespoon anise extract

Begin heating the pizzelle iron. Measure the flour into a large electric mixer bowl. In a small bowl, stir together the melted butter, sweetener, and water, and anise flavoring and pour them into the bowl with the flour. Beat the dough on low speed until all of the flour is moistened, then beat it on medium speed for one minute. (Do not over beat or your pizzelles may be tough). Brush the top and bottom grids of the iron with melted butter. When the iron's light goes off, indicating that it is sufficiently heated, put one heaping tablespoon of dough in the iron. (You may need more – this is a starting point as you determine how much dough you should put in to fill the iron when you close it). Cook each pizzelle for 20 to 30 seconds or until it is golden brown, remove it from the iron using two forks, and lay it on a paper towel to cool.

You may have to experiment to determine what cooking time makes the cookies easiest to remove. If the pizzelles stick, brush the iron with melted butter oil before cooking each set of cookies. Makes about 2 to 3 dozen 6-inch pizzelles or about 15 pizzelles which are 8-inch circles that break apart into quarter-circles.

*Note on butter versus coconut oil: If you wish to make pizzelles just like Grandma's but cannot have butter, you can substitute melted coconut oil for the butter. You may find it easier to bake them in a krumkake iron rather than a pizzelle iron because the grooves in the pattern are not as deep, and they tend to stick more tenaciously in a pizzelle iron. Be sure to oil both plates of the iron with melted coconut oil before beginning and between each set of cookies. Also be prepared to carefully pull the cookie from the top plate of the iron with a pair of forks if needed. Shortening or margarine will not work in this recipe. I spent over an hour scraping and cleaning my pizzelle iron after trying this recipe with Spectrum Naturals™ non-hydrogenated shortening!

PREMIUM ICE CREAM

Here is ice cream that is better than Hagan Dazs™ but without the sugar. These recipes are made with cream or milk and eggs. However, if you cannot have those foods, you don't have to miss out on ice cream. See the recipes on pages 37 to 38 and 100 to 113.

Custard Base for Ice Cream

Gluten-Free

Remember the days of frozen custard sold at amusement parks? Adding egg yolks to your homemade ice cream improves the texture tremendously if you are going to keep it in the freezer for a few days before you finish eating the batch. The wonderful taste and texture of ice cream made with this base is worth planning ahead to allow time for the custard to cool.

2 cups cream, half-and-half or milk of any kind (cow, goat, gluten-free soy, etc.)
⅜ cup agave, Fruit Sweet™ or honey
2 egg yolks

Heat the cream or milk and sweetener over medium heat until they are hot. In a bowl, briefly whisk the egg yolks. Add 1 cup of the hot milk mixture to the yolks very gradually while whisking. Then gradually add the yolk mixture to the hot milk in the pan while whisking. Cook the mixture over low to medium heat, whisking continually, for 4 to 8 minutes, or until it just begins to coat a spoon. (Test for this by dipping the spoon in the custard base and then running your finger across the back of the spoon. When it leaves a clean swath, the custard base is done cooking). At no time should the mixture boil! If it begins to bubble, remove it from the heat immediately or it will curdle. Pour the hot mixture through a wire mesh strainer into a jar and chill thoroughly, at least several hours or overnight. Use it to make your favorite ice cream recipes on the following pages. Or if you wish to make a richer variation of any of the ice cream recipes on pages 100 to 105, substitute this base for the milk and sweetener and omit the methylcellulose.

Rich Vanilla Ice Cream

Gluten-Free

1 batch (about 2½ cups) "Custard Base," above
1 tablespoon vanilla extract or a 2-inch piece of vanilla bean, cut open

Combine the chilled custard base and vanilla. If you are using vanilla bean, put the bean into the custard base and let the mixture sit overnight in the refrigerator, scrape the seeds out of the bean into the custard mixture, and discard the bean pod. Freeze the mixture as your ice cream machine directions suggest or use the food processor method on page 99. This ice cream keeps well in the freezer without becoming extremely hard, but you may wish to move it to the refrigerator about 15 to 20 minutes before you plan to serve it. Makes about 1½ pints of ice cream.

Rich Chocolate Ice Cream

Gluten-Free

1 batch (about 2½ cups) "Custard Base," page 224
3 tablespoons cocoa OR 1 ounce unsweetened baking chocolate
2 tablespoons additional agave, honey or Fruit Sweet™ only if you are using
 the baking chocolate rather than the cocoa

If you are using the cocoa, combine it with the cold custard base using a hand blender or electric mixer. If you are using the baking chocolate, chop it finely and add it to the custard base at the beginning of the final cooking period when you are making the base along with an additional 2 tablespoons of honey or Fruit Sweet™. Beat the mixture briefly after cooking with a hand blender or electric mixer to disperse the chocolate. Chill the mixture thoroughly.

Freeze the mixture as your ice cream machine directions suggest or use the food processor method on page 99. This recipe keeps well in the freezer without becoming extremely hard, but you may wish to move it to the refrigerator about 15 to 20 minutes before you plan to serve it. Makes about 1½ pints of ice cream.

Rich Strawberry Ice Cream

Gluten-Free

1 batch (about 2½ cups) "Custard Base," page 224
1½ cups puree of ripe strawberries (about 2 pints strawberries)

Wash, stem, and puree the strawberries. Measure out 1½ cups of puree and combine it with the chilled custard base. Freeze the mixture as your ice cream machine directions suggest or use the food processor method on page 99. This recipe keeps very well in the freezer without becoming extremely hard because of the strawberry fiber, but you may wish to move it to the refrigerator about 15 to 20 minutes before you plan to serve it. Makes about 2 pints of ice cream.

Rich Peach Ice Cream

Gluten-Free

1 batch (about 2½ cups) "Custard Base," page 224
1½ cups puree of ripe peaches (about 4 peaches)

Wash, peel, pit and puree the peaches. Measure out 1½ cups of puree and combine it with the chilled custard base. Freeze the mixture as your ice cream machine directions suggest or use the food processor method on page 99. This recipe keeps very well in the freezer without becoming extremely hard due to the peach fiber but you may wish to move it to the refrigerator about 15 to 20 minutes before you plan to serve it. Makes about 2 pints of ice cream.

Rich Lemon Ice Cream

Gluten-Free

1 batch (about 2½ cups) "Custard Base," page 224
1½ teaspoons lemon zest
¼ cup freshly squeezed lemon juice

Remove the zest from a lemon, being careful to take only the yellow layer. Squeeze the lemon juice. Combine the custard base, lemon zest, and lemon juice. Freeze the mixture as your ice cream machine directions suggest or use the food processor method on page 99. This recipe keeps well in the freezer without becoming extremely hard, but you may wish to move it to the refrigerator about 15 to 20 minutes before you plan to serve it. Makes about 1½ pints of ice cream.

Eggnog Ice Cream

Gluten-Free

1 batch (about 2½ cups) "Custard Base," page 224
2½ teaspoons rum flavoring

Combine the custard base and flavoring. Freeze the mixture as your ice cream machine directions suggest or use the food processor method on page 99. This recipe keeps well in the freezer without becoming extremely hard, but you may wish to move it to the refrigerator about 15 to 20 minutes before you plan to serve it. Makes about 1½ pints of ice cream.

Chocolate Mint Ice Cream

To have this ice cream made without eggs, see the "Mint Chocolate Chip Ice Cream" recipe on page 102.

> 1 batch (about 2½ cups) "Custard Base," page 224
> ½ teaspoon peppermint extract
> ¼ cup chocolate chips or mini-chips (preferably sugar-free*), carob chips, or milk-free chocolate or carob chips, page 201, or 1 batch of "Chocolate Chips for Ice Cream," page 202

Combine the custard base and peppermint extract. If you must have your ice cream green, add 3 to 4 drops of green food coloring. Freeze the mixture as your ice cream machine directions suggest or use the food processor method on page 99. When frozen, stir in the chocolate chips. This recipe keeps well in the freezer without becoming extremely hard, but you may wish to move it to the refrigerator about 15 to 20 minutes before you plan to serve it. Makes about 1½ pints of ice cream.

*Note on chocolate chips: This recipe contains sugar in commercially-made chocolate chips unless sugar-free chips are used. Grain-sweetened chips are usually not gluten-free however. See "Sources," page 228, to purchase maltitol sweetened chocolate chips.

Sources of Special Ingredients and Products

This section lists sources of special ingredients and products needed for desserts and which may not always be easy to find locally. Most of these companies sell products and services in addition to those listed below. Visit their websites for up-to-date information about all of their products and services.

BANANA POWDER

King Arthur Flour Baker's Catalogue
P.O. Box 876
Norwich, Vermont 05055
(800) 827-6836
www.kingarthurflour.com

CAROB POWDER

Bob's Red Mill
Natural Foods Inc.
5209 S.E. International Way
Milwaukie, OR 97222
(800) 349-2173 or (503) 654-3215
www.bobsredmill.com

CHOCOLATE and COCOA

Chocolate chips, sugar-free
(sweetened with maltitol)

King Arthur Flour Baker's Catalogue
P.O. Box 876
Norwich, Vermont 05055
(800) 827-6836
www.kingarthurflour.com

Chocolate chips, dairy, soy and gluten-free

Enjoy Life™ Semi-Sweet Chocolate Chips
Enjoy Life™ Natural Brands, LLC
3810 N. River Road
Schiller Park, IL 60176
(888-503-6569 (888-50-ENJOY)
www.enjoylifenb.com

Although gluten-containing ingredients are not used in making chocolate or chocolate chips, Enjoy Life™ chocolate chips are processed in a facility guaranteed to be gluten, dairy, and soy free.

Cocoa, Dutch process

King Arthur Flour Baker's Catalogue
P.O. Box 876
Norwich, Vermont 05055
(800) 827-6836
www.kingarthurflour.com

FLAVORINGS, NATURAL

(gluten, corn and alcohol-free)

Extracts

Frontier Natural Flavorings*
Frontier Natural Products Co-op
P.O. Box 299
3021 78th Street
Norway, IA 52318
(800) 669-3275
www.frontierherb.com

***Note:** Some Frontier flavorings such as vanilla are corn-, alcohol-, and gluten-free; others are not.

**The Spicery Shoppe Natural
    Flavorings**
The Spicery Shoppe
1525 Brook Drive
Downers Grove, IL 60515
(800) 323-1301 or (630) 932-8100

Citrus oils

King Arthur Flour Baker's Catalogue
P.O. Box 876
Norwich, Vermont 05055
(800) 827-6836
www.kingarthurflour.com

Vanilla beans, whole

King Arthur Flour Baker's Catalogue
P.O. Box 876
Norwich, VT 05055
(800) 827-6836
www.kingarthurflour.com

FLOURS, GRAINS, and GRAIN ALTERNATIVES

Amaranth flour

Nu-World Amaranth, Inc.
P. O. Box 2202
Naperville, IL 60540
(630) 369-6819
www.nuworldfoods.com

Arrowroot

Authentic Foods
1850 W. 168th Street, Suite B
Gardena, CA 90247
(800) 806-4737 or (310) 366-7612
www.authenticfoods.com

Bob's Red Mill Natural Foods Inc.
5209 S.E. International Way
Milwaukie, OR 97222
(800) 349-2173 or (503) 654-3215
www.bobsredmill.com

Barley flour

Arrowhead Mills
The Hain Celestial Group, Inc.
4600 Sleepytime Drive
Boulder, CO 80301
(800) 434-4246
www.hain-celestial.com

Buckwheat flour

Arrowhead Mills
The Hain Celestial Group, Inc.
4600 Sleepytime Drive
Boulder, CO 80301
(800) 434-4246
www.hain-celestial.com

Kamut flour

Arrowhead Mills
The Hain Celestial Group, Inc.
4600 Sleepytime Drive
Boulder, CO 80301
(800) 434-4246
www.hain-celestial.com

Millet flour

Bob's Red Mill Natural Foods Inc.
5209 S.E. International Way
Milwaukie, OR 97222
(800) 349-2173 or (503) 654-3215
www.bobsredmill.com

Potato starch

Bob's Red Mill Natural Foods Inc.
5209 S.E. International Way
Milwaukie, OR 97222
(800) 349-2173 or (503) 654-3215
www.bobsredmill.com

Quinoa flakes

Purcell Mountain Farms
393 Firehouse Road
Moyie Springs, ID 83845
(866) 440-BEAN or 208-267-0627
www.purcellmountainfarms.com

Quinoa flour and grain

The Quinoa Corporation
P.O. Box 279
Gardena, CA. 90248
(310) 217-8125
www.quinoa.net

Rice flour, brown or white

Arrowhead Mills
The Hain Celestial Group, Inc.
4600 Sleepytime Drive
Boulder, CO 80301
(800) 434-4246
www.hain-celestial.com

Rye flour

Arrowhead Mills
The Hain Celestial Group, Inc.
4600 Sleepytime Drive
Boulder, CO 80301
(800) 434-4246
www.hain-celestial.com

Sorghum (milo) flour, super-fine

Authentic Foods
1850 W. 168th Street, Suite B
Gardena, CA 90247
(800) 806-4737 or (310) 366-7612
www.authenticfoods.com

Spelt flour, whole or white (sifted)

Purity Foods, Inc.
2871 W. Jolly Road
Okemos, MI 48864
(517) 351-9231
www.purityfoods.com

Tapioca starch/flour

Authentic Foods
1850 W. 168th Street, Suite B
Gardena, CA 90247
(800) 806-4737 or (310) 366-7612
www.authenticfoods.com

Bob's Red Mill Natural Foods Inc.
5209 S.E. International Way
Milwaukie, OR 97222
(800) 349-2173 or (503) 654-3215
www.bobsredmill.com

Teff flour

Bob's Red Mill Natural Foods Inc.
5209 S.E. International Way
Milwaukie, OR 97222
(800) 349-2173 or (503) 654-3215
www.bobsredmill.com

GRAHAM CRACKERS (gluten-free)

Outside the Bread Box
2027 W. Colorado Avenue
Colorado Springs, CO 80904
(719) 633-3434
www.outsidethebreadbox.com

(Also free of wheat, nuts, corn, dairy, soy)

JUICE CONCENTRATES

Apple, frozen organic
 (containing the natural apple fiber)

Cascadian Farm
719 Metcalf
Sedro Wolley, WA 98284
(800) 249-0562
www.cascadianfarm.com

Blueberry, cranberry and cherry, bottled

R. W. Knudsen and Sons, Inc.
1 Strawberry Lane
Orrville, Ohio 44667-0280
(888) 569 6993
www.knudsenjuices.com

Pomegranate, bottled

**Pomegranate Molasses
Cortas USA Ltd.**
5925 McShann Road
Dallas, TX 75230
 972) 387-5529
www.cortas.com.lb

**PomeGreat™ Pomegranate Juice
Jarrow Formulas**
1824 S. Robertson Blvd.
Los Angeles, CA 90035
(310) 204-6936
www.jarrow.com

(Although I prefer Cortas™ pomegranate molasses for both flavor and price, this pomegranate concentrate is given as an alternative).

KITCHEN EQUIPMENT

Apple peeler/corer, crank-style

Progressive International Corp.
6111 S. 228th Street
Kent, WA 98032
(800) 426-7101 or (253) 850-6111
www.progressiveintl.com
Also sold on **Amazon.com.**

Bread machines, measuring cups, Microplane™ grater/zester, pie crust spatula, doughnut pans, etc.

King Arthur Flour Baker's Catalogue
P.O. Box 876
Norwich, Vermont 05055
(800) 827-6836
www.kingarthurflour.com

LEAVENING INGREDIENTS

Baking powder, corn-free

Featherweight Baking Powder
The Hain Celestial Group, Inc.
4600 Sleepytime Drive
Boulder, CO 80301
(800) 434-4246
www.hain-celestial.com

Unbuffered vitamin C powder, cassava source
(Made by Allergy Research Group)

Professional Supplement Center
2427 Porter Lake Drive
Sarasota, FL 34230
(888) 245-5000
www.professionalsupplementcenter.com

Yeast, active dry and quick-rise
(gluten-, corn- and preservative-free,
in 1 or 2 pound bags)

Red Star Yeast and SAF Yeast
King Arthur Flour Baker's Catalogue
P.O. Box 876
Norwich, Vermont 05055
(800) 827-6836
www.kingarthurflour.com

METHYLCELLULOSE

Ener-G Foods
5960 First Avenue South
P.O. Box 84487
Seattle, WA 98124-5787
(800) 331-5222
www.ener-g.com

MISCELLANEOUS INGREDIENTS FOR BAKING

Gum, guar and xanthum

Authentic Foods
1850 W. 168th Street, Suite B
Gardena, CA 90247
(800) 806-4737 or (310) 366-7612
www.authenticfoods.com

Non-hydrogenated, trans-fat free shortening

**Spectrum Naturals™ Organic All
Vegetable Shortening**
Spectrum Organic Products, Inc.
The Hain Celestial Group, Inc.
4600 Sleepytime Drive
Boulder, CO 80301
(800) 434-4246
www.spectrumorganics.com

This shortening is soy-free and contains palm oil only.

NUT PRODUCTS

Almond flour/meal

King Arthur Flour Baker's Catalogue
P.O. Box 876
Norwich, VT 05055
(800) 827-6836
www.kingarthurflour.com

Authentic Foods
1850 W. 168th Street, Suite B
Gardena, CA 90247
(800) 806-4737 or (310) 366-7612
www.authenticfoods.com

Bob's Red Mill Natural Foods Inc.
5209 S.E. International Way
Milwaukie, OR 97222
(800) 349-2173 or (503) 654-3215
www.bobsredmill.com

Coconut, unsweetened, finely shredded

Jerry's Nut House, Inc.
2101 Humboldt Street
Denver, CO 80205
(303) 861-2262

Coconut milk, free of guar gum

Natural Value™ Coconut Milk
Natural Value
Email: Gary@NaturalValue.com
www.naturalvalue.com

Purchase Natural Value™ coconut milk through your health food store. To find out which stores near you have or can order it and how they can get it, email Gary@NaturalValue.com. Natural Value "regular" coconut milk is free of guar gum. Their organic coconut milk contains guar.

Pecan meal

King Arthur Flour Baker's Catalogue
P.O. Box 876
Norwich, VT 05055
(800) 827-6836
www.kingarthurflour.com

SWEETENERS

Agave

Madhava agave nectar, light, dark, amber, and raw
Madhava Honey
4689 Ute Highway
Lyons, CO 80540
(303) 823-5166
www.madhavasagave.com

Date sugar

NOW Natural Foods
395 S. Glen Ellyn Road
Bloomingdale, IL 60108
(800) 283-3500
www.nowfoods.com

Order from NOW Foods through your health food store.

Fruit Sweet™, Grape Sweet™, and Pear Sweet™

Wax Orchards, Inc.
P.O. Box 25448
Seattle, WA 98665
(800) 634-6132
www.waxorchards.com

Maple sugar, finely ground

India Tree™ Maple Sugar
India Tree Gourmet Spices and Specialties
1421 Elliott Avenue West
Seattle, WA 98119
(800) 369-4848 or (206) 270-0293
www.indiatree.com

Stevia, pure white powder

NOW Natural Foods
395 S. Glen Ellyn Road
Bloomingdale, IL 60108
(800) 283-3500
www.nowfoods.com

Order from NOW Foods through your health food store.

Protocol for Life Balance
(877) 776-8610
Email: sales@protocolforlife.com
www.protocolforlife.com

This stevia has been treated with an enzyme to remove the licorice-like after taste. Use the powder rather than the packets for baking. This product is gluten-free but the packets contain maltodextrin from corn. Protocol for Life Balance products are available from health care practitioners only. If your health care practitioner does not carry this stevia, email the company for information on where to get it.

Xylitol, corn-free
(from birch trees)

The Ultimate Sweetener™ Xylitol
The Ultimate Life
Box 4308
Santa Barbara, CA 93140
(800) 843-6325 or (805) 962-2221
www.ultimatelife.com/CatSweet.htm

Table of Measurements

For some of these recipes you will need to measure less-common amounts of ingredients such as ⅜ cup or ⅛ teaspoon. The easiest and most accurate way to do this is to have a liquid measuring cup with ⅛ cup markings, a set of dry measuring cups that contains a ⅛ cup measure, and a set of measuring spoons that has a ⅛ teaspoon. Such kitchen equipment is available from the King Arthur Flour Baker's Catalogue (See "Sources," page 231). But while you are waiting for your measuring cups and spoons to arrive or if you need to halve, double, or triple recipes, use this table.

⅛ teaspoon	= ½ of your ¼ teaspoon measure	
⅜ teaspoon	= ¼ teaspoon + ⅛ teaspoon	
⅝ teaspoon	= ½ teaspoon + ⅛ teaspoon	
¾ teaspoon	= ½ teaspoon + ¼ teaspoon	
⅞ teaspoon	= ½ teaspoon + ¼ teaspoon + ⅛ teaspoon	
1 teaspoon	= ⅓ tablespoon	= ⅙ fluid ounce
1½ teaspoons	= ½ tablespoon	= ¼ fluid ounce
3 teaspoons	= 1 tablespoon	= ½ fluid ounce
½ tablespoon	= 1½ teaspoons	= ¼ fluid ounce
1 tablespoon	= 3 teaspoons	= ½ fluid ounce
2 tablespoons*	= ⅛ cup	= 1 fluid ounce
4 tablespoons	= ¼ cup	= 2 fluid ounces
5⅓ tablespoons	= ⅓ cup	= 2⅔ fluid ounces
8 tablespoons	= ½ cup	= 4 fluid ounces
16 tablespoons	= 1 cup	= 8 fluid ounces
⅛ cup	= 2 tablespoons*	= 1 fluid ounce
¼ cup	= 4 tablespoons	= 2 fluid ounces
⅜ cup	= ¼ cup + 2 tablespoons*	= 3 fluid ounces
⅝ cup	= ½ cup + 2 tablespoons*	= 5 fluid ounces
¾ cup	= ½ cup + ¼ cup	= 6 fluid ounces
⅞ cup	= ¾ cup + 2 tablespoons*	= 7 fluid ounces
	OR ½ cup + ¼ cup + 2 tablespoons*	
1 cup	= ½ pint	= 8 fluid ounces
1 pint	= 2 cups	= 16 fluid ounces
1 quart	= 4 cups OR 2 pints	= 32 fluid ounces
1 gallon	= 4 quarts	= 128 fluid ounces

*Note: In my experience, measuring tablespoons are all a little scanty of ¹⁄₁₆ cup so 2 tablespoons is a little short of ⅛ cup. Therefore, if you need to measure, for example, ⅜ cup of liquid and do not have a measuring cup with ⅛ cup markings, it will probably be more accurate to eyeball an amount halfway between ¼ cup and ½ cup than to use ¼ cup plus two tablespoons.

About Sweeteners, Health and Life

What about sweeteners? We love them because they make the sweet treats which bring us pleasure, help build relationships, and make special occasions more special. But if we want ideal health, should we eat them often? Are they good or bad for our health? The answer is – it depends.

Whether, how much, which sweeteners you use, and how often you use them depends, most importantly, on your body. The bottom line answer to the question above is **ASK YOUR DOCTOR** whether and how often you should have desserts and sweet treats and what kinds of sweeteners are acceptable for your medical condition. Perhaps he or she will say that you can eat fresh fruit every day or have or a cookie or two daily if sweetened with the healthier sweeteners used in this book. Maybe it is even all right for you to have a conventional treat made with sugar occasionally. Or perhaps you need to save all desserts made with caloric sweeteners for special occasions only. Maybe you should have treats made with stevia only. See the medical conditions section on page 238 for some of the reasons which may be behind your doctor's answer.

Another factor that determines whether a sweetener is good or bad for health is the sweetener itself. Is it minimally or highly processed? What is the source of the sweetener? What types of sugar(s) does it contain? How does our body use those types of sugars? A brief discussion of sugars and carbohydrates in general and how our bodies handle them is essential here.

Glucose is the single sugar (monosaccharide) which is the main source of fuel for the cells in our bodies. All sugars and starches must be converted to glucose before we can use them for energy. Fructose, or fruit sugar, is a monosaccharide that goes directly to the liver from the digestive system and is converted to glucose there before it enters the general circulation for our cells to use. This conversion slows the impact fructose has on blood sugar levels.

Complex carbohydrates are a major source of the glucose our bodies use for energy. There are several types of complex carbohydrates including amylose (non-branching chains of glucose molecules), amylopectin (branching chains and more complex groups of glucose molecules), and fructans (chains of fructose or fructose with some glucose molecules included). Complex carbohydrates require digestion before the sugars they are composed of enter the bloodstream. However, if a starch is very finely ground or partially pre-digested by rigorous modern food processing techniques, the amount of digestion our bodies need to do may be minimal and a flood of glucose molecules can enter the bloodstream rapidly.

White table sugar is sucrose, a disaccharide (two single sugars joined together by a chemical bond) made of one molecule of glucose and one of fructose. Molasses, maple syrup and sugar, and some varieties of dates also contain sucrose. Barley malt or other types of malt contain maltose, which is a disaccharide made of two molecules of glucose. All disaccharides must be broken down into single sugars in the intestine before they can be properly absorbed and be used by our bodies.

The least processed sweetening agents used in this book are whole fruits. The sugar in them is usually mostly fructose. Fruit is allowed on the diets of many people because it contains fiber, vitamins and minerals in addition to the natural sugar. The fructose contained in whole fruit is absorbed slowly because it is accompanied by fiber and then must be processed by the liver before we can use it for energy. Therefore the sugar from fruit does not enter the bloodstream rapidly and thus does not cause a major spike in blood sugar or insulin levels. If you can have desserts made with whole fruit, use recipes from this book that contain whole fruit as the major ingredient or use it for sweetening. See the "Simple Fruit Desserts" chapter on pages 34 to 38, the cantaloupe or mango sorbet recipes on page 112, and the recipes for "Sorghum Banana Cookies" on page 158 and "Fiber-Full Oatmeal Cookies" on page 160.

Liquid fruit sweeteners are more processed than whole fruits. If you are making a recipe sweetened with apple juice concentrate, use natural apple juice which retains the fiber such as Cascadian Farm™ organic apple juice concentrate. Sweeteners such as Fruit Sweet™ and Pear Sweet™ are more concentrated than apple juice concentrate but the sugar in them is mostly fructose, so their effect on blood sugar levels is more moderate than for some sweeteners.

Date sugar is ground dried dates and thus contains all the fiber and minerals of the dates themselves. Some types of dates, such as the Deglet Noor variety, contain mostly sucrose. Other varieties, such as Halawy, Zahidi, and Khadrawy, contain a mixture of glucose and fructose. Several recipes in this book use date sugar.

Agave is a sweetener derived from a plant in the cactus family. The plant contains fructans which, by treatment with moderate heat, are broken down into a mixture of simple sugars that is usually about 90% fructose. Because the sugar from agave is mostly fructose and must be processed by the liver into glucose before we can use it, the impact on blood sugar levels is low and slow. This gives it a very low score on the glycemic index. Thus agave may be better for diabetics and weight watchers than other sweeteners. It is used in many recipes in this book. See pages 21 to 22 for more about agave.

Honey is a mixture of glucose and fructose. Some types of honey, such as pure floral honey, contain a fair amount of fructose and thus have a low-moderate score on the glycemic index. Other types of honey may contain more glucose and have a higher glycemic score.

High fructose corn syrup is also a mixture of glucose and fructose, but it has been chemically refined to break cornstarch into sugars and may contain remnants of that processing history such as mercury.[1] It is often made from genetically modified corn. Because it is highly refined and the sugar it contains is a mixture of monosaccharides – so there are no chemical bonds that need to be broken by digestion – the glucose portion of high fructose corn syrup enters the bloodstream very rapidly. (The fructose must be processed by the liver first). Also, high fructose corn syrup is usually consumed in large quantities by those who drink non-diet sodas and eat commercially made sweets. The quantity factor is undoubtedly part of the health risk associated with this sweetener. Because it is 55% fructose and 45% glucose, some have erroneously tried to associate the risks of high fructose corn syrup with fructose itself. For more about high fructose corn syrup see page 21 and the medical conditions section below. This is a sweetener to avoid!

Sugar alcohols usually are chemically produced from corn. They are poorly absorbed by the digestive system so may cause diarrhea. However, they tend to be low on the glycemic index so are often recommended for diabetics and weight watchers. For more about sugar alcohols, see page 24.

Stevia is a non-caloric natural sweetener which comes from an herb in the lettuce (composite) family. Although classified by the FDA as a supplement, it has been used as a sweetener in South America for hundreds of years and in diet foods in Japan for several decades without causing problems. Since it is an herb rather than a nutritive sweetener, it does not affect blood sugar levels or intestinal flora. For more about stevia, see page 24. See the "Stevia-sweetened recipes" entry on page 257 of the general index for a list of the recipes in this book which use stevia.

MEDICAL CONDITIONS AND SWEETENERS

DIABETES, OVERWEIGHT, INSULIN RESISTANCE, METABOLIC SYN-DROME and preliminary stages of these conditions are exacerbated by over-consumption of sweeteners. When sweeteners (especially highly refined sweeteners such as high fructose corn syrup) and highly processed starches are consumed as a large part of the diet, blood sugar levels may rise rapidly several times per day. This rapid rise is followed by a rapid output of insulin by the pancreas. Once the pancreas has been worn out by repetition of this pattern, overt diabetes develops. Obesity, insulin resistance, and metabolic syndrome may be steps along the way to diabetes.

High levels of blood insulin can lead to detrimental health effects. High insulin causes blood sugar to plummet rapidly as it drives the insulin into our cells. Confronted with this overabundance of glucose, the cells store it either as glycogen or as fat.[2] The rapid rise in insulin may also cause blood glucose levels may drop to below normal, which can lead to uncontrollable hunger. Thus a vicious cycle of overeating and fat storage may develop and lead to weight gain. The rapidly falling blood sugar level that can follow a "sugar high" may also cause symptoms of reactive hypoglycemia.

High levels of insulin raise blood pressure and detrimental blood fats while suppressing LDL (good) cholesterol.[3] High blood pressure, high blood fats such as triglycerides and HDL (bad) cholesterol, disordered blood glucose regulation, and obesity are the four hallmarks of metabolic syndrome. Thus, it is sensible for those with any indication of metabolic syndrome, obesity or blood sugar problems to avoid over-consumption of sweeteners, especially highly refined sweeteners, and to eat dessert sparingly with a protein-containing meal to moderate its impact on blood sugar and insulin levels.

The use of sweeteners also should be carefully controlled by those with **INFLAMMATORY BOWEL DISEASE,** other **DIGESTIVE DISORDERS,** and **DYSBIOSIS**. (Dysbiosis is a state of imbalance in the intestinal flora which often involves the presence of harmful organisms and/or the absence of beneficial bacteria. For more information its relationship to food allergies, see *The Ultimate Food Allergy Cookbook and Survival Guide* as described on the last pages of this book). With these conditions, the digestion of disaccharides and amylopectin may be impaired. When these carbohydrates are consumed, rather than being digested and absorbed, they may become food for large populations of intestinal microorganisms such as unfriendly bacteria and/or yeast.[4] Because they are easily absorbed, sweeteners that contain monosaccharides, such as honey, fruit, and agave, are allowed on the Specific Carbohydrate Diet (SCD) for inflammatory bowel disease. Most starches are not allowed. (Thankfully, amylose, which is allowed on the SCD, is also the best type of starch for low glycemic index diets). Those who follow the SCD will find recipes in this book which they can use such as "Baked Apples or Pears," page 33, "Old Fashioned Applesauce," page 35, the fruit sorbets on pages 37 to 38 and 109 to 113, "Frozen Yogurt," page 106, if made with completely fermented SCD yogurt, the ice cream and sherbet recipes on pages 100 to 108 if made with pure additive-free coconut milk, and "No Bake Pumpkin Pie," page 72, if sweetened with stevia and the filling is put into a "Coconut Pie Crust," page 67.

So should we eat sweeteners? Should dessert be an experience that enhances our enjoyment of life and our relationships? Many of you will be able to use the healthy recipes in this book often. For some, however, your doctor's answer may be "rarely," "only whole fruit," or "only if sweetened with stevia." If you hear this type of answer, I would encourage you to focus on what you can have rather than what you cannot and on improving your health. Develop a taste for stevia starting with recipes that contain other highly flavored ingredients. Eat in-season fresh fruit which is delicious and no work to prepare! Take advantage of the recipes in this book that use whole fruit in special ways for special occasion desserts. Enjoy the social aspects of those occasions as you satisfy your hunger with a healthy treat. My hope is that all readers will find a few recipes which they can eat in this book and that those recipes will add to their enjoyment of life.

Endnotes:

1. *Environmental Health,* 2009 Jan 26;8:2. For more information about problems with high fructose corn syrup alsoe see www.chemicalfreekids.com/updates.htm, January 30, 2009 posting.

2. Brand-Miller, Jennie, PhD, Kate Marshall, RD, CDE, and Phillppa Sandall. *The New Glucose Revolution: Low GI Gluten-Free Eating Made Easy.* DaCapo Press/Perseus Books Group, Philadelphia, copyright 2007, page 23.

3. Brand-Miller, Jennie, PhD, Kate Marshall, RD, CDE, and Phillppa Sandall. *The New Glucose Revolution: Low GI Gluten-Free Eating Made Easy.* DaCapo Press/Perseus Books Group, Philadelphia, copyright 2007, page 22.

4. Gottschall, Elaine, BA, MSc. *Breaking the Vicious Cycle: Intestinal Health Through Diet.* The Kirkton Press, Baltimore, copyright 1994, pages 28-30.

About Spelt

If you have celiac disease, an allergy to gluten itself, or gluten intolerance of any kind, you should eat neither spelt nor wheat because both contain gluten. The information in this section is of no personal value to you, so skip ahead if you wish. However, if you are allergic to wheat but do not have gluten intolerance, you may – or may not – be able to eat spelt. Have your doctor test you for it and advise you based on the test results.

When shopping for spelt products, be aware that a great deal of confusion has risen concerning spelt recently. The United States Government now requires that foods be labeled to indicate whether the food contains any of eight food allergens. As part of the implementation of this law, the FDA has declared that spelt is wheat. Although spelt and wheat are indeed closely related, they are two different species in the same genus. Spelt is *Triticum spelta* and wheat is *Triticum aestivum*. When asked why they had decided that spelt is wheat, an FDA official said that it was because spelt contains gluten. (They had no answer to the question of whether rye would also be considered wheat because it contains gluten, and indeed, bags of rye flour in the health food store are still labeled "wheat-free"). Spelt does indeed contain gluten and should not be eaten by anyone who is gluten-sensitive or has celiac disease, but the presence of gluten does not make spelt wheat. However, under the new law, packages of spelt products must be labeled "Contains wheat."

There are a variety of reasons for the tolerance some wheat-allergic patients have for spelt. All grains contain components in addition to gluten to which a person may develop an allergy. If you are allergic to one of them, but not gluten, you may tolerate spelt.

There are other differences between wheat and spelt. The gluten in spelt behaves differently than the gluten in wheat in cooking. It is extremely difficult to make seitan from spelt. (Seitan is a meat substitute that is almost pure gluten). When making it from wheat, a process of soaking in hot water is used to remove the starch from the gluten protein. If the same process is followed with spelt, the protein structure also dissolves in the hot water. Spelt seitan must be washed by hand very carefully under running cold water.

Because the gluten in spelt is more soluble than wheat gluten, making yeast bread with spelt is also different than making it with wheat. The individual gluten molecules join up more readily to form long chains and sheets that trap the gas produced by yeast. This means that it is possible to over-knead spelt bread. There are some bread machines that work quite well for wheat and even other allergy breads but are unacceptable for spelt bread because they knead so vigorously that they over-develop the gluten. See pages 41 to 42 of this book and pages 32 to 33 of *Easy Breadmaking for Special Diets* (described on the last pages of this book) for recommendations about bread machines to use for making spelt bread.

It is possible that the greater solubility of spelt protein makes it easier to digest than wheat. Undoubtedly, most people have had much less prior exposure to spelt than to wheat resulting in less opportunity to become allergic to spelt. Whatever the reason, there are many people who suffer allergic reactions after eating wheat but do not react to spelt. (I have talked to hundreds of them). Restricting one's diet unnecessarily, as the confusion generated by new labeling law will undoubtedly lead people to do, is counterproductive to good nutrition. Consult your doctor about your own food allergy test results and follow the diet recommended for you, but do not unnecessarily restrict spelt consumption based on the faulty logic behind the new government labeling requirements.

References
Helpful Books and Websites

BOOKS

Burrows, Nancy. *Allergy Cooking Tricks and Treasures.* Burrows Publishing, 526 Belmont Road, Grand Forks, ND 58201, 1987.

Dumke, Nicolette M. *Allergy and Celiac Diets With Ease: Money and Time Saving Solutions for Food Allergy and Gluten-Free Diets.* Allergy Adapt, Inc., 1877 Polk Avenue, Louisville, CO 80027, 2008; Revised edition, 2009.

Dumke, Nicolette M. *Allergy Cooking With Ease.* Starburst Publishers, Lancaster, PA, 1992; Allergy Adapt, Inc., 1877 Polk Avenue, Louisville, CO 80027, Revised edition, 2007.

Dumke, Nicolette M. *Easy Breadmaking for Special Diets.* Allergy Adapt, Inc., 1877 Polk Avenue, Louisville, CO 80027, 1995; Revised edition, 2007.

Dumke, Nicolette M. *Gluten-Free Without Rice.* Allergy Adapt, Inc., 1877 Polk Avenue, Louisville, CO 80027, 2007.

Dumke, Nicolette M. *The Ultimate Food Allergy Cookbook and Survival Guide.* Allergy Adapt, Inc., 1877 Polk Avenue, Louisville, CO 80027, 2007.

Hagman, Bette. *The Gluten-Free Gourmet: Living Well Without Wheat.* Henry Holt and Company, New York, NY, 1990. Revised edition, 2000.

Jones, Marjorie Hurt, R.N. *The Allergy Self-Help Cookbook.* Rodale Press, Emmaus, PA 1984, Revised edition, 2001.

Lewis, Sondra K. with Lonette Dietrich Blakely. *Allergy and Candida Cooking: Understanding and Implementing Plans for Healing.* Canary Connect Publications, 605 Holiday Road, Coralville, IA 52241-1016, 2006.

Rudoff, Carol. *The Allergy Baker, New Expanded Edition.* Prologue Publications, P.O. Box 640, Menlo Park, CA 94206, 1984.

Sahelian, Ray, M.D. and Donna Gates. *The Stevia Cookbook: Cooking with Nature's Calorie-Free Sweetener.* Avery, New York, NY, 1999.

WEBSITES

Help for celiacs:

> Gluten Intolerance Group of North America – www.gluten.net
> Celiac.com – www.celiac.com

Help for those with food allergies:

> Food Allergy.org – www.food-allergy.org
> Optimal Health Resource Laboratories – www.yorkallergyusa.com
>   (for allergy testing)

Products that can be used on celiac and food allergy diets:

See pages 231 to 234 for websites of companies that produce special foods and products for food allergy and gluten-free diets.

Index to Recipes by Grain Use

To help those on rotation diets find recipes made with the grain they need for each diet day, this index lists the recipes for baked goods according to the major grain or grain alternative that they contain. The recipes that do not contain a grain or grain alternative, such as those for ice creams, etc., are not listed in this index but can be found by name in the "General Index," page 250. Arrowroot and tapioca are used as binders or thickeners in many recipes in this book but are included in the listing below only for recipes in which they are the main flour-type ingredient. Headings which contain **GF** indicate that the grain or grain alternative is gluten-free.

AMARANTH (GF)

Double Cherry-Berry Seed Cake
    Cobbler. 47
Traditional Fruit Cobbler Topping . . 49
One Layer "Shortcake" 58
Quick-Mix No-Roll Pie Crust. 63
Oil Pastry 64
Shoo Fly Pie Cake. 76
Gingerbread 80
Amaranth Spice Cake 83
Stevia-Sweetened Amaranth Spice Cake. 83
Amaranth Chocolate Cake 87
German Chocolate or Carob Cake . . 88
Ice Cream Cones. 118
Banana Bread 150
Amaranth Chocolate or Carob Chip
    Cookies. 155
Vanilla Cookies 158
Cashew Butter Cookies 162
Gingersnaps 168
Amaranth Chocolate Brownies 170
Amaranth Carob Brownies 171
Stevia-Sweetened Amaranth Carob
    Brownies. 172
Shortbread. 174
Gluten-Free Gingerbread Diamonds. 176
Drop "Sugar" Cookies. 178
Cookie Press Cookies 180

Fig Bars 182
Pfeffernusse. 184
Amaranth Biscotti 185
Pizzelles. 186
Traditional German Chocolate Cake. 215

ARROWROOT (GF)

See the starch listing on page 249.

BARLEY

Traditional Fruit Cobbler Topping . . 49
One Layer "Shortcake" 58
Oil Pastry 64
Barley Pineapple Upside-Down Cake. 75
Banana Spice Cake 81
Barley Vanilla Cake. 84
Barley Lemon Cake. 89
Barley Sweet Roll Dough. 133
Streusel Coffee Cake 134
Fruit Kuchen. 135
Easy Lattice Coffee Cake. 135
Barley Cake Doughnuts 146
Chocolate Barley Cake Doughnuts . 148
Banana Bread 150
Barley Date-Nut Bread 152
Barley Chocolate or Carob Chip
    Cookies. 156
Vanilla Cookies 158

Barley Lemon Cookies 166
Gingersnaps 168
Barley Chocolate Brownies 171
Shortbread. 174
Cut-Out "Sugar" Cookies 178
Sumptuous Shortcake 206

BUCKWHEAT (GF)

Traditional Fruit Cobbler Topping . . 49
One Layer "Shortcake" 58
Oil Pastry 64
Buckwheat Sweet Roll Dough 132
Streusel Coffee Cake 134
Fruit Kuchen. 135
Easy Lattice Coffee Cake. 135
Buckwheat Chocolate Brownies . . . 169

CORN (GF)

Caramel Corn 198
Nutty Caramel Corn. 199
Good and Healthy Popcorn. 199

KAMUT

Traditional Fruit Cobbler Topping . . 49
One Layer "Shortcake" 58
Oil Pastry 64
Kamut Sweet Roll Dough 133
Streusel Coffee Cake 134
Fruit Kuchen. 135
Easy Lattice Coffee Cake. 135
Monkey Bread. 136
Jam Crescents or Tea Ring. 137
Sticky Buns 138
Cinnamon Rolls 140
Low-fat Danish 141
Hot Cross Buns. 141
Cinnamon Crisps 142
Orange Rolls 143
Lemon Rolls 144
No-Fry Raised Doughnuts 144

Kamut Chocolate or Carob Chip Cookies . . 158
Vanilla Cookies. 158
Tropical Delights. 164
Gingerbread Men 177

MILLET (GF)

Easy Fruit Crumble. 56
Banana Bread 150
Gluten-Free Applesauce Cookies. . . 164

NUTS ONLY (GF)

Nutty Cherry Cobbler. 55
"Instant" Nutty Cobbler 55
Coconut Pie Crust 67
Nutty Topping 195

OAT (Ask your doctor about eating oats on a gluten-free diet).

Easy Apple Crisp (with spelt or rice) . 45
Fresh Peach Crisp (with spelt or rice) . 46
Blueberry Crisp (with spelt or rice) . . 46
Fresh Apple Crisp (with spelt or rice) . 46
Easy Fruit Crumble. 56
Blueberry Squares (with spelt) 61
Oil Pastry 64
Date-Nut Bundt Cake 77
Banana Spice Cake 81
Ice Cream Cones. 118
Fiber-Full Oatmeal Raisin Cookies . 160
Oatmeal Treasures (with spelt). 161
Peanut Butter Oatmeal Cookies (with
    spelt) 161
Oat Lemon Cookies 167
Oatmeal Bars (with spelt) 172
Date Squares (with spelt). 173
Apple Butter Squares (with spelt) . . 173
Shortbread. 174
Cookie Press Cookies 180
Sumptuous Shortcake 206

QUINOA (GF)

Traditional Fruit Cobbler Topping . . 49
Easy Fruit Crumble. 56
One Layer "Shortcake" 58
Oil Pastry 64
Quinoa Carrot Cake 79
Gingerbread 80
Dark Carob Cake 85
Carob Cake. 86
Stevia-Sweetened Carob Cake 86
German Chocolate or Carob Cake . . 88
Ice Cream Cones. 118
Quinoa Cinnamon Raisin Bread . . . 124
No-Fry Raised Doughnuts 144
Quinoa Chocolate or Carob Chip
    Cookies 156
Stevia-Sweetened Quinoa Chocolate
    or Carob Chip Cookies 156
Vanilla Cookies 158
Quinoa Almond Cookies 163
Carrot Cookies 166
Stevia-Sweetened Carrot Cookies . . 166
Shortbread. 174
Cookie Press Cookies 180
Pizzelles. 186
Carob Pizzelles 188
Traditional German Chocolate Cake.215

RICE (GF)

Easy Apple Crisp (with oats) 45
Fresh Peach Crisp (with oats) 46
Blueberry Crisp (with oats) 46
Fresh Apple Crisp (with oats) 46
Traditional Fruit Cobbler Topping . . 49
One Layer "Shortcake" 58
Quick-Mix No-Roll Pie Crust. 63
Oil Pastry 64
"Graham" Cracker Pie Crust 68
Rice Banana Spice Cake 82
Rice Vanilla Cake 84

Rice Chocolate Cake. 88
German Chocolate or Carob Cake . . 88
Rice Lemon Cake 90
Rice Cinnamon Raisin Bread 126
Cranberry Orange Bread 128
Blueberry Lemon Bread. 128
Rice Sweet Roll Dough 132
Streusel Coffee Cake 134
Fruit Kuchen. 135
Easy Lattice Coffee Cake 135
Monkey Bread. 136
Sticky Buns 138
Cinnamon Rolls 140
Hot Cross Buns. 141
Orange Rolls 143
Lemon Rolls 144
No-Fry Raised Doughnuts 144
Rice Cake Doughnuts 146
Chocolate Rice Cake Doughnuts. . . 147
Rice Chocolate or Carob Chip Cookies.154
Vanilla Cookies 158
Shortbread. 174
Wickedly Rich Cheesecake 205
Traditional German Chocolate Cake.215

RYE

Traditional Fruit Cobbler Topping . . 49
One Layer "Shortcake" 58
Oil Pastry 64
Rye Carrot Cake 78
Carob Cake. 86
Stevia-Sweetened Carob Cake 86
German Chocolate or Carob Cake . . 88
Ice Cream Cones. 118
No-Fry Raised Doughnuts 144
Cashew Butter Cookies 162
Tropical Delights. 164
Pfeffernusse. 184
Pizzelles. 186
Traditional German Chocolate Cake.215

SORGHUM (also called MILO) (GF)

Banana Spice Cake 81
Dessert Pancakes 114
Sorghum Banana Cookies 158
Gluten-Free Banana Chocolate
    Cookies 165
Gluten-Free Lemon Cookies 168

SPELT

Easy Apple Crisp (with oats) 45
Fresh Peach Crisp (with oats) 46
Blueberry Crisp (with oats) 46
Fresh Apple Crisp (with oats) 46
Double Cherry-Berry Seed Cake
    Cobbler 47
Traditional Fruit Cobbler Topping . . 49
One Layer "Shortcake" 58
Traditional Strawberry Shortcake 60
Blueberry Squares (with oats) 61
Quick-Mix No-Roll Pie Crust 63
Oil Pastry 64
"Graham" Cracker Pie Crust 68
White Spelt Carrot Cake 78
Gingerbread 80
White Spelt Carob or Chocolate Cake. 86
German Chocolate or Carob Cake . . 88
Dessert Waffles 115
Ice Cream Cones 118
White Spelt Cinnamon Raisin Bread.126
Whole Spelt Cinnamon Raisin Bread.127
Cranberry Orange Bread 128
Blueberry Lemon Bread 128
Sugarplum Bread 128
Mexican Holiday Bread 129
Pannetone 130
Hawaiian Bread 130
White Spelt Sweet Roll Dough 131
Whole Spelt Sweet Roll Dough 133
Streusel Coffee Cake 134

Fruit Kuchen 135
Easy Lattice Coffee Cake 135
Monkey Bread 136
Jam Crescents or Tea Ring 137
Sticky Buns 138
Cinnamon Rolls 140
Low-fat Danish 141
Hot Cross Buns 141
Cinnamon Crisps 142
Orange Rolls 143
Lemon Rolls 144
No-Fry Raised Doughnuts 144
Banana Bread 150
Spelt Date-Nut Bread 151
White Spelt Chocolate or Carob Chip
    Cookies 154
Whole Spelt Chocolate or Carob Chip
    Cookies 157
Vanilla Cookies 158
White Spelt Banana Cookies 159
Oatmeal Treasures (with oats) 161
Peanut Butter Oatmeal Cookies
    (with oats) 161
Tropical Delights 164
Carrot Cookies 166
Stevia-Sweetened Carrot Cookies . . 166
Oatmeal Bars (with oats) 172
Date Squares (with oats) 173
Apple Butter Squares (with oats) . . . 173
Shortbread 174
Gingerbread Men 177
Cut-Out "Sugar" Cookies 178
Cookie Press Cookies 180
Fig Bars 182
Pfeffernusse 184
Pizzelles 186
Spelt "Graham" Crackers 203
Wickedly Rich Cheesecake 205
Sumptuous Shortcake 206
Extra Flaky Pie Crust 208

White Spelt Pineapple Upside-Down
   Cake 212
Luscious Lemon Layer Cake 213
Orange Layer Cake 213
Devils Tower Fudge Cake 214
Traditional German Chocolate Cake.215
Almond Cookies 216
Rich Chocolate Brownies 217
Favorite Chocolate Chip Cookies . . 218
Easy Shortbread. 218
Lively Lemon Drops 219
Double Chocolate Cookies 220
White Spelt Biscotti 221
Spritz. 222
Pizzelles Just Like Grandma's. 223

STARCH ONLY or STARCH PLUS NUTS (GF)

No-Grain Easy Fruit Crumble. 57
Nutty Waffles 116
Stevia-Sweetened Nutty Waffles. . . . 116
Easy Almond Waffles. 117
Stevia-Sweetened Easy Almond Waffles .117
No Grain Coconut Cookies 179
Carob Wafers or Sandwich Cookies   181
Stevia-Sweetened Carob Wafers or
   Sandwich Cookies. 182
Cookies Like "Oreos™" 182

TAPIOCA (GF)

See the starch listing above.

TEFF (GF)

Traditional Fruit Cobbler Topping . . 49
One Layer "Shortcake" 58
Oil Pastry 64
Gluten-Free Applesauce Cookies. . . 164
Shortbread 174

General Index

Recipes appear in *italics*. Informational sections appear in standard type.

A

Agave 21-22, 237
  In light colored cakes. 22, 75
Almond Cookies, Quinoa 163
Almond Cookies (spelt) 216
Almond Waffles, Easy 117
Amaranth 27
Amaranth Biscotti. 185
Amaranth Carob Brownies 171
Amaranth Chocolate Brownies. 170
Amaranth Chocolate Cake. 87
Amaranth Chocolate or Carob Chip
  Cookies 155
Amaranth Spice Cake 83
Apple Butter Squares. 173
Apple Cobbler. 52
Applesauce Cookies, Gluten-Free 164
Apple Crisp, Easy 45
Apple Crisp, Fresh. 46
Apple Pie 68
Apples, Baked. 34
Apple Sauce, Old Fashioned 35
Applesauce Tapioca, Easy. 37
Apple Topping. 194
Arrowroot 28

B

Baked Apples or Pears 34
Baked goods
  Fragile, removing from pans 15
  Storage 15
  Testing for doneness 14-15
Bakeware. 15
Baking powder 30

Baking soda. 30
Banana Bread 150
Banana Carob Frosting. 92
Banana-Cherry or Berry Sorbet, Easy. . . 38
Banana Chocolate Cookies, Gluten-Free . 165
Banana Cookies, Sorghum. 158
Banana Cookies, White Spelt. 159
Banana Sherbet 107
Banana Sorbet 112
Banana Spice Cake. 81
Banana Spice Cake, Rice. 82
Barley 26
Barley Cake Doughnuts. 146
Barley Chocolate Brownies. 171
Barley Chocolate or Carob Chip Cookies. 156
Barley Date-Nut Bread 152
Barley Lemon Cake. 89
Barley Lemon Cookies. 166
Barley Pineapple Upside-Down Cake. . . 75
Barley Sweet Roll Dough 133
Barley Vanilla Cake 84
Binders 30, 31
Bing Cherry Cobbler. 53
Biscotti, Amaranth 185
Biscotti, White Spelt 221
Blood sugar, effect of food processing
  on 236
Blueberry Pie 69
Blueberry Cobbler. 51
Blueberry Crisp. 46
Blueberry Lemon Bread. 128
Blueberry or Raspberry Sauce. 193
Blueberry Squares. 61
Blueberry Tapioca Pudding, Best 39
Bread machines 17-18, 120, 124

Bread making with high-gluten flours
   Hand method 121-123
   Mixer method 122-123
   Bread machine method 124
Bread making with low-gluten
   flours. 123
Bread recipes. 124-131
Bread storage. 124
Broiled Nut-Coconut Cake Topping. . . 92
Brownie recipes. 169-172
Buckwheat 28
Buckwheat Chocolate Brownies 169
Buckwheat Sweet Roll Dough 132
Butter Pecan Ice Cream. 102
Butterscotch Sauce 190

C

Café au Lait Ice Cream. 103
Cakes
   Chocolate and carob, prevention of
    over-baking 75
   Fragility. 74
   Method to remove fragile cakes from
    pans 74-75
Cake Doughnuts, Barley 146
Cake Doughnuts, Rice. 146
Cake Doughnuts, Chocolate Barley . . 148
Cake Doughnuts, Chocolate Rice 147
Cake recipes 75-90, 212-215
   Especially for guests recipes. . . . 212-215
Cantaloupe Sorbet 112
Caramel Corn 198
Caramel Corn, Nutty 199
Carbohydrates
   Effect of food processing on blood
    sugar level. 236
   Types of. 236
Carob and carob chips. 19, 20
Carob Cake 86
Carob Cake, Dark 85

Carob cake recipes. 85-86
Carob Ice Cream, Easy 101
Carob or Chocolate Cake, White Spelt . 86
Carob Pizzelles. 188
Carob Pudding. 44
Carob Syrup. 190
Carob Wafers or Sandwich Cookies . . 181
Carrot Cake, Quinoa 79
Carrot Cake, Rye 78
Carrot Cake, White Spelt 78
Carrot Cookies 166
Carrot Cookies, Stevia-Sweetened . . . 166
Cashew Butter Cookies 162
Cheesecake, Wickedly Rich. 205
Cherry-Berry Seed Cake Cobbler,
   Double. 47
Cherry Cobbler, Bing 53
Cherry Cobbler, Nutty 55
Cherry Cobbler, Tart. 52
Cherry Pie 70
Cherry Sauce 193
Cherry Tapioca Pudding, Delightful
   Dark 40
Cherry Vanilla Ice Cream 103
Chocolate and chocolate chips 19
   Melting. 15
Chocolate Barley Cake Doughnuts . . . 148
Chocolate Brownies, Amaranth 170
Chocolate Brownies, Barley 171
Chocolate Brownies, Buckwheat. 169
Chocolate Brownies, Rich 217
Chocolate Cake, Amaranth 87
Chocolate cake recipes 86-88
Chocolate Cake, Rice. 88
Chocolate Cake, White Spelt 86
Chocolate Chip Cookies, Favorite. . . . 218
Chocolate Chips for Ice Cream. 202
Chocolate Chip Ice Cream. 102
Chocolate Cookies, Double 220
Chocolate Cream Cheese Frosting. 94

Chocolate Frosting, Dairy-Free 94
Chocolate Ice Cream, Easy. 100
Chocolate Ice Cream, Rich. 225
Chocolate Mint Ice Cream. 227
Chocolate or Carob Chip Cookies,
    Amaranth 155
Chocolate or Carob Chip Cookies,
    Barley 156
Chocolate or Carob Chip Cookies,
    Kamut. 158
Chocolate or Carob Chip Cookies,
    Quinoa 156
Chocolate or Carob Chip Cookies,
    Rice 154
Chocolate or Carob Chip Cookies,
    Sorghum Banana 158
Chocolate or Carob Chip Cookies,
    White Spelt 154
Chocolate or Carob Chip Cookies,
    Whole Spelt. 157
Chocolate or Carob Chips, Milk-free . 201
Chocolate or Carob Pudding 44
Chocolate Syrup 189
Cinnamon Crisps 142
Cinnamon Raisin Bread, Rice 126
Cinnamon Raisin Bread, Quinoa . . . 124
Cinnamon Raisin Bread, White Spelt .126
Cinnamon Raisin Bread, Whole Spelt .127
Chocolate Barley Cake Doughnuts . . . 148
Chocolate Rice Cake Doughnuts 147
Cinnamon Rolls 140
Cinnamon "Sugar" Doughnut Topping .149
Cobbler and crisp recipes. 45-57
Cobbler, "Instant" Nutty. 55
Cobbler Topping. 49
Cocoa 19-20
Coconut Cookies, No Grain. 179
Coconut Frosting 90
Coconut Pie Crust 67
Coconut Pudding, Fancy. 44
Coconut Tapioca Pudding 41

Coconut Topping, Easy 194
Coffee cake recipes. 134-137
Confections and snack recipes
    . . . . .197-200, 203
Cookie Press Cookies 180
Cookie recipes 153-188, 216-223
    Bar cookie recipes 169-173, 217
    Drop cookie recipes
        . . . . 154-168, 216, 218-220
    Especially for guests recipes. . . . 216-223
    Holiday cookie recipes
        . . . . 184-188, 221-223
    Rolled cookie recipes 174-178, 218
    Shaped cookie recipes. . . . 179-183, 221
Cookware 16
Cranberry Orange Bread. 128
Cranberry Sorbet 110
Cranberry Tapioca Pudding, Holiday
    Special 40
Cream Cheese Frosting 93
Cream Cheese Frosting, Chocolate 94
Cream Cheese Glaze 93
Creaming fat with liquid sweeteners . 15
Cream Pies. 73
Creamy Cake Topping. 96
Creamy Glaze for Doughnuts and Sweet
    Rolls. 148
Custard Base for Ice Cream 224
Cut-Out "Sugar" Cookies 178

D

Dairy-Free Chocolate Frosting. 94
Danish, Low-fat. 141
Dark Carob Cake. 85
Dark Cherry Tapioca Pudding. 40
Date Frosting. 91
Date Glaze. 91
Date-Nut Bread, Barley 152
Date-Nut Bread, Spelt 151
Date-Nut Bundt Cake 77
Date Squares 173

Date sugar. 23, 237
Desserts, functions of:
   Build memories 9-10
   Build relationships 8
   Connect us to friends and family. 7, 9, 10
   Enjoyment. 9
   Express love 7
   Give comfort 9-10
   Help us maintain a positive outlook. 9
Dessert Pancakes. 114
Dessert Waffles 115
Devils Tower Fudge Cake 214
Diabetes 238
Dietary restrictions
   and feelings of deprivation. 11
   ask your doctor about 12
   desserts to fit 11-12
Digestive disorders and diet. 239
Double Cherry-Berry Seed Cake
   Cobbler. 47
Double Chocolate Cookies. 220
Doughnut recipes 144-149
Doughnut topping recipes 148-149
Dysbiosis. 23, 239

E

Easy Almond Waffles. 117
Easy Lattice Coffee Cake. 135
Easy Fruit Crumble 56
Eggs
   as binders 31
   warming for yeast breads. 31
   substitutions for eggs. 33
Eggnog Ice Cream 226
Equipment for making desserts . . 15-18
   Bakeware 15
   Bread machines 17-18
   Cookware. 16
   Food processors 17
   Griddles and irons 17

   Hand blenders 17
   Ice cream makers 17, 99
   Mixers 17
   Rolling pins 16
   Strainers. 16
   Thermometers 16
   Zesters 17
Extra Flaky Pie Crust 208

F

Fats, types of 29-30
Fiber-Full Oatmeal Raisin Cookies . . 160
Fig Bars 182
Flavorings 20, 229
Flour. 24-28
Flour substitutions 32-33
Food allergies, prevention of
   Ingredient choices 12
   Number of ingredients in recipes and
     frequency of use 13
Food processors. 17
Frozen Yogurt. 106
Frosting recipes 90-96, 215
Fructose 236, 237
   Impact on blood sugar.20-21, 236, 237
Fruit 19
   Role in diet 237
Fruit Cobbler Topping, Traditional . . . 49
Fruit Crumble, Easy 56
Fruit Crumble, No-Grain Easy 57
Fruit dessert recipes . 34-38, 45-61, 68-73
Fruit Kuchen 135
Fruit sauce recipes. 191-194
Fruit Sorbet, Quick 38
Fruit sweeteners. 22-23, 237
Fruit Tapioca, Quick and Easy 36
Fruit Tapioca, Fresh 36
Fudge Cake, Devils Tower. 214
Fudge Sauce. 189
Fudgey Nut Balls 200

G

Gingerbread. 80
Gingerbread Men 177
German Chocolate Cake, Traditional . 215
German Chocolate or Carob Cake. . . . 88
German Chocolate Frosting, Dairy Free.95
Gingerbread Diamonds, Gluten-Free . 176
Gingersnaps 168
Glazed Nuts, Spicy 197
Glucose. 236
Gluten-Free Applesauce Cookies. 164
Gluten-Free Banana Chocolate Cookies.165
Gluten-Free Gingerbread Diamonds . 176
Gluten-Free Lemon Cookies. 168
Good and Healthy Popcorn 199
"Graham" Cracker Pie Crust. 68
"Graham" Crackers, Spelt 203
Grape Pie. 71
Griddles and irons. 17
Guar gum 31
  In low-gluten breads 121
Guest worthy desserts 205-227

H

Hand blenders. 17
Hawaiian Bread 130
High fructose corn syrup. . . 20-21, 238
Honey. 23, 237
Hot Cross Buns. 141

I

Ice cream
  Ingredients for. 97-98
  Serving and storage 98
  Stabilizers for. 97-98
  Sweeteners for 97
Ice Cream Cones. 118
Ice cream freezing methods
  Food processor or blender method . 99

Ice cream machine method 99
  Still freezing method 98-99
Ice cream makers 17, 99
Ice cream recipes 100-105, 224-227
Ice cream recipes, custard-based . .224-227
Inflammatory bowel disease. 239
Ingredients for desserts 12, 19-33
Ingredient substitutions 32-33
Insulin. 238-239
Insulin resistance. 238

J

Jam Crescents or Tea Ring 137

K

Kamut. 25
Kamut Chocolate or Carob Chip
  Cookies 158
Kamut Sweet Roll Dough 133
Kiwi Sorbet 109

L

Lattice Coffee Cake, Easy 135
Leavening ingredients 30-31
Lemon Cake, Barley 89
Lemon Cake, Rice. 90
Lemon Cookies, Barley 166
Lemon Cookies, Gluten-Free 168
Lemon Cookies, Oat 167
Lemon Drops, Lively 219
Lemon Ice Cream, Rich. 226
Lemon Layer Cake, Luscious 213
Lemon Rolls. 144
Lemon Sherbet 107
Lemon Sorbet, Quick 113
Lively Lemon Drops 219
Low-fat Danish 141
Luscious Lemon Layer Cake 213

M

Mango Sorbet. 112
Maple sugar and syrup 23, 237
Measuring 13-14, 235
Metabolic syndrome 238-239
Methylcellulose for ice cream 98
Mexican Holiday Bread 129
Milk-free Chocolate or Carob Chips. . 201
Milk substitutions 33
Millet 27
Mint Chocolate Chip Ice Cream 102
Mixers. 17
Mixing, correct technique for 14
Molasses 23, 237
Monkey Bread 136

N

No-Bake Pumpkin Pie 72
No-Fry Raised Doughnuts 144
No-Bake Strawberry Pie 72
No Grain Coconut Cookies 179
No-Grain Easy Fruit Crumble. 57
Nut Balls 200
Nut Balls, Fudgey. 200
Nut-Coconut Cake Topping, Broiled . . 92
Nut flour or meal 28
Nutty Caramel Corn. 199
Nutty Cherry Cobbler. 55
Nutty Cobbler, "Instant". 55
Nutty Topping 195
Nutty Waffles 116
Nutty "Whipped Cream" 196

O

Oat Lemon Cookies 167
Oatmeal Bars. 172
Oatmeal Raisin Cookies, Fiber-Full. . 160
Oatmeal Cookies, Peanut Butter 161
Oatmeal Treasures. 161

Oats 27
Oil Pastry 64
Orange Ice Cream. 105
Orange Layer Cake. 213
Orange Rolls. 143
Orange Sherbet. 106
"Oreos™", cookies similar to 182
Overweight and obesity 238-239

P

Pancakes, Dessert 114
Pannetone 130
Parchment paper 16
Pastry, Oil 64
Peach Cobbler 54
Peach Crisp, Fresh. 46
Peach Ice Cream. 104
Peach Ice Cream, Rich. 226
Peach Pie. 70
Peach Sauce 192
Peach Shortcake, Traditional. 60
Peach Sorbet. 110
Peanut Butter Oatmeal Cookies. 161
Pears, Baked. 34
Pfeffernusse. 184
Phytonutrients in dark fruit juices . . 39
Pie Crust, Coconut 67
Pie Crust, Extra Flaky. 208
Pie crust, methods of handling 62
   Pressing into the dish. 62
   Rolling with a pastry cloth 62
Pie Crust, Quick-Mix No-Roll. 63
Pie crust recipes. 63-68, 208
Pie recipes 68-73, 209-211
Piña Colada Ice Cream. 104
Pineapple Sauce 192
Pineapple Sorbet, Easy 37
Pineapple Upside-Down Cake, Barley . 75
*Pineapple Upside-Down Cake, White
   Spelt.* 212

Pizzelles 186
Pizzelles, Carob 188
Pizzelles Just Like Grandma's 223
Pomegranate Tapioca Pudding, Tangy . 41
Popcorn, Good and Healthy 199
Potato flour or starch 28
Powdered "Sugar" Doughnut Topping . 149
Prevention of new food allergies 12
    Ingredient choices 12
    Number of ingredients in recipes and
        frequency of use 13
Pudding recipes 39-44
Pumpkin Pie, No-Bake 72

Q

Quick bread recipes 150-152
Quick Lemon Sorbet 113
Quick-Mix No-Roll Pie Crust 63
Quick Fruit Sorbet 38
Quinoa 27-28
Quinoa Almond Cookies 163
Quinoa Carrot Cake 79
Quinoa Chocolate or Carob Chip
    Cookies 156
Quinoa Cinnamon Raisin Bread 124
Quinoa Pudding 43

R

Raised Doughnuts, No-Fry 144
Raspberry Sauce 193
Raspberry Sherbet 108
Raspberry Sorbet 111
References 243
Rhubarb Cobbler 54
Rice 26
Rice Banana Spice Cake 82
Rice Cake Doughnuts 146
Rice Cinnamon Raisin Bread 126
Rice Chocolate Cake 88

Rice Chocolate or Carob Chip Cookies . 154
Rice Lemon Cake 90
Rice Pudding 43
Rice Sweet Roll Dough 132
Rice syrup 23
Rice Vanilla Cake 84
Rich Chocolate Brownies 217
Rolling pins 16
Rye 25
Rye Carrot Cake 78

S

Sauce recipes 189-194
Sherbet recipes 106-108
Shoo Fly Pie Cake 76
Shortbread (many grains) 174
Shortbread, Easy (white spelt) 218
"Shortcake," One Layer 58
Shortcake, Sumptuous 206
Shortcake, Traditional Strawberry 60
Shortcake recipes 58-60, 206
Shortening, healthy vs. unhealthy . . . 30
Simple fruit dessert recipes 34-37
Simplified recipes 12, 13
Sorbet recipes 37-38, 109-113
Sorghum 27
Sorghum Banana Cookies 158
Sources of special ingredients and
    products 228-234
Specific carbohydrate diet (SCD) . . 239
Spelt 24-25, 241-242
    Confusion about due to FDA-required
        labeling 241, 242
    Solubility of 241-242
    Use in bread making 121
Spelt Date-Nut Bread 151
Spelt "Graham" Crackers 203
Spice cake recipes 80-83
Spice Cream 105
Spicy Glazed Nuts 197

Spritz. 222
Starches. 28
Stevia 24, 234, 238
Stevia-sweetened recipes:
  Stevia-Sweetened Amaranth Carob
    Brownies. 172
  Stevia-Sweetened Amaranth Spice Cake.83
  Stevia-Sweetened Carob Cake 86
  Stevia-Sweetened Carob Wafers or
    Sandwich Cookies 182
  Stevia-Sweetened Carrot Cookies . . . 166
  Stevia-Sweetened Quinoa Chocolate or
    Carob Chip Cookies. 156
  Stevia-Sweetened Cranberry Sorbet . 110
  Stevia-Sweetened Easy Almond Waffles .117
  Stevia-Sweetened Kiwi Sorbet 109
  Stevia- Sweetened Nutty Waffles. . . . 116
Sticky Agave. 139
Sticky Buns. 138
Strainers 16
Strawberry Cobbler. 53
Strawberry Ice Cream, Easy. 101
Strawberry Ice Cream, Rich. 225
Strawberry Pie, No-Bake. 72
Strawberry Sauce 191
Strawberry Shortcake, Traditional 60
Strawberry Sherbet 108
Strawberry Sorbet. 111
Streusel Coffee Cake 134
Substitutions, ingredient 32-33
Sucrose 23, 237
  Role in dysbiosis 23, 239
Sugar. 21
Sugar alcohols 23-24, 238
"Sugar" Cookies, Cut-Out. 178
"Sugar" Cookies, Drop 178
Sugar-Free Whipped Cream. 196
Sugarplum Bread 128
Sumptuous Shortcake 206
Sweet bread recipes 124-130

Sweet dough recipes. 131-133
Sweet roll recipes. 138-144
Sweeteners. 20-24
  Health implications of. 236-240
Sweetener substitutions 33

T

Table of measurements 235
Tapioca Parfaits, Elegant. 42
Tapioca Pudding Made with Alternative
  Milks. 42
Tapioca starch 28
Tart Cherry Cobbler 52
Tea Ring 137
Teff. 26
Thermometers. 16
Time saving. 12
Topping recipes 194-196
Traditional German Chocolate Cake . 214
Tropical Delights 164

V

Vanilla Cake, Barley. 84
Vanilla Cake, Rice 84
Vanilla Cookies. 158
Vanilla Ice Cream, Easy 100
Vanilla Ice Cream, Rich 224
Vanilla Pudding. 44
Vitamin C, unbuffered, for leavening .30-31

W

Waffles, Dessert. 115
Waffles, Easy Almond 117
Waffles, Nutty. 116
Weight control 238-239
Whipped Cream, Sugar-Free 196
"Whipped Cream," Nutty 196
White Spelt Biscotti. 221

White Spelt Banana Cookies 159
White Spelt Carrot Cake 78
White Spelt Carob or Chocolate Cake . 86
White Spelt Chocolate or Carob Chip
   Cookies 154
White Spelt Cinnamon Raisin Bread . 126
White Spelt Pineapple Upside-Down
   Cake 212
White Spelt Sweet Roll Dough 131
Whole Spelt Chocolate or Carob Chip
   Cookies 157
Whole Spelt Cinnamon Raisin Bread . 127
Whole Spelt Sweet Roll Dough 133
Wickedly Rich Cheesecake 205

X

Xanthum gum 31
   Use in low-gluten bread 121
Xylitol 24, 234

Y

Yeast 31
Yogurt, Frozen 106

Z

Zesters 17

Books to Help With Your Special Diet

Do you need more fun in your life? ***I Love Dessert but NOT Sugar, Wheat, Milk, Gluten, Corn, Soy, Unhealthy Fat...*** can help you rediscover the enjoyment of simple pleasures. If you are on a restricted diet due to food allergies or gluten intolerance, you don't have to miss out on your favorite desserts any more. The book contains more than 300 easily-made recipes for almost any dessert you might want, all free of sugar, wheat, corn, soy, and unhealthy fats. Many of them are gluten-free. A very few of the desserts contain dairy products or eggs, but there are egg and milk-free alternatives for the same desserts. Many recipes are made with healthy new sweeteners such as agave. When your friends or family are having a treat, now you can join in. Don't deprive yourself any more!

ISBN 978-1-887624-18-3 . . . .$22.95

In these times of economic downturn, what is a person on a special diet to do? ***Allergy and Celiac Diets With Ease: Money and Time Saving Solutions for Food Allergy and Celiac Diets*** provides solutions to both the economic and time challenges you face on your diet. It shows how to shop economically, cook without spending all day in the kitchen, stock your kitchen for efficiency and good health, make the best use of your appliances, have good times with friends and family without breaking the bank, get organized, and be able to do this in limited time. This book contains over 160 money-saving, quick and easy recipes for allergy and celiac diets. Over 140 of them are gluten-free. It includes extensive reference sections including "Sources" and "Special Diet Resources" sections to help you find the foods you need. A list of helpful books and websites (even an online celiac/special diet restaurant search database) is also included.

ISBN 978-1-887624-17-6 . . . .$19.95

The Ultimate Food Allergy Cookbook and Survival Guide: How to Cook with Ease for Food Allergies and Recover Good Health gives you everything you need to survive and recover from food allergies. It contains medical information about the diagnosis of food allergies, health problems that can be caused by food allergies, and your options for treatment. The book includes a rotation diet that is free from common food allergens such as wheat, milk, eggs, corn, soy, yeast, beef, legumes, citrus fruits, potatoes, tomatoes, and more. Instructions are given on how to personalize the standard rotation diet to meet your individual needs and fit your food preferences. It contains 500 recipes that can be used with (or independently of) the diet. Extensive reference sections include a listing of commercially prepared foods for allergy diets and sources for special foods, services, and products.

ISBN 978-1-887624-08-4 . . . .$24.95

Gluten-Free Without Rice introduces you to gluten-free grains and grain alternatives other than rice such as teff, millet, sorghum, amaranth, quinoa, buckwheat, tapioca, arrowroot, corn, potato starch, and more. It gives you over 75 delicious recipes for muffins, crackers, bread, pancakes, waffles, granola, main and side dishes, cookies, and desserts. With this book you can cook easily for a gluten-free diet without relying on rice. Whether you have celiac disease or food allergies, this book will make it easier and more enjoyable to stay on your diet and will help you to improve your health.

ISBN 978-1-887624-15-2 . . . .$9.95

Allergy Cooking With Ease (**Revised Edition**). This classic all-purpose allergy cookbook was out of print and now is back in a revised edition. It includes all the old favorite recipes of the first edition plus many new recipes and new foods. It contains over 300 recipes for baked goods, main dishes, soups, salads, vegetables, ethnic dishes, desserts, and more. Informational sections of the book are also totally updated, including the extensive "Sources" section.

ISBN 978-1-887624-10-7 . . . .$19.95

Easy Breadmaking for Special Diets contains over 200 recipes for allergy, heart healthy, low fat, low sodium, yeast-free, controlled carbohydrate, diabetic, celiac, and low calorie diets. It includes recipes for breads of all kinds, tortillas, bread and tortilla based main dishes, and desserts. Use your bread machine, food processor, mixer, or electric tortilla maker to make the bread YOU need quickly and easily.

Revised Edition – ISBN 978-1-887624-11-4 . . . . $19.95

Original Edition Bargain Book – ISBN 1-887624-02-3 . . . . **SALE!** - $9.95

   With the bargain book we will include an insert of updated pages about current bread machines and the tortilla recipes from the new edition.

Easy Cooking for Special Diets: How to Cook for Weight Loss/Blood Sugar Control, Food Allergy, Heart Healthy, Diabetic and "Just Healthy" Diets – Even if You've Never Cooked Before. This book contains everything you need to know to stay on your diet plus 265 recipes complete with nutritional analyses and diabetic exchanges. It also includes basics such as how to grocery shop, equip your kitchen, handle food safely, time management, information on nutrition, and sources of special foods.

ISBN 978-1-887624-09-1 . . . . $24.95

The Low Dose Immunotherapy Handbook: Recipes and Lifestyle Tips for Patients on LDA and EPD Treatment gives 80 recipes for patients on low dose immunotherapy treatment for their food allergies. It also includes organizational information to help you get ready for your shots.

ISBN: 978-1-887624-07-7 . . . .$9.95

How to Cope With Food Allergies When You're Short on Time is a booklet of time saving tips and recipes to help you stick to your allergy or gluten-free diet with the least amount of time and effort.

. . . . $4.95 or FREE with the order of two other books on these pages

Order these books on-line by going to
www.food-allergy.org,
by mail using the order form on the next page
or from Amazon.com at **www.amazon.com**.

Mail your order form and check to:
Allergy Adapt, Inc.
1877 Polk Avenue
Louisville, CO 80027

Questions? Call 303-666-8253
or email foodalle@food-allergy.org.

Shipping for mail-in orders:

IF YOU ARE ORDERING JUST ONE BOOK, FOR SHIPPING ADD:
$5.00 for any one of the starred (*) books
$2.50 for any one of the non-starred books

TO ORDER MORE THAN ONE BOOK, FOR SHIPPING ADD:
$7.00 for up to three starred* and up to two non-starred books
$9.00 for up to four starred* and up to two non-starred books
$11.00 for up to eight starred* and up to three non-starred books

Call 303-666-8253 for international shipping rates or if you have questions about shipping calculations or large quantity orders.

Thank you for your order!

Order Form

Send to:

Name: _____

Street address: _____

City, State, ZIP code: _____

Phone number (for questions about order): _____

Item	Quantity	Price	Total
I Love Dessert but NOT Sugar, Wheat, Gluten, Milk, Corn, Soy, Unhealthy Fat...*		$22.95	
Allergy and Celiac Diets With Ease*		$19.95	
The Ultimate Food Allergy Cookbook and Survival Guide*		$24.95	
Gluten-Free Without Rice		$9.95	
Allergy Cooking With Ease*		$19.95	
Easy Breadmaking for Special Diets* – Original Edition Bargain Book Revised Edition		$9.95 $19.95	
Easy Cooking for Special Diets*		$24.95	
The Low Dose How Immunotherapy Handbook		$9.95	
How to Cope with Food Allergies When You're Short on Time		$4.95 or **FREE**	
Order any TWO of the first eight books above and get ***How to Cope* FREE!**	Subtotal		
	Shipping – See chart on page 261		
	Colorado residents add 4.1% sales tax		
	Total		